Completely
Staged

Completely Staged

The Complete Illustrated Scripts

Created by
SIMON EVANS & PHIN GLYNN

Written by
SIMON EVANS

Compiled & edited by
**VICTOR GLYNN &
SOPHIE GOLDSWORTHY**

unbound

First published in 2021

Unbound
Level 1, Devonshire House, One Mayfair Place, London W1J 8AJ
WWW.UNBOUND.COM

Text design by Amazing15

A CIP record for this book is available from the British Library

ISBN 978-1-80018-091-8 (hardback)
ISBN 978-1-80018-092-5 (ebook)

Printed in Barcelona by Novoprint

1 3 5 7 9 8 6 4 2

In tribute to the extraordinary, dedicated and brilliant people in our hospitals, care homes, university medical research departments and beyond.

For your unstinting commitment and diligence during the pandemic, which helped protect and look after the rest of us so selflessly.

Thank you.

Contents

Foreword

Staged is a phenomenon. Other than the arrival of the coronavirus vaccines and the heroism of all those in the front line in the battle against Covid-19, I reckon *Staged* is quite the best thing to come out of the horror of the global pandemic of 2020/21.

What is *Staged*? In a nutshell it's two short TV series created by Simon Evans and Phin Glynn and starring Michael Sheen and David Tennant. In the first series, set during Britain's first national lockdown, and first shown by the BBC in June 2020, the actors Sheen and Tennant play fictionalised versions of themselves, meeting up via videoconference to rehearse from their homes a production of Luigi Pirandello's *Six Characters in Search of an Author*, while the play's director, Simon Evans (also playing a version of himself), does what he can to keep control of the proceedings. The second series picks up from the success of the first series and explores what happens when Evans begins work on an American remake of the first series and Tennant and Sheen are not asked to reprise their roles.

Why is it so enjoyable? Because it is ingeniously constructed, beautifully observed, brilliantly played, deftly edited and says something (quite a lot, actually) about actors and life, about men and women, about vanity and insecurity. The casting is impeccable. Alongside the leads, there is Georgia Tennant, David's wife, Anna Lundberg, Michael's partner, and Lucy Eaton, Simon's sister, all appearing as versions of themselves and, as the series evolves, a growing *galère* of international stars zooming in for cameo moments. It's very clever. Pirandello's play explores illusion and reality and so does *Staged*. It's very touching. We buy into all the relationships on show. We care about these people, however ridiculous they seem at times. Best of all, it's very funny.

Why is it so special? It's wholly original. Yes, other TV series have explored the world and ways of actors (*Call My Agent!/Dix Pour Cent* is my particular favourite) and Steve Coogan and Rob Brydon played entertaining versions of themselves in *The Trip,* but *Staged* is unique. It was conceived and made in lockdown. It is born of its time and uses the challenges and limitations of that time quite dazzlingly. Just as we were all beginning to get to grips with Zoom meetings in our own lives, we found Michael Sheen and David Tennant doing the same thing on TV. This was art reflecting reality and giving us something more as well – something revelatory and life-enhancing, as well as delightfully droll. Charlotte Moore, the BBC's Chief Content Officer, believes *Staged* 'will be seen as one of the defining cultural legacies of 2020'. She is right.

On the day the first lockdown was introduced in Britain in March 2020 I was due to open in a two-handed show at the Bridge Theatre in London starring and celebrating the career of the great Dame Judi Dench. When our first night was cancelled, Dame Judi looked at me sadly and asked, 'I wonder, will we ever appear on a real stage again?'

Who knows when our theatres will be fully open once more? Once upon a time, during Oliver Cromwell's rule in the seventeenth century, theatres in England were closed for eighteen long years. When they reopened in 1660, with the Restoration of King Charles II, there was a renaissance in English drama. Something new and extraordinary was born: Restoration comedy. Three hundred and sixty years later, when theatres around the world were in shutdown, Simon Evans and Phin Glynn created something new and extraordinary, too: Zoom comedy. And, happily, they even invited Judi Dench to make a guest appearance.

Staged was written and directed by Simon Evans. It was fully scripted, but given the nature of the stars, I have no doubt they occasionally went off-piste. I have been lucky enough to see several of Simon's stage productions and even to be in one of them. The guy is a bit of a genius. He is also a magician – yes, an old-fashioned conjuror, who can do card tricks and make rabbits appear out of hats. In my book, *Staged* is magic. Everyone involved in the enterprise needs to be saluted: the writer, the director, the stars, the whole creative team (notably the ace editor, Dan Gage, and Alex Baranowski, the composer) and, of course, the people who had the faith to put up the money and make it happen.

Staged is landmark television. That's why you need to have these scripts in your hand. Enjoy.

Gyles Brandreth
London, 2021

Director's Note

I worry how much I have in common with the character of 'Simon'.

It's a concern, because he's not an attractive human: a soggy-Rich-Tea-biscuit of a man, meerkat-ing opportunistically and grasping at a career which seems entirely unearned. However, there are clearly similarities between him and me, so I'm keen to draw a line between us, if only to distance myself from any damage 'he' might do in the future.

Physical appearance seems the biggest overlap: we're the same height and weight; we both have green eyes and beards (of varying length); we both wear glasses for reading, trainers for running; we're both magicians (to a degree) and share a taste for pale blue shirts and pale blue notebooks. In addition to these shared aesthetics, we are, I'd imagine, close in age (although 'Simon' seems more Pisces than Capricorn); we both have a younger sister called Lucy (or 'Lucy'); and we both overuse semi-colons under the misguided impression that it makes us look sophisticated.

And we were both supposed to be directing a play.

'Simon' had found himself responsible for wrestling Pirandello's incomprehensible meta-drama *Six Characters in Search of an Author* to the ground (*Staged* didn't address how he'd managed to get 'David' and 'Michael' on board, but I couldn't swear that he's above crying down the phone). Meanwhile I was preparing to direct Tom Stoppard's *The Real Thing*, for the Chichester Festival Theatre.

This was February 2020, and rumours were beginning to swirl about people getting sick. Words like 'pandemic' and 'lockdown' were being whispered in the corners of emptying restaurants, and Artistic Directors (responsible for programming and running the nation's theatres) were getting nervous about their spring seasons. Theatre is a sociable industry (the requirement to meet new people one day and bare your soul to them in rehearsals the next makes for accelerated intimacy) so rehearsal rooms presented the perfect petri dish, and the people in them were starting to realise it. A friend of mine, already in rehearsals, was fighting back a revolution from cast-members-turned-doomsday-preppers, and his stories of bloodshed and terror were at the front of my mind when I found myself looking into the worried eyes of my prospective leading lady at a bustling party: 'We'll be fine.'

'Simon's' *Six Characters* suffered the same fate as my *Real Thing* (and hundreds of other projects and plans across the country), and so it was that both versions of me drove back to Oxfordshire: a greener, wider, quieter part of the world in which to spend three months.

And here 'Simon' and Simon deviate.

For all his failings (and they are plentiful), 'Simon' is the more tenacious. The depths he might plumb have yet to be mapped or morally judged (my godsend of an editor, Dan Gage, is convinced 'Simon' was behind 'Michael' and 'David' being dropped from Series Two's American remake). So it's no surprise 'Simon' was calling 'David' en route from the car, choreographing his ducks into a row with his eyes on a West End takeover, before I'd even unpacked.

I needed a bit longer to get going. And I needed Phin Glynn.

Phin is dynamite. A film (and now television) producer, with a unique ability to mine for silver linings. We'd known each other for years, but only recently started working together when he asked me to adapt and direct the film of Lawrence Osborne's *Hunters in the Dark*. We'd been struggling to cast the final roles, so the project seemed destined to share the same fate as my theatrical ambitions, if not for Phin's silver mine. It was no surprise to me that he rang just as I was investing time in YouTube videos of Bob Ross: 'Could we use this window to make something which might (at least) show potential actors that you know which end of the camera should be pointing forward?'*

Cast had to be small. Story had to be housebound. Technical practicalities had to be basic… Even with our expectations lowered in light of all that, there were still some genuinely awful ideas (the *Blair Witch*'s ears were burning) before we saw the lemonade in the lemons of my *Real Thing* experience.

Phin had worked with David Tennant before, so we took our fledgling idea ('A hapless director uses Zoom to try and keep rehearsals going with his two leading actors') to him and his wife Georgia. Their reply: 'Yeah, don't hate it. A comedy?' David took the idea to Michael Sheen (a relationship already cemented in the public consciousness by their magnificent work on Neil Gaiman's *Good Omens*). Michael didn't hate it either.

I wrote the pilot over a weekend in April, in the tea-soaked fervour of creative terror. Sharing scenes with Phin as I went, I built a script fuelled by the quick impressions I got of David and Michael during one video call, the jealousy I felt at friends who'd managed to master the Bob Ross landscape method already, a smattering of Welsh, and the hope that a gag about a stop-start video call might still be funny in a month.

The paths of 'Simon' and Simon came together again.

Both joined a Zoom call with David/'David' and Michael/'Michael' to read a script, and make a thing. But while 'Simon' was caught up in the terrible shockwave of an immoveable object meeting an unstoppable force, I got on with the joyful job of making (what Georgia Tennant had recently titled) *Staged*, with two of the most extraordinary collaborators I could have hoped for.

---

* The irony that, throughout *Staged*, I never pointed a film camera at anyone, is not lost on me.

Despite Michael Palin's assertion to the contrary, David and Michael are very, *very* funny. Phin and I had initially planned for more 'technically sophisticated' sections: Sorkin-esque walk-and-talks, iPhone-filmed through the corridors of David's and Michael's houses as they discussed the matters of the day. We were worried that entire episodes of side by-side faces (even of those two) might prove tiring to even the most devoted of fans. We were wrong.

David and Michael are addictive: completely natural, and absurd, and charming, and monstrous, and kind, with a quicksilver ability to move from the ridiculous to the profound which somehow (I hope) smuggles a real story about real things in amongst the endless bickering. They're not technically minded (Michael managed to send his audio files to the wrong Simon on our first day of filming and we've yet to get them back), but I remember the first take of 'Michael's' presentation of *Port Talbot at Dawn*: two Zoom boxes and nothing else but Michael's painting and pride, and David's pineapple and fury. It was the moment I thought, *We might get away with this.*

Add to them the most astonishing team: their partners, Georgia and Anna, who steal every scene they're in; my inspiration of a sister, Lucy ('Simon' and 'Lucy' aren't close, but Simon and Lucy are the closest); her fiancée Tristam Kaye, who was in lockdown with us and captured the remarkable drone footage; the genius of Dan Gage, our Editor, who gave our show its visual identity, suffering through my own technical illiteracy to somehow cut together a thing of style; then Alex Baranowski, writing a theme for us which was sad and silly, tying together the disparate elements we'd cooked up around our respective kitchen tables, and filmed in our living rooms; then our guest stars. I owe everything to my parents, Russell and Janet Evans, who bought me a book on magic when I was twelve and stood back as the ripples became waves, but they were enjoying their retirement from dentistry and not looking to take up acting. So, we looked further afield: Nina Sosanya, Adrian Lester, Samuel L Jackson, Dame Judi Dench.

'Simon' suffered on, trying to finish rehearsing even one scene, volunteering to read all the animals mentioned in 'David's' screenplay if it would buy him another day, while I held my breath as Victor Glynn showed our pilot to Charlotte Moore at the BBC…

This book is a collection of the scripts which followed: six episodes of Series One and eight episodes of Series Two. It seems wholly unoriginal to say it's been 'a strange time', but the responsibility of making something through it has added to that strangeness. It's been a tragic time for so many, and with the future of our industry (and hundreds of others) hanging in the balance, it wasn't always easy to see the funny side. But I tried to handle it with care alongside the irony, avoiding those words which were whispered in restaurants, touching on the love we feel for those we miss, looking inwards at the effect it's having on us all.

If I've managed that, it's thanks in huge amount to Phin Glynn, who co-created the story for every single episode. Also Charlotte, Shane Allen and Gregor Sharp at the BBC who told us not to change a thing, to leave it at fifteen minutes, to trust that it was what it was (which I took as a compliment). Also my long-suffering agent, Robert Taylor, and my friends DHW Mildon and Tom Weijand, who read the scripts and gave such brilliant feedback; and Helen Sartory, who is kind enough both to love me (a feeling very much reciprocated) *and* lend me her more sophisticated sense of humour. Finally the cast: a list of actors which beggars belief, all of whom offered themselves up for ridicule and dissection, and allowed me to borrow their ideas and pepper them through the pages that follow.

I don't know where 'Simon' is now, or what he's up to. Last I heard, he was in Los Angeles, waiting for a taxi to take him to the airport where a plane would bring him back to London. I don't know what he would have done if his tenacity had paid off: if his production of *Six Characters* had made it to the stage, or his ideas for the American remake had made it into production. I imagine he'd have wallowed indulgently in his success. He's that kind of guy.

Actually, he'd have probably published a book, detailing how it all came about. I bet he'd have written the introduction to it too.

And that, I suppose, is the final difference between me and 'Simon'.

I have a book. He doesn't.

Simon Evans
Oxford, 2021

An Appreciation

What a beautiful thing *Staged* is. Such a mischievous idea and shows what great sports David and Michael are in sending themselves up. Somehow the show captured our shared feelings of frustration and confusion and the absurdities of our new lockdown lives. I don't think any of us thought it would become such a massive hit – but only eight weeks after Victor brought the idea to us, the show hit our screens and immediately struck a chord, bringing joy to millions at such a challenging time. The performances are excellent, crackling with snide chemistry. It's compulsive viewing, full of glorious twists and turns, not to mention stellar casting. And the response from all quarters has been overwhelming. I really can't remember seeing so much positive press across the board – and then the second series arrived just in the nick of time as we plunged into lockdown once again. Perhaps not such a surprise then that *Staged* has connected profoundly with people not just at home but around the world too, finding audiences in North and South America, Australia, Israel, Russia and now Japan and China.

Staged brought entertainment to a nation facing unprecedented adversity together – and in years to come I have no doubt it will be seen as one of the defining cultural legacies of this difficult time.

Charlotte Moore
Chief Content Officer, BBC

Staged

Series One

STAGED SERIES ONE CAST

In order of appearance

Michael Sheen	Michael Sheen
David Tennant	David Tennant
Simon Evans	Simon Evans
Georgia Tennant	Georgia Tennant
Anna Lundberg	Anna Lundberg
Lucy Eaton	Lucy Eaton
Nina Sosanya	Jo
Rebecca Gage	Janine
Samuel L. Jackson	Samuel L. Jackson
Adrian Lester	Adrian Lester
Judi Dench	Judi Dench
Ryan Gage	Judi's Assistant

PRODUCTION NOTE
Almost all of the characters included are real people. Except they
are not real people. They are, if you like, Pirandellian versions
of themselves, as imagined by me, the author. They are, as it were,
trapped in a Pirandellian universe, and are therefore exaggerated
and highly skewed, and not to be taken at face value. At all.

Episode One
Cachu Hwch

DAVID TENNANT's and MICHAEL SHEEN's faces sit in boxes side by
side. Quiet and still and bored, staring into the oblivion.

At some point, the credits appear. White letters on a black
screen: STAGED

> **DAVID**
> The Welsh must have a good phrase for
> the end of the world.

> **MICHAEL**
> Why do you have to say that?

> **DAVID**
> Dylan Thomas must have written about it?
> A poem, I mean.

> **MICHAEL**
> Of course. He wrote 'Do not go gentle
> into that good night.'

> **DAVID**
> There you go.

> **MICHAEL**
> I did a bit of it for the BBC.

> **DAVID**
> Did you?

> **MICHAEL**
> 'Rage, rage, against the dying of the
> light.'

> **DAVID**
> Do you know what it was in the original
> Welsh?

> **MICHAEL**
> How do you mean?

> **DAVID**
> Before it was translated.

> **MICHAEL**
> Translated?

> **DAVID**
> What did he originally write?

> **MICHAEL**
> He originally wrote 'Do not go gentle
> into that good night.'

> **DAVID**
> In English?

> **MICHAEL**
> Yes.

                              DAVID
              That's disappointing.

                              MICHAEL
              Cachu hwch.

                              DAVID
              What does that mean?

                              MICHAEL
              Total fucking disaster.

                              DAVID
                        (repeating)
              Cachu hwch.

                              MICHAEL
              Sounds like you're throwing up.

                              DAVID
                        (trying)
              Cachu hwch.

                              MICHAEL
                        (correct pronunciation)
              Cachu hwch.

                              DAVID
                        (no better)
              Cachu fucking hwch.

                              MICHAEL
              Now you've gone Scouse.
                        (trying again)
              Cachu hwch.

                              DAVID
              Cachu hwch.
                        (giving up)
              I could be Welsh. I could definitely be
              Welsh.

                              MICHAEL
              We would never let you in.

                              DAVID
              You'd love to have me. You'd beg to have
              me.

                              MICHAEL
              We've been fighting the Scots off for
              centuries. We're not going to let you in
              now.

                              DAVID
              Cachu hwch.

      They laugh. The laugh fades. They sigh and look away.

                                                    CUT TO --

SIMON has pulled up outside his sister's house. He sits there in silence for a second. Then takes out his phone and makes a call. Deep breath.

                              SIMON
          David? Can you hear me?

                         DAVID (V.O.)
          I can. I can't see you though. Have you
          got the camera turned on?

                              SIMON
          No. I've been driving, so this is an old
          fashioned phone call.

                         DAVID (V.O.)
          No video?

                              SIMON
          No video.

                         DAVID (V.O.)
          Primitive.

                              SIMON
          Can I moot an idea?

                              DAVID
          I think you might be the only person I
          know who uses that word.

                              SIMON
          What word? Moot?

                              DAVID
                    (not really hearing)
          You also use semi-colons in your emails.

                              SIMON
          I'm trying to cut back on that. Is there
          a version of this lockdown where we
          carry on with rehearsals?

Beat. David clocks what Simon said.

                         DAVID (V.O.)
          Rehearsals?

                              SIMON
          Yes. Bear with me. What if we spend a
          couple of hours a day working on the
          play. Then, when the theatres reopen,
          we're ready to go. Everyone else wastes
          six weeks, we swan into town. The
          British public will need entertainment.

                          DAVID
              You think the British public need Six
              Characters in Search of an Author?

                          SIMON
              It's funny.

                       DAVID (V.O.)
              It's Italian.

                          SIMON
              We can make it funnier. If we rehearse.

    Beat.

                       DAVID (V.O.)
              Speak fluent Italian, do you?

                          SIMON
              Si, ho studiato Italiano all'università.

                       DAVID (V.O.)
              I speak a little German. Tiny bit of
              French. How do we do it?

                          SIMON
              Do you have Zoom?

                          DAVID
              I've got Portal.

                          SIMON
              I'm simonevans1983. If you find me, and
              add me ... we can chat.

                          DAVID
                       (shouting off camera)
              Georgia!
                       (back to Simon)
              Give me a minute. Just going to go
              inside.
                                                CUT TO --

3 INT. LUCY EVANS' HOUSE AND DAVID TENNANT'S HOUSE - DAY   3

    DAVID is already on the video call, talking to his wife GEORGIA
    (O.S.). She is trying to tell him how to use it.

                         GEORGIA
              Look on the screen.

                          DAVID
                       (looking at her)
              Yeah.

                         GEORGIA
              No. Look at the screen. Top right-hand
              corner. There's a preferences bar ...

                          DAVID
              I'll just let you do it.

Simon appears.

                    SIMON
          David.

                    DAVID
                (turning back to the screen)
          Hi Simon!

                    SIMON
          Like this.

                    DAVID
                (overlapping)
          It worked.

                    SIMON
          We do it like this.

                    GEORGIA (O.S.)
          Is it working?

                    DAVID
                (to Georgia)
          So far.
                (back to Simon)
          That's Georgia. She's here.

                    SIMON
                (trying to lean around)
          Hi.

Georgia's face appears on the screen next to David's.

                    GEORGIA
          Hi Simon, nice to meet you.

                    SIMON
          Lovely to meet you too.

                    GEORGIA
                (overlapping)
          Sorry to hear about the play. That's a
          shame, Simon.

                    SIMON
          Thank you.

                    GEORGIA
          A real fucking shame.

                    DAVID
                (to Georgia)
          Simon wants to keep rehearsing.

                    GEORGIA
          How?

                    DAVID
                (wafting at the screen)
          Like ... this.

                              SIMON
                  Like this.

Beat.

                             GEORGIA
                  Have you spoken to Michael?

Both of them turn to look at Simon.

                              DAVID
                  Have you?

Simon takes a breath.

                              SIMON
                  Well ...

                                                    CUT TO --

4 INT. KITCHEN - DAVID AND GEORGIA TENNANT'S HOUSE — DAY   4

   GEORGIA and DAVID sit at the corner of their kitchen table. A
   laptop sits closed on the table in front of them. A beat.

                             GEORGIA
                  It will be better coming from you.

                              DAVID
                  I'm not the director.

                             GEORGIA
                  Yes, but he's your friend.

                              DAVID
                  He's not going to like it.

                             GEORGIA
                  You don't know that.

   We hear David and Georgia's children sporadically.

                          VOICE (O.S.)
                  Mum!

                             GEORGIA
                       (shouting back)
                  Yeah, okay. Hold on.

                              DAVID
                  He never really warmed to the play.

                             GEORGIA
                  That'll change.

                              DAVID
                  Or to Simon.

                             GEORGIA
                  Why was he doing it then?

                              DAVID
Well for me. I think.

                             GEORGIA
Then maybe he'll do this for you too.

                          VOICE (O.S.)
Dad!

                              DAVID
                     (also shouting back)
Yes, just coming!
                     (back to Georgia)
You seem weirdly keen on this idea?

                             GEORGIA
Not 'weirdly keen'. I just think it
might be good for you.

                              DAVID
Good for me?

                             GEORGIA
Do you remember when we went away for
the weekend, and got snowed in? Just
us and the kids. You went a little bit
mad and started spelling everything
backwards in your head.

                              DAVID
                   (remembering with concern)
Yeah.

                             GEORGIA
I don't think I could deal with it
again. So, I think the distraction might
be good for ...

                              DAVID
For you.

                             GEORGIA
For me, yeah.

                      MULTIPLE VOICES (O.S.)
Mum! Dad!

                      DAVID & GEORGIA
                     (shouting back)
JUST A MINUTE!

Georgia drops her head onto the table and David stares vacantly
in front of him. Georgia sits up and sees David.

                             GEORGIA
It's started already, hasn't it!

                              DAVID
I'll call him.
                                                   CUT TO --

ZOOM RINGING TONE. THEN --

5 INT. MICHAEL'S HOUSE AND DAVID'S HOUSE - AFTERNOON   5

MICHAEL SHEEN's face appears on the monitor, next to DAVID's
face. DAVID is looking directly into the camera. MICHAEL is at
ninety degrees to the camera, in profile, staring at something off
screen.

> **DAVID**
> Michael.

Beat.

> **DAVID (CONT'D)**
> Michael?

> **MICHAEL**
> David.

> **DAVID**
> You alright?

> **MICHAEL**
> Give me a minute.

He's still staring off screen.

> **DAVID**
> What are you looking at?

> **MICHAEL**
> I worry I'm in a Hitchcock film.

> **DAVID**
> What do you mean?

> **MICHAEL**
> The birds are coming back to Port
> Talbot.

> **DAVID**
> That's nice. Are you alright?

Michael turns to the camera. Smiles.

> **MICHAEL**
> Just adjusting. You alright?

> **DAVID**
> Yeah. Not bad.

> **MICHAEL**
> Started spelling the words backwards in
> your head yet?

> **DAVID**
> I have, yeah.

> **MICHAEL**
> Can you do 'Finsbury Park'?

I see you,
you little
feathred
Shit!

David's eyes look up as his brain works through it. It seems like a struggle.

> MICHAEL (CONT'D)
> (losing patience)
> It's Krapy Rubsnif!

> DAVID
> I nearly had it.

> MICHAEL
> I shouldn't be telling you this, you're the one who does it.

> DAVID
> It's not a skill set. It's a compulsion.

> MICHAEL
> Anna's got me painting.

> DAVID
> Is she there with you?

> MICHAEL
> She is. We were up early this morning to capture the dawn.

> DAVID
> Our family got together to sketch pineapples yesterday.

> MICHAEL
> How did you do?

> DAVID
> I'll show you mine if you show me yours.

> MICHAEL
> Seems fair.

David rises and leaves the frame to collect the sketch. Maybe we hear him on his journey. Michael turns back to his view.

He sees something, stands and steps out of frame.

> MICHAEL (O.S.) (CONT'D)
> I see you, you little feathered shit!

Michael returns to the frame and sits, passive again. David returns with a piece of paper and shows it to the camera with (perhaps) a little fanfare. It is a rudimentary sketch of a pineapple. It looks a lot like it was drawn by a child.

> MICHAEL (CONT'D)
> Very good.

> DAVID
> And yours?

Michael stoops slightly and brings up a canvas. It is a stunning oil painting of Port Talbot and the countryside around lit by an early dawn sun. The colours burn.

                    DAVID (CONT'D)
          You did that?

                    MICHAEL
          Just this morning.

                    DAVID
               (after a beat)
          Fuck off.

                    MICHAEL
          What?

                    DAVID
          You did not paint that this morning.

                    MICHAEL
          Yes I did.

                    DAVID
          You DID NOT paint that this morning.

                    MICHAEL
          I did.

                    DAVID
          I don't believe you.

                    MICHAEL
          You drew a pineapple.

                    DAVID
          My pineapple's shit.

                    MICHAEL
          It just needs some shading.

                    DAVID
          Shut up.

                    MICHAEL
          A little charcoal.

                    DAVID
          How do you know this much about art?

                    MICHAEL
          I learned about it for a role.

                    DAVID
          What role?

                    MICHAEL
          David Frost.

                    DAVID
          Could he paint?

HOW TO DRAW A PINEAPPLE

1. FIND nearest pineapple.

2. Place at eye level.

pineapple rays

3. FIND your INNER pineapple.

2m

4. Looking straight ahead, DRAW a pineapple shape.

5. Remember, keep it simple!

Delicious!

                    MICHAEL
          Are you angry at me for having a hobby?

                    DAVID
          Evidently.

Beat. They smile at each other.

                    DAVID (CONT'D)
                    (deep breath)
          Can I moot an idea with you?

Michael's eyes find David's. He's suspicious.

                    MICHAEL
          You don't use the word 'moot'.

                    DAVID
          Yes I do.

                    MICHAEL
          I've never heard you use that word.

                    DAVID
          I have, historically, used it.

                    MICHAEL
          Simon uses that word.

                    DAVID
          Does he?

Michael's eyes bore into him.

6   INT./EXT. LUCY'S HOUSE - DAY   6

    SIMON is doing his best to stave off boredom. He stares into
    space, he checks his phone, he tries to exercise, he washes his
    hands.

7   INT. MICHAEL'S HOUSE AND DAVID'S HOUSE - AFTERNOON   7

                    MICHAEL
          Simon wants to rehearse a play over the
          internet?

                    DAVID
          It's funny.

                    MICHAEL
          Is it?

                    DAVID
          We'll make it funnier. You know Simon
          speaks Italian.

                    MICHAEL
          I speak Italian.

                         DAVID
          We all speak Italian. Everybody speaks
          Italian. So, come on, what do you think?
          Are you up for it?

Suddenly Anna sets a glass of wine down in front of Michael. We
don't see her yet.

                        MICHAEL
                   (to David)
          Hang on a minute.
                   (to Anna)
          Thanks, babe.

Michael sips the wine.

                         DAVID
          Is that ... Did Anna just bring you
          wine, Michael?

Anna leans into frame.

                          ANNA
          Hi David!

                         DAVID
          Hi Anna!

                          ANNA
          Hi. Good to see you.

                         DAVID
          And you. Bit early isn't it?

                        MICHAEL
          What time did you wake up this morning?

                         DAVID
          About eight.

                        MICHAEL
          I was up at five for the dawn, so I'm
          three hours ahead of you. So it's after
          six. Cheers.

He takes a sip.

                          ANNA
          Did Michael show you his painting,
          David?

                         DAVID
          He did, yes.

                          ANNA
          Isn't it stunning.

                         DAVID
          I can scarcely believe it.

MICHAEL

We're discussing Six Characters in
Search of an Author.

ANNA

I heard about the cancellation, David.
That's such a shame.

MICHAEL

David isn't ready to give up on it yet.
He has an idea to cast it and rehearse
like this.

ANNA

Could that work?

DAVID

In theory. And then we're ahead of
everyone. When the theatres reopen, we
get our pick of the West End houses.

MICHAEL

If the birds haven't taken over by then.

He stands and walks to the window.

ANNA
                    (to David)
Has he told you about the birds?

DAVID

He mentioned a growing militia.

Michael paces behind Anna.

MICHAEL

What are we going to do, just meet up
every day ad infinitum? 'Morning David',
'Morning Michael', 'Nothing to be done',
'I'm beginning to come round to that
opinion'. It's like something out of the
damn play.

He sits. Anna runs her fingers through his hair affectionately.

ANNA

You don't do well in confinement do you.

She stands and leaves the frame.

DAVID

Look, here's how I see it. First: we're
not going anywhere. So it's a good way
to exercise our brains for a couple of
hours a day. Second ...
                    (a new thought)
Nice to see Anna, by the way.

MICHAEL

She's still here. Rooting in a cupboard
for something.

He stands to see what Anna's looking for.

> **MICHAEL (CONT'D)**
> (to David)
> So don't say anything rude.

> **DAVID**
> Your flies are open.

Michael sits.

> **MICHAEL**
> Lucky you.

> **DAVID**
> Second, I get to spend some time with a
> mate. If something comes out of it at
> the end, that's wonderful. If not, we've
> read a play a few times and got to know
> a great author.

> **MICHAEL**
> Pirandello was a fascist.

> **DAVID**
> Was he?

> **MICHAEL**
> Yes.

> **DAVID**
> Well most writers are very dubious
> people. Look at the Marquis de Sade.

> **MICHAEL**
> Look at Nabokov ...

> **DAVID**
> Hemingway ...

> **MICHAEL**
> Orwell ...

> **DAVID**
> Adolf Hitler.

> **MICHAEL**
> Shakespeare.

> **DAVID**
> Shakespeare?

> **MICHAEL**
> He was a rapacious, litigious landlord.

> **DAVID**
> But he'd stopped writing by then, hadn't
> he?

> **MICHAEL**
> Maybe.

Anna comes back into frame. She brings some extraordinary accompaniment for the wine: olives, fruit, something enviable. David reacts to it. Michael and Anna don't.

                    MICHAEL (CONT'D)
          Pirandello was a fascist, you know.

                         ANNA
          Why do you say that?

                       MICHAEL
          The play was first performed under
          Mussolini in 1921.

                         ANNA
          Mussolini only came to power in 1922.

Michael turns to her in astonishment.

                    ANNA (CONT'D)
          So Pirandello couldn't have been a
          fascist in 1921. The National Fascist
          Party didn't exist in Italy until a year
          later.

Michael looks back to David.

                       MICHAEL
          Well I still don't think he's very
          funny.

                        DAVID
          Simon's worked really hard on this. It's
          a big deal for him. Working with you. He
          said that.

                       MICHAEL
          Really?

                        DAVID
          He's always saying that. He's always
          banging on about your Hamlet. You should
          hear him. Life changing, it was, for
          him, he said, when he saw it. He was
          absolutely thrilled when you said you'd
          come on board.

                       MICHAEL
                    (softening)
          Really.

                        DAVID
          Yeah.

Michael turns back to the birds, a smile forming.

                                              CUT TO --

8 INT. KITCHEN. LUCY EVANS' HOUSE - AFTERNOON.   8

SIMON is on the phone, talking to DAVID.

> SIMON (V.O.)
> David. Hi.

> DAVID (V.O.)
> I'm going to set up a video call for all
> three of us.

> SIMON
> Is Michael on board?

> DAVID
> He wants to hear about it from you.

> SIMON
> Okay.

> DAVID
> Did you see his Hamlet?

> SIMON
> (worried)
> No.

> DAVID
> (after a beat)
> Alright. Never mind. Stand by. I'll sort
> it out.

9 INT. MICHAEL'S HOUSE, SIMON'S HOUSE AND DAVID'S HOUSE –   9

AFTERNOON

All three faces appear side by side.

> SIMON
> Hi, everyone.

> DAVID
> (at the same time)
> Afternoon, all.

> MICHAEL
> (at the same time)
> Hello, both.

Beat.

Beat.

> DAVID
> I said, 'Afternoon, all.'

> MICHAEL
> (at the same time)
> Can you hear me?

> SIMON
> (at the same time)
> Great to see you.

                         MICHAEL
              Good to see you, Simon.

                          DAVID
                    (at the same time)
              We can hear you, Michael.

                          SIMON
              Afternoon, David.

Beat.

Beat.

                       SIMON (CONT'D)
              Should I start?

                          DAVID
                    (at the same time)
              Why don't you start, Simon.

Beat.

Beat.

                      DAVID (CONT'D)
              Yes, you start.

                          SIMON
                    (at the same time)
              Sorry, David, you go ahead.

Beat.

Beat.

Beat.

                          DAVID
              Simon?

                          SIMON
                    (at the same time)
              David?

Beat.

Beat.

Beat.

Beat.

                         MICHAEL
              Well this is hardly Shakespearean.

                          SIMON
                    (taking over)
              I'll talk. David, thank you for sorting
              this. Michael, it's great to see you
              again. I'm sure you've got some

questions, but let me summarize what I'm
thinking, then we can go from there.
Sound okay?

MICHAEL

Fine by me.

DAVID

And me.

SIMON

I propose we continue casting the play,
then we rehearse the play. Like this. It
won't feel natural, but I think we might
be able to make something which people
need when this whole thing passes.

Beat. Michael leans in to the camera. Simon backs away.

MICHAEL

Why do you want to do this, Simon?

SIMON

Honestly?

MICHAEL

Honestly.

Simon opens his mouth to speak, but his image freezes. Open-
mouthed and grotesque. David and Michael continue to shuffle
slightly. Suddenly Simon's picture goes black and the words
'Connection Lost' appear.

DAVID

I think he was about to talk about your
Hamlet.

CUT TO --

10 INT. MICHAEL'S HOUSE AND DAVID'S HOUSE - AFTERNOON   10

DAVID's and MICHAEL's faces sit side by side again. Perhaps
SIMON's face is there too. Still frozen. They sit in silence for
a few seconds, waiting. Drumming fingers, etc. The end credits
play over this.

MICHAEL

I want my name first.

DAVID

What?

MICHAEL

On the poster.

DAVID

There is no poster.

MICHAEL

'Michael Sheen and David Tennant in Six
Characters.'

Connection Lost

                    DAVID
No.

                  MICHAEL
Why not?

                    DAVID
You were first on Good Omens.

                  MICHAEL
So?

                    DAVID
So it's my turn.

                  MICHAEL
God, that is so childish. It's not about
turns.

                    DAVID
Yes it is.

                  MICHAEL
No it isn't.

                    DAVID
Yes it is.

                  MICHAEL
It's about alphabetical order.

                    DAVID
No it isn't.

                  MICHAEL
Yes it is. 'Sheen' comes before
'Tennant'.

                    DAVID
'David' comes before 'Michael'.

                  MICHAEL
That's not how it works.

                    DAVID
          (continuing)
So that's one point all.

                  MICHAEL
Have you got a middle name?

                    DAVID
Yes.

                  MICHAEL
What is it?

                    DAVID
John.

                    MICHAEL
                  (victory)
          Christopher!

                     DAVID
                  (disbelieving)
          Christopher? Fuck off.

                    MICHAEL
          Two points to moi. Un point to you.

                     DAVID
          You made that up.

                    MICHAEL
          No I didn't.

David leans into the screen, typing something into a keyboard.

                MICHAEL (CONT'D)
          What are you doing?

                     DAVID
          Checking Wikipedia.

Beat. David finds the relevant information.

                DAVID (CONT'D)
          Dammit.

                    MICHAEL
                  (with relish)
          'Michael Christopher Sheen and David
          John Tennant in Six Characters ...'

                     DAVID
          It also says you're a cu--

                                        BLACK SCREEN

Episode Two
Up to No Good

MICHAEL SHEEN's and DAVID TENNANT's faces sit in boxes side by side. Over this, the credits: white letters on black.

> **MICHAEL**
> Do you know what I did yesterday?

> **DAVID**
> I do not.

> **MICHAEL**
> I walked out into the middle of the field next to us. And I screamed.

> **DAVID**
> Why?

> **MICHAEL**
> I wanted to see if anyone heard.

> **DAVID**
> Did they?

> **MICHAEL**
> Well no one came to my aid.

> **DAVID**
> Do people scream a lot up there?

> **MICHAEL**
> We do. It's how we say hello.

He lets out a short scream.

> **DAVID**
> (as if replying)
> 'Yeah, not bad thanks. How are you?'

> **MICHAEL**
> Do you scream much in Scotland?

> **DAVID**
> It's how we summon the haggis.

> **MICHAEL**
> Is that still happening in contemporary Scotland?

> **DAVID**
> It's like a rite of passage. You go onto a blasted heath, and you strip down to your tartan undercrackers, and you ...

He howls. Michael responds with professional interest.

> **DAVID (CONT'D)**
> It's a very open thing.

He howls again, sustaining it for longer this time.

                              MICHAEL
                    It's got a meaty timbre.

     They both howl together. David pauses.

                              DAVID
                    I'm hearing Tarzan with you. You know,
                    the haggis doesn't come unless you get
                    it right. We train for this for years.

                              MICHAEL
                    Listen, if the haggis doesn't come, no
                    one's going to be happy.

                              DAVID
                    Exactly.

                              MICHAEL
                    That's the Scottish tourism campaign
                    right there.

                              DAVID
                    That's true. Nicola Sturgeon can often
                    be seen on the top of a hillock.

     He demonstrates, howling again.

                              MICHAEL
                    Making her haggis come.

                              DAVID
                    Did it help? The screaming?

                              MICHAEL
                    A bit.

                              DAVID
                    I don't think I've ever tried it.

                              MICHAEL
                    Well, now's the time.

     Beat. David walks out of frame. There's a pause. From the
     distance we hear him screaming.
                                                        CUT TO --

2   EPISODE TITLE CARD   2

     Over this we hear a phone ringing somewhere.

                           MICHAEL (V.O.)
                    Can you hear that?

3   INT. MICHAEL'S, SIMON'S AND DAVID'S - MORNING   3

     SIMON, DAVID and MICHAEL are ready to rehearse for the first
     time. SIMON has made some effort: shirt and jacket. DAVID and
     MICHAEL are less committed. SIMON doodles as he speaks.

     The phone is still ringing.

                    MICHAEL
          Whose phone is that?

                    DAVID
          It's not mine.

                    SIMON
          Mine neither.

They listen together for a beat.

                    SIMON (CONT'D)
          Could we start.

But Michael holds up a finger. They wait. The ringing stops.

                    DAVID
          Yes.

                    MICHAEL
          Fine.

                    SIMON
              (deep breath)
          Great. Thanks. Well, welcome to
          rehearsals. I appreciate this is an
          unusual first day. I don't have a
          creative team to introduce you to, or a
          model box to show you. We've all got a
          copy of the play, yes?

David and Michael waft a leaf of pages at the camera.

                    SIMON (CONT'D)
          And I've got one of these.

He waves a notebook and makes an excited little gesture.

                    SIMON (CONT'D)
          Great. So, I'd like to suggest we start
          by reading the first scene through and
          asking some questions.

                    DAVID
          Sounds good to me.

                    SIMON
          But first, because we obviously don't
          know each other very well, maybe we
          could start with something to break the
          ice. So ...
              (he sings)
          'Who stole the cookie from the cookie
          jar?'
              (he takes a breath)
          'Michael stole the cookie from the
          cookie jar.'

Michael looks at him with something like horror. He might be
about to say something but the phone starts ringing again.
Michael is up in a flash and out of frame, searching.

                    DAVID
                 (leaning in)
        What the fuck was that?

                    SIMON
        I'm sorry, it's a rehearsal exercise.
        I'm nervous.

                    DAVID
        We're not at fucking Sylvia Young's.
        What are you doing?

                    SIMON
        I sing, then Michael sings.

                    DAVID
        Just be normal, for fuck's sake. He's a
        pussycat but you've got to ... You can't
        roll that shit out.

Michael is suddenly back on the screen, frighteningly close to
the camera. The phone sound is still going.

                   MICHAEL
        It's definitely from one of you.

                    DAVID
                 (showing his phone)
        It's not me.

                    SIMON
        Nor me.

But Simon turns towards the door behind him.

                   MICHAEL
        Simon?

Lucy enters behind Simon, carrying his ringing phone.

                    LUCY
        Simon. Phone. 'Jo'?

Beat. He stands, takes the phone and leaves.

                    SIMON
                 (leaving)
        Hi Jo.

Lucy remains.

                    LUCY
                 (after a pause)
        I'm Lucy, Simon's sister.

                    DAVID
        David.

                   MICHAEL
        Michael.

                         DAVID
          You live with Simon?

                         LUCY
          Actually he's living with me. This is my
          place.

                         DAVID
          It looks lovely. From here.

                         LUCY
          Thank you.

Slight awkward beat.

                      LUCY (CONT'D)
          I'm a big fan.

                        MICHAEL
          That's very kind.

                         LUCY
          I saw The Pillowman.

                         DAVID
          That was a long time ago.

                         LUCY
          Never left me.

                         DAVID
          You should say something nice to
          Michael, or he'll get jealous.

                        MICHAEL
          That is true.

                         LUCY
                   (to Michael)
          I saw your Hamlet. Twice.

                         DAVID
          Twice?

                         LUCY
          You seemed so heartbreakingly conscious
          of human potential.

Beat.

                        MICHAEL
          Well that's what I was going for.

                         DAVID
          You lying shit.

                        MICHAEL
          David. Lucy is not the first person to
          notice my heartbreaking consciousness of
          human potential.

                         DAVID
          Name one other person who has used that
          collection of words about you.

                        MICHAEL
          Tim Burton.

                         LUCY
                    (interrupting)
          I've got to get back to work.

                         DAVID
          Is Simon coming back?

                        MICHAEL
          We've earned a break.

                         LUCY
          It was lovely to meet you both.

                        MICHAEL
          You too.

                         DAVID
          Nice to chat with a theatre fan.

                        MICHAEL
          Have you seen much of Simon's work?

                         LUCY
                    (no judgement, just a fact)
          No.

Beat. Is she going to expand? No.

                        MICHAEL
          Oh.

                         DAVID
          Fair enough.

Lucy smiles and is gone.

                    DAVID (CONT'D)
                    (about Lucy)
          Lovely. Big fan of yours.

                        MICHAEL
          Yes. And your Pillowman has never left
          her. Like some sort of 18th-century STD.

                         DAVID
          Well, she had to come and see you twice.

                        MICHAEL
          Couldn't believe it the first time.

                         DAVID
          Couldn't believe it. 'That can't be what's
          passing for Hamlet these days!' she
          thought. 'I'd better go back and check.'

                              MICHAEL
                    Not only did it not leave her, she had
                    to come back. She didn't want to leave
                    it.

                              DAVID
                    What was it Tim Burton said?

                              MICHAEL
                    Word for word.
                              (imitating Tim Burton)
                    'Michael, I loved how heartbreaking your
                    consciousness of human potential was.'

                              DAVID
                    You've never actually met Tim Burton,
                    have you?

                              MICHAEL
                    No. I mean, I worked with him, but he
                    wasn't there. When's Simon coming back.

                              DAVID
                    I think we're done for the day.

He begins to pack up.

                              DAVID (CONT'D)
                    Pleasure working with you, Michael.

                              MICHAEL
                    You too, David. Never leave.

                                                    CUT TO --

4 INT. LUCY'S HOUSE AND JO'S HOUSE - DAY   4

JO is a powerful woman in the male-dominated world of theatre
producing. It's clear she doesn't suffer fools gladly.

                              JO
                    I have three questions.

                              SIMON
                    Sure.

                              JO
                    One: why is this fucking actor's agent
                    calling me every fucking hour of the
                    fucking day? He left the fucking
                    project.

                              SIMON
                    His film's been cancelled, so he wants
                    back in.

                              JO
                    And he can't be?

                              SIMON
                    No.

                              JO
Why?

                           SIMON
Michael.

                              JO
Can't they both be in it?

                           SIMON
No, there's just the two lead roles.

                              JO
What are the next biggest roles?

                           SIMON
The Mother and the Stepdaughter.

                              JO
Can you write another character?

                           STMON
No.

                              JO
Why not?

                           SIMON
It's a one-hundred-year-old
masterpiece.

                              JO
Two: how did he get my fucking number?

                           SIMON
I don't know.

                              JO
Did you give it to him?

                           SIMON
Yes.

                              JO
          (shouting O.S.)
Janine!

                        JANINE (O.S.)
Yes!

                              JO
Come here.

                           SIMON
Your assistant's with you?

                              JO
Yes.

SIMON

At your home?

JO

What benefit would she be at hers?

Jo registers Janine O.S.

JANINE (O.S.)

What do you need?

JO
(to Janine)

Cancel my phone, get me a new number.

SIMON
(to Janine)

Sorry, Janine.

JO
(back to Simon)

Three: can you handle this?

SIMON

Yep.

CUT TO --

5 INT. DAVID AND GEORGIA TENNANT'S HOUSE — MORNING   5

GEORGIA is sitting on the floor with an iPad, staring at
something on the screen. She is picking at a piece of cake.

DAVID joins her. He seems restless, in need of attention.

DAVID
(after a beat)

What are you doing?

GEORGIA

Yoga.

Beat. He looks at the iPad.

DAVID

You got some good options?

GEORGIA

I've narrowed it down to five.

DAVID

Well done. You must be exhausted.

GEORGIA

That's why I'm having cake.

DAVID

How are the kids?

GEORGIA

Quiet.

                    DAVID
Are they okay?

                  GEORGIA
I don't know.

                    DAVID
Shouldn't they be doing school?

                  GEORGIA
They're finished for the day.

                    DAVID
Really.

                  GEORGIA
Okay, I'm finished for the day. How many
fucking rainbows does a four-year-old
need to make. How are rehearsals?

                    DAVID
We've just finished for the day.

                  GEORGIA
You've only been at it an hour.

                    DAVID
It was a really intense hour.

                  GEORGIA
Well done. You must be exhausted.

                    DAVID
I am.

She feeds him a bit of the cake.

                DAVID (CONT'D)
Simon had a call with Jo. We're going to
pick up tomorrow.

                  GEORGIA
So you're done for the day?

                    DAVID
Was quite looking forward to doing
something today. Maybe I'll cook.

                  GEORGIA
Could you look after the kids?

                    DAVID
I'll cook, maybe.

                  GEORGIA
Seriously. I need to finish that final
draft.

                    DAVID
I'll cook as well.

She smiles patiently, and turns back to the cake.

CUT TO --

6 INT. MICHAEL'S HOUSE AND DAVID'S HOUSE - AFTERNOON   6

MICHAEL's and DAVID's faces next to each other. DAVID has a baby
monitor with him, which he checks occasionally. DAVID is reading
from a list, MICHAEL is scribbling things down.

> **DAVID**
> Coconut water, one bagel, grapes, pitta
> bread, leftover lasagne, two carrots,
> feta cheese and the remains of an Easter
> egg.

> **MICHAEL**
> What sort of Easter egg?

> **DAVID**
> Milky Bar.

Michael stares at his piece of paper, then screws it up.

> **MICHAEL**
> Nope.

> **DAVID**
> Nothing?

> **MICHAEL**
> Just warm up the lasagne.

> **DAVID**
> She cooked the lasagne.

> **MICHAEL**
> Garnish it with some white chocolate
> shavings.

> **DAVID**
> I promised I'd cook.

> **MICHAEL**
> You have nothing of culinary value.

> **DAVID**
> I've got two carrots.

> **MICHAEL**
> Then cook the carrots.

> **DAVID**
> You're no help.

> **MICHAEL**
> What's this in aid of?

> **DAVID**
> Georgia's novel.

> **MICHAEL**
> Yes of course.

                              DAVID
          I've been in charge of the kids this
          afternoon.

He indicates the baby monitor.

          Wanted to give her time to finish editing
          the last chapter.
          Thought 'Wouldn't it be lovely if there
          was a lovely meal prepared for her at
          the end of it?'

                            MICHAEL
          That is nice.

David takes a sip from a mug. There's a photo on it. It looks a
lot like him. Michael notices.

                        MICHAEL (CONT'D)
          Is that you on that mug?

                              DAVID
          No. Homeschooling was slowing her down.
          So ...

                            MICHAEL
          I'd jack it in. Teach them a craft
          instead. Send them up a chimney.

Beat. They try to think of another helpful craft.

                        MICHAEL (CONT'D)
          Pick-pocketing?

                              DAVID
          Like Oliver Twist?

                            MICHAEL
          You could send them out across London,
          and back they would come. Their little
          withered arms full of plunder.

                              DAVID
                    (as a Dickensian boy)
          'I bring home some neckerchiefs and
          wristwatches!'

                            MICHAEL
                    (the same)
          'I sold my legs, Father. Can I have a
          little morsel.'

                              DAVID
          That's not a bad idea.

                            MICHAEL
          Just planting seeds.

                              DAVID
          Though it is in stark contravention of
          social distancing laws.

Beat.

> **MICHAEL**
> I assumed, if you were okay with your
> children robbing total strangers, you'd
> be fine with them ignoring the two-metre
> rule too.

> **DAVID**
> Maybe. It's an ethical grey area.

> **DAVID (CONT'D)**
> You'd be a good Fagin.

> **MICHAEL**
> You'd be a good Nancy.

> **DAVID**
> Thank you. I only really see it now, but
> if I met you now for the first time, I'd
> think, 'He's up to no good.'

Michael leans into the camera.

> **MICHAEL**
> (whispers)
> I am actually up to no good.

David leans in too.

> **DAVID**
> Tell me more.

> **MICHAEL**
> It's not that bad. Really. During the
> lockdown, Anna and I have been drinking
> a little more than usual.

> **DAVID**
> That's understandable.

> **MICHAEL**
> It's not excessive.

> **DAVID**
> Of course not.

> **MICHAEL**
> But when we emptied the recycling this
> morning and got ready to take the
> bottles out to the wheelie bin on the
> road, it did look a bit ...

> **DAVID**
> Excessive.

> **MICHAEL**
> Yes. Which is why I'm nervous to leave
> the pile by the side of the road.
> Outside the house. People know it's me
> who lives here.

                              DAVID
          So? What's the plan?

                            MICHAEL
          I'm going to sneak out tonight and put
          it in my neighbour's bin.

Beat.

                              DAVID
          You can't do that?

                            MICHAEL
          Yes I can.

                              DAVID
          What if their bin's full too?

                            MICHAEL
          It won't be. She's eighty. Probably
          doesn't even recycle.

                              DAVID
          So you're sneaking out, under cover
          of night, to leave a bacchanalian
          embarrassment in your octogenarian
          neighbour's bin.

                            MICHAEL
          'Bacchanalian embarrassment'?

                              DAVID
          That's right.

                            MICHAEL
          Yes I am.

Beat.

                              DAVID
                    (shouting)
          Anna!

                            MICHAEL
          Don't even try. She knows about it.

                              DAVID
                    (shouting again)
          ANNA!

Anna appears on screen.

                             ANNA
          What?

                            MICHAEL
          David doesn't agree with our recycling
          plan.

                              DAVID
          Do you know about the plan, Anna?

                              ANNA
            I do.

                              DAVID
            And you're happy with this?

                              ANNA
            Would you rather we didn't recycle?

The absurdity of this reply stops David in his tracks. Michael
leaps on the opportunity to divert.

                            MICHAEL
                    (to Anna)
            Did you know Georgia was writing a
            novel? She's finishing today.

                              ANNA
            No! What's it about?

                              DAVID
                    (a little unsure)
            A Spanish queen and Columbus?

                              ANNA
            Isabella di Castile?

                              DAVID
                    (no idea)
            Maybe?

                              ANNA
            Wonderful.

                            MICHAEL
            I don't have the patience to write.

                              ANNA
            Of course you do.

                              DAVID
            I've been thinking about it.

                            MICHAEL
            You should. Put me in it.

                              DAVID
            I'm really proud of Georgia.

                              ANNA
            Have you told her that?

                              DAVID
            I was going to cook her dinner.

                            MICHAEL
            Something with carrots.

Suddenly a sound from the baby monitor. A slight whimper.

                              DAVID
            Hang on a sec.

The baby starts to cry.

> **MICHAEL**
> Do you need to go?

> **DAVID**
> Looks like it.

But he hears Georgia on the baby monitor, soothing the baby.

> **DAVID (CONT'D)**
> Ah, Georgia's beaten me to it.

> **GEORGIA (O.S.)**
> Sorry, just checking on the baby.

> **DAVID**
> (to Michael and Anna)
> I think she's on the phone.

He listens. We can hear Georgia too. Quiet, but clear.

> **GEORGIA (O.S.)**
> David was brilliant. So supportive.

> **DAVID**
> (whispered to the camera)
> She's saying nice things about me.

Michael and Anna lean in too.

> **MICHAEL**
> We can hear.

> **GEORGIA (O.S.)**
> It's just that he's not been the same
> since lockdown started. He's listless.
> Can't focus or get anything done.

David tries to turn the baby monitor off.

> **GEORGIA (CONT'D)**
> Yesterday he went out into the garden
> and just screamed. I'm sure it's not
> serious. Just not like him.

David tries to remove the batteries.

> The kids have noticed, which is sad.

Michael and Anna look embarrassed.

> **DAVID**
> I'm not sure how to turn this off.

CUT TO --

7   INT. MICHAEL'S, SIMON'S AND DAVID'S - MORNING   7

The next day. Three faces sit side by side. They're mid-call.

DAVID has taken GEORGIA's words to heart. He is more active.

                          DAVID
          It's not good enough, Simon.

                          SIMON
          I know.

                         MICHAEL
          You spent no small amount of effort
          persuading us to do this, then you
          disappear for a day and a night.

                          SIMON
          I'm sorry. I've been trying to solve a
          small problem.

                          DAVID
          What problem?

                          SIMON
          And I wanted to wait and come back to
          you when it was resolved.

                         MICHAEL
          And is it resolved?

                          SIMON
          Not yet.

                         MICHAEL
          What is it?

                          DAVID
          And if your face freezes like a punched
          quiche again, I'm done.

Beat. Simon takes a deep breath. He opens his mouth to speak,
but is interrupted by a doorbell. Michael leans in.

                         MICHAEL
          Do not answer that door, Simon.

                          SIMON
          It's not my door.

                          DAVID
          Well it's not mine.

It sounds again.

                         MICHAEL
          I am getting very tired of this.

Anna's voice comes from elsewhere in the house.

                       ANNA (O.S.)
          Michael. Door.

Michael stays where he is for a second.

                         MICHAEL
          I will be right back.

And he's gone. David and Simon are left.

> SIMON
>
> I'm sorry, David. I'll explain
> everything when Michael gets back.

> DAVID
>
> I just want us to focus. This has all
> been a little listless so far.

> SIMON
>
> I know, but it's the other actor. From
> before. He's been calling again and
> again. He wants to get back involved.

David's face registers horror, but Michael is suddenly back.

> MICHAEL
>
> I've got to go.

> DAVID
>
> What is it?

> MICHAEL
>
> My neighbour's at the gate. She's
> brought my fucking bottles back.

CUT TO --

8 INT. MICHAEL'S HOUSE AND DAVID'S HOUSE - AFTERNOON   8

DAVID's and MICHAEL's faces sit side by side again. The end
credits play over this.

> DAVID
>
> I've been thinking about what Georgia
> was saying, and what you were saying.
> About writing.

> MICHAEL
>
> Thinking of dipping your toe in those
> murky waters?

> DAVID
>
> Maybe. I don't think I'd want to use my
> actual name though.

> MICHAEL
>
> A nom de plume?

> DAVID
>
> Oui. Oui.

> MICHAEL
>
> Très bien. Any ideas?

> DAVID
>
> Well, my birth name is McDonald.

> MICHAEL
> (trying it out)
> 'McDonald.'

DAVID

'McDonald.'

MICHAEL

'Written by David McDonald.'

DAVID

'A novel by David McDonald.'

MICHAEL

'A play by David McDonald.'

DAVID

What do you think?

MICHAEL

I like it! Very much.

DAVID

Yeah?

MICHAEL

It's got history. It's got nobility.

DAVID

Maybe I should rebrand completely?

MICHAEL

Acting too?

DAVID

Maybe.

MICHAEL

That's bold.

DAVID

Too bold?

MICHAEL

Well now's the time.

DAVID

'Starring David McDonald.'

MICHAEL

'Starring David McDonald.'

DAVID

Of course, you know what that means.

Beat. Michael realises.

MICHAEL
(rushing at the camera)

No!

BLACK SCREEN

Episode Three

Who the F#!k Is
Michael Sheen?

1 OPENING CREDITS.   1

MICHAEL SHEEN's and DAVID TENNANT's faces sit in boxes side by
side. Over this, the credits: white letters on black.

> **DAVID**
> I think I'm losing my authority.

> **MICHAEL**
> You have authority?

> **DAVID**
> I thought so, but the children have
> started to answer back.

> **MICHAEL**
> Slippery slope.

> **DAVID**
> We're days away from a mutiny.

> **MICHAEL**
> You won't stand a chance. There are more
> of them than of you. How many have you
> got now?

> **DAVID**
> I can't quite remember. There's a couple
> I feel like I haven't seen for weeks.

> **MICHAEL**
> Understandable.

> **DAVID**
> Did your parents punish you for
> swearing?

> **MICHAEL**
> Only if they caught me.

> **DAVID**
> What would have happened?

> **MICHAEL**
> Depended on the severity.

> **DAVID**
> The low end?

> **MICHAEL**
> My mother made me drink soapy water.

> **DAVID**
> I don't think the kids would go for it.

> **MICHAEL**
> It's not supposed to be voluntary.

David sips from his mug. The picture on it still looks like him.

                    MICHAEL (CONT'D)
Are you sure that's not you on that mug?

                         DAVID
No.

                       MICHAEL
It looks like you.

                         DAVID
It's not.

                       MICHAEL
What happened?

                         DAVID
One of them swore at me.

                       MICHAEL
What did he say?

                         DAVID
She.

                       MICHAEL
                (correcting himself)
What did she say?

David tries to communicate what it is without saying it.

                    MICHAEL (CONT'D)
How old is she?

                         DAVID
Four.

                       MICHAEL
Does she know what that means?

                         DAVID
I don't think so. She just picked it up
from somewhere.

                       MICHAEL
Where?

                         DAVID
Our eldest is the obvious suspect. When
I was a kid, my dad, if we lied, made us
stand in the corner for half an hour.

                       MICHAEL
Did it stop you lying?

                         DAVID
For half an hour.
                (remembers)
What happened with your neighbour?

                       MICHAEL
She brought my bottles back.

                              DAVID
            What did you do?

                             MICHAEL
            Denied it. Told her she must be
            mistaken. Said I would be happy to
            put them outside my house, but that I
            wouldn't cover up for her again.

                              DAVID
            So you lied.

                             MICHAEL
            Yes.

                              DAVID
            I think you should stand in the corner
            for half an hour.

     Beat.

                             MICHAEL
            Alright.

     He stands and leaves the frame.

                                                    CUT TO --

2   INT. MICHAEL'S, SIMON'S AND DAVID'S - MORNING   2

     DAVID's and MICHAEL's faces are on either side of SIMON's while
     he tries to explain the problem he alluded to in Episode 2.

     Simon is doodling nervously throughout.

                              SIMON
            David knows some of this. Before we cast
            you, Michael, we were talking to someone
            else.

     Michael says nothing. His eyes bore into Simon.

                          SIMON (CONT'D)
            He's quite a big deal and always wanted
            to do a play in London. I was riding
            quite high after Killer Joe. In fact it
            was my idea to take it to David.

                              DAVID
                     (trying to help)
            And they got it to me.

                              SIMON
            Yup, and we got it to David. David
            said ...

                              DAVID
            Yes. I said yes.

                              SIMON
            We were ready to announce.

Michael still says nothing.

> **SIMON (CONT'D)**
> But then this other actor got offered a
> film so had to drop out of the project.
> We couldn't postpone so we chose to find
> someone else. David suggested you.

> **DAVID**
> Of course I did.

> **SIMON**
> Now that film he went to do has been
> cancelled, because of all this. So he's
> been calling, a lot, to ask if he can be
> involved.
> Again.

Silence. Michael takes all this in.

> **MICHAEL**
> Well. Thank you for 'suggesting me',
> David.

> **DAVID**
> Not just a suggestion. A strong
> recommendation.

> **MICHAEL**
> I was unaware you'd been submitting me
> for roles over the years.

> **DAVID**
> Advocating!

> **MICHAEL**
> Do you take a nice bit of commission on
> that?

> **DAVID**
> I just really wanted to do it with you!

> **SIMON**
> He did.

> **DAVID**
> I was thrilled when you said yes.

> **SIMON**
> We both were. Ecstatic ...

> **MICHAEL**
> (interrupting)
> I don't like you, Simon.

> **SIMON**
> No.

> **MICHAEL**
> I find you weaselly.

                              SIMON
          I understand.

                             MICHAEL
          Who is it?

                              SIMON
          I'd rather not say.

                             MICHAEL
          Does he know about me?

                              SIMON
          No. Not yet.

                             MICHAEL
          Then how exactly have you told him no?

                              SIMON
          I haven't.

                             MICHAEL
          Your reason being?

                              SIMON
          He scares me.

                             MICHAEL
          He scares you?

                              DAVID
                    (trying to help)
          He's quite an intimidating personality.

                             MICHAEL
          I can be intimidating.

                              DAVID
          I know. Yes, yes, you can.

                             MICHAEL
          I feel a very strong urge to be
          intimidating.

                              DAVID
          Yup yup yup. Well, just resist it, okay?

                              SIMON
          Please. Please.

                              DAVID
          Listen, I'm going to suggest I just
          call him up and we have a conversation,
          actor to actor.

     Simon nods and smiles, encouraged.

                          DAVID (CONT'D)
          I just tell him it's done, he had his
          chance, but we have Michael now and we
          are over the moon.

> MICHAEL
> Don't you think that we should, we
> deserve, a director who is brave enough
> to have difficult conversations like
> that?

> DAVID
> Well, we are where we are, aren't we?
> So ...

Simon's face falls.

> DAVID (CONT'D)
> ... these are exceptional times. I
> think we have to allow our individual
> exceptionalism to catch up with the
> moment. Yes?

Beat.

> MICHAEL
> Do you know how to get people to trust
> you, Simon? Honesty.

> SIMON
> Yes.

Michael signs off.

> DAVID
> And if you can't be honest ... just
> don't get caught.

Lucy enters behind Simon.

> DAVID (CONT'D)
> (seeing Lucy)
> Oh, hi Lucy!

Lucy waves, and David signs off. Simon and Lucy are alone.

> SIMON
> David's going to phone Sam.

> LUCY
> Right.

> SIMON
> I'm not doing very good at this.

Lucy pats him on the shoulder.

3 INT. DAVID'S AND THE OTHER ACTOR'S — MORNING   3

DAVID's face appears. He prepares himself for the appearance of
SAM. We will hear SAM's voice before we see him.

> SAM (V.O.)
> David.

> DAVID
> I can't see your face.

                          SAM (V.O.)
          That's a choice. Hate these fucking
          things.

                            DAVID
          Video calls?

                          SAM (V.O.)
          Everyone was happy with a fucking phone
          call before all this shit, now suddenly
          they feel this need to share a fucking
          close-up with me.

                            DAVID
          Right. Can we talk about Six Characters
          in Search of an Author?

Sam suddenly appears.

                             SAM
          You know, I've been trying to get Simon
          on the fucking phone for days. That
          motherfucker's not picking up.

                            DAVID
          He's a cock. What happened to the film?

                             SAM
          Unofficially?

                            DAVID
          Yes.

                             SAM
          The script is a mess. Then the director
          starts fucking the co-star. Her husband
          finds out. Husband stomps his ass out.
          He's in the hospital. That bitch goes to
          rehab and we lost half our locations.

                            DAVID
          And officially?

                             SAM
          They're saying global pandemic.

                            DAVID
          Silver lining. Are you still in LA?

                             SAM
          For now. I'm bored as shit.

                            DAVID
          Right.

                             SAM
          I've been trying to get hold of this
          goddamn Simon on his fucking phone, but
          like I tell you, he's not goddamn picking
          up.

                              DAVID
              I know. He said you'd called.

                               SAM
                         (interrogative)
              You talked to that motherfucker?

                              DAVID
                         (covering quickly)
              Voicemails.

                               SAM
              Alright, you know, fuck it. I say we use
              the time to work on the play. I get that
              it's strange, but we'll have something
              while everyone else is running around
              with their dick in their hand.

                              DAVID
              Right.

                               SAM
              What do you think?

                              DAVID
              What do I think?

                               SAM
              Yeah.

                              DAVID
                         (buying time)
              What do I think.

                               SAM
              Yes!

Beat. David takes a deep breath.

                              DAVID
                     (with Herculean courage)
              I think you're too late. I think you left
              the project, and us, in real trouble. I
              know why you did it, and I understand,
              but we had to pick up the pieces, and we
              did that by finding someone else. I wish
              you the best, but we've moved on.

Beat.

                               SAM
              David?

                              DAVID
              Yes?

                               SAM
              You froze. I heard, 'I think ...' then
              nothing. Could you run through all that
              shit again, please?

DAVID
(losing his nerve)
I said I think ... I think that ... I
think ...

SAM
What? You think what?

DAVID
Jo won't allow it.

SAM
What the fuck is his problem? I don't
even know this fucking Joe. Why would
that motherfucker be mad with me?

DAVID
Well, because you left the production,
she was ...

SAM
(interrupting)
She? It's a she?

DAVID
Yes.

SAM
A woman named Jo?

DAVID
Yeah.

SAM
Like Joanne? Or Josephine? Or is it just
fucking plain old Jo?

DAVID
I have no idea.

SAM
You know her, I don't even know who the
fuck she is and she's pissed off with me.

DAVID
I just know her as Jo.

SAM
I'll talk to my assistant and I'll call
her.

DAVID
Well, I wouldn't, because she doesn't
like you very much now. She doesn't want
you to derail the show, so she went
straight out and she hired another actor.

SAM
Who?

DAVID

Michael Sheen.

SAM

Who the fuck is Michael Sheen?

DAVID

Some Welsh ... British ... You'll know
him. He was in Good Omens with me?

No response from Sam.

DAVID (CONT'D)

Frost/Nixon? Passengers? Twilight?

SAM

Any of these movies make any goddamn
money?

David looks helpless.

SAM (CONT'D)

Do you want to do this with him?

DAVID

Of course not. I've worked with him
once, and I want to do it with you. But
here we are, we're stuck. Jo won't let
us change.

SAM

Tell you what. I'll call Jo.

DAVID

I wouldn't. She's not easy to talk to.
She's angry, I'd let her cool down. In
the fullness of time, when the dust is
settled, you and me will move on and we'll
do something else, something better.

Sam eyes David a little suspiciously.

4   INT. DAVID'S AND MICHAEL'S - AFTERNOON   4

Two windows side by side. GEORGIA is in one with tea. The other
is empty. GEORGIA takes a minute to herself, breathes in and out
again. ANNA comes into the empty frame and sits.

ANNA
(whispering)

Sorry.

GEORGIA
(also whispering)

Don't worry.

ANNA

Got to keep a bit quiet. Nap time.

GEORGIA

I get it. Is she down?

                              ANNA
               Not Lyra. Michael.

                              GEORGIA
               Michael has nap time?

                              ANNA
               He was a little angry earlier.

                              GEORGIA
               I heard.

                              ANNA
               So he let off some steam in the garden.
               Then he sat in the sun with his script.
               Then he fell asleep.

                              GEORGIA
               David does that. Then he pretends he was
               awake the whole time.

                              ANNA
               Michael's strangely proud of it. Claims
               he can sleep anywhere.

                              GEORGIA
               Good to have a hobby.

                              ANNA
               How are you all?

                              GEORGIA
               Good. Good. Fine.

Beat.

                              GEORGIA (CONT'D)
               There's seven of us.
                       (moving on)
               You?

                              ANNA
               We're fine. Lyra's pretty low
               maintenance.

The sound of a loud yawn and stretch from Anna's screen. She
turns and waves at Michael (O.S.).

                              ANNA (CONT'D)
               So things could be worse.

                              GEORGIA
               A friend of mine's pregnant.

Anna turns back.

                              GEORGIA (CONT'D)
               And alone.

                              ANNA
               The father not around?

                    GEORGIA
Couldn't get away from his wife.

                    ANNA
            (understanding)
Ah.

                    GEORGIA
I've offered to be her birthing partner.

                    ANNA
Is that allowed?

                    GEORGIA
I'd worry about leaving David alone.

                    ANNA
How's he doing?

                    GEORGIA
Good days and bad. I'd hoped these
rehearsals would help, but they seem
more of a hindrance so far.

Michael walks past the screen behind Anna.

                    ANNA
            (to Michael)
Just talking to Georgia.

                MICHAEL (O.S.)
            (with real pride)
Did you tell her I was asleep?

                    ANNA
I did.

                    GEORGIA
            (so Michael can hear)
Well done, Michael.

                MICHAEL (O.S.)
            (shouting)
Thank you.

                    GEORGIA
            (to Anna)
David's trying to write. I'm hoping
it'll give him something to focus on.

                    ANNA
            (remembering)
How's your novel?

                    GEORGIA
            (a little proud)
I've sold it.

                    ANNA
            (loudly)
What?

> MICHAEL (O.S.)
> What?

> ANNA
> (to Michael)
> Georgia's sold her novel.

Michael leans into shot.

> MICHAEL
> That's fantastic.

> GEORGIA
> It actually only just happened. I
> haven't told David yet.

> MICHAEL
> Mum's the word.

5 INT. MICHAEL'S HOUSE AND DAVID'S HOUSE - AFTERNOON   5

MICHAEL's and DAVID's faces next to each other. We are joining
them mid-conversation.

> DAVID
> It's all fine.

> MICHAEL
> Really?

> DAVID
> Really.

> MICHAEL
> What did you say to him?

Beat.

> DAVID
> I stood up to him. Told him he missed
> his shot. Told him we had a superior
> actor and that you weren't going
> anywhere.

> MICHAEL
> How did he take it?

> DAVID
> Well no one likes getting bad news.

> MICHAEL
> I wouldn't know.

> DAVID
> Of course not.

> MICHAEL
> But you stood your ground.

                    DAVID

I channelled Henry V: 'When the blast
of war blows in our ears, imitate the
action of the tiger.'

                   MICHAEL

You said that to him?

                    DAVID

Not out loud.

                   MICHAEL

Of course not.
Have you ever played Henry V?

                    DAVID

I have not. Have you?

                   MICHAEL

For the RSC.

                    DAVID

Of course you did. I gave the RSC my
Richard II.

                   MICHAEL

I saw it. I don't know if I would trust
Richard II in a formal negotiation
setting though.

                    DAVID

He's impassioned.

                   MICHAEL

That's true.

                    DAVID

Eloquent.

                   MICHAEL

Undeniably.

                    DAVID

Snappy dresser.

                   MICHAEL

So history would have us believe, but
perhaps not a temperamental fit for the
artistic battlefield.

                    DAVID

Perhaps not.

                   MICHAEL

I'm just saying I think you channelled
the right Shakespearean monarch.

                    DAVID

Thank you. I need to tell Simon.

                    MICHAEL
He'll be delighted.

                    DAVID
Do you have a window this afternoon to
rehearse?

                    MICHAEL
I'm afraid not. I have errands.

                    DAVID
Groceries?

                    MICHAEL
The library.

                    DAVID
Picking up or dropping off?

                    MICHAEL
Dropping off. For my neighbour.

                    DAVID
I thought that was dealt with?

                    MICHAEL
I thought so too.

                    DAVID
You denied it. You lied to a poor little
old lady.

                    MICHAEL
          (vehement)
There is nothing poor or little about
her. I'm beginning to doubt she's even
old!

                    DAVID
She rumbled you?

                    MICHAEL
She has a CCTV camera on her garage.
She was kind enough to email me a short
video clip.

This delights David.

                    DAVID
          (laughing)
What? With your arms full of bottles?
Shoving them in her bin?

                    MICHAEL
So now I do her chores.

                    DAVID
You're being blackmailed by a wee little
old lady!

                    MICHAEL
Blackmail is a strong word.

                              DAVID
                Well, it'll be nice for people to
                see you. Around the community. Local
                celebrity, Michael Sheen, visits the
                library.

    He mimes waving at the crowd.

                              MICHAEL
                Not returning books like Passion on the
                Plantation, The Smell of the Poacher,
                Ivory on Ebony. There's a sort of theme,
                isn't there.

                              DAVID
                Do you know how to get people to trust
                you, Michael?

                              MICHAEL
                Oh, piss off.

                                                CUT TO --

6 INT. SAM'S HOUSE - AFTERNOON   6

    SAM is speaking on the phone to DAVID. We can't see DAVID yet,
    but his voice can be heard coming out of a speakerphone.

                              SAM
                You said not to speak to Jo.

                         DAVID (V.O.)
                Yes.

                              SAM
                Well, I spoke to Jo.

                         DAVID (V.O.)
                Why?

                              SAM
                You told me she was furious.

                         DAVID (V.O.)
                She was!

                              SAM
                She seemed fine.

                         DAVID (V.O.)
                She's quick to forgive.

                              SAM
                Did you lie to me?

                         DAVID (V.O.)
                No.

                              SAM
                Do you want to do this play with Michael?

                         DAVID (V.O.)
                No!

We cut to our computer camera angle. Sam is still speaking to
David on the phone, but he's obviously on a Zoom call too.

> SAM
>
> Tell me again.

> DAVID (V.O.)
>
> I want to do this with you. That was
> always the plan. I was excited about the
> plan. Michael is fine. Better than fine.
> But he's not you.

As David continues, the other side of the Zoom call opens out.
Michael is there, listening.

> SAM
>
> How so?

> DAVID (V.O.)
>
> He's overbearing. He drinks too much. He
> thinks Henry V is better than Richard
> II. I've worked with him once and I'd do
> anything not to do it again.

Sam looks at Michael.

> DAVID (V.O.)
>
> But it's too late. We're in it now. I
> know you're upset but spare a thought
> for me. I'm stuck with him.

> SAM
>
> But if the situation was different?

> DAVID
>
> Are you kidding? I'd do it with you. In
> a heartbeat.

Sam nods, then holds the phone out near his computer speaker.

> MICHAEL
> (to David across computers
> and phone)
> Hello David.

Silence.

> DAVID
>
> Michael?

> MICHAEL
>
> Yes.

> DAVID
>
> Back from the library?

> MICHAEL
>
> I am.

> DAVID
>
> All the books safe.

                    MICHAEL
         No major issues.

                    SAM
         I wanted to give Michael a call. Clear
         the air.

                    DAVID
         Good of you.

                    SAM
         We had lots to talk about.

David mouths 'Fuuu' and shakes phone. Silence. Sam checks his
phone.

                    MICHAEL
         Has he gone?

                    SAM
         That motherfucker is ghost. Probably
         tucked his tail between his legs and
         ran his spineless spindly ass down the
         street like a wounded dog.

                    MICHAEL
         Give him a second.

Michael's phone starts to ring. He looks at it with disgust.

                    SAM
         Is that him?

                    MICHAEL
         It is, yeah.

The phone stops ringing. He throws it to one side.

                    SAM
         It's been nice to meet you. Big fan.

                    MICHAEL
         Thank you.

                    SAM
         Strange circumstances. Can't believe our
         paths haven't crossed before.

                    MICHAEL
         We did a movie together actually?

                    SAM
         Really. When? Were you, like, a younger
         actor? Doing background or something?

                    MICHAEL
         I had a bag over my head for most of it.

                    SAM
         A bag over your head?

                    MICHAEL
    You were torturing me all the way through?

                    SAM
                (remembering)
    Get the fuck out of here. That was you?
    You were in that film?

                    MICHAEL
    Yep.

                    SAM
    That was a great fucking movie. You were
    awesome in it. Remember the night Obama
    won his first presidency and we were
    torturing the fuck out of you.

The phone rings again.

                  SAM (CONT'D)
              (in reference to the phone)
    Do you need to get that?

Michael answers it, puts it on speakerphone.

                    MICHAEL
    David.

                  DAVID (V.O.)
    Look, I'll admit I was cowardly.

                    MICHAEL
    And you were caught.

                  DAVID (V.O.)
    And I was caught.

                    MICHAEL
    Lying.

                  DAVID (V.O.)
    Felt like the day for it.

                    MICHAEL
    So where do we go from here?

                  DAVID (V.O.)
    I want to do this with you. Sam has got
    an ego the size of a fucking tour bus,
    and I needed to manage that, and I did
    that badly, but he's not who I want to
    do this with. You've got passion. You've
    got integrity. He's got a mansion in the
    Hollywood Hills and zero imagination. I'd
    do anything not to do it with him.

Michael holds the phone out near his computer speaker.

                    SAM
    David.

Silence.

> **DAVID**
> I should have seen that coming.

> **SAM**
> Yes, motherfucker. You should have.
> What's wrong with you?

> **DAVID**
> Sorry.

> **SAM**
> Do you know how to get people to trust
> you?

> **DAVID**
> Honesty?

> **SAM**
> No! You grow a brain, and a pair of
> balls. Fuck you, David, goodbye.

Michael hangs up.

> **SAM (CONT'D)**
> Nice talking with you Michael.

                                              CUT TO --

7 INT. MICHAEL'S HOUSE AND DAVID'S HOUSE - AFTERNOON   7

MICHAEL sits in his window, looking off-screen. DAVID's window is
empty. Silence. The end credits play over this.

DAVID walks into his window and sits. He looks into the camera,
waiting, hoping for MICHAEL to acknowledge him.

> **DAVID**
> That's half an hour.

Michael doesn't answer, keeps staring off screen.

> **DAVID (CONT'D)**
> I could do another one?

Silence.

Silence.

Silence.

Michael turns to the camera.

> **MICHAEL**
> The credits will be: Michael Sheen and
> 'that fucking liar David Tennant'.

> **DAVID**
> Seems fair.

                                              BLACK SCREEN

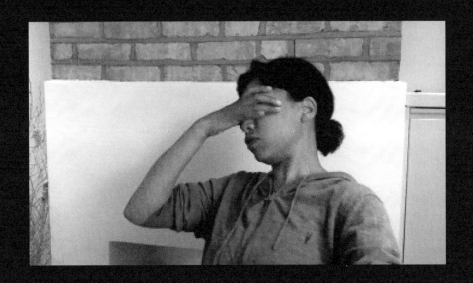

Episode Four
Bara Brith

MICHAEL SHEEN's and DAVID TENNANT's faces sit in boxes side by side. Over this, the credits: white letters on black.

> **DAVID**
> Have the photos come through?

> **MICHAEL**
> They have. Some.

> **DAVID**
> Simon says we have to pick three.

> **MICHAEL**
> Er, two zero eight nine. Mmm.

> **DAVID**
> I'm not in two zero eight nine.

> **MICHAEL**
> Oh, are you not?

> **DAVID**
> You know I'm not.

> **MICHAEL**
> I hadn't noticed.

> **DAVID**
> Needs to have both of us in it.

> **MICHAEL**
> Where were you for two zero eight nine?

> **DAVID**
> I don't know, choosing a new shirt, I think.

> **MICHAEL**
> You chose that shirt?

> **DAVID**
> Yeah, you were rude about it then. You don't get to be rude about it now.

> **MICHAEL**
> Oh, was I rude about it?

> **DAVID**
> Yeah, you were rude about it. Yeah.

> **MICHAEL**
> What did I say?

> **DAVID**
> You said I looked like a J-cloth.

> **MICHAEL**
> Huh.

Michael looks closely at his phone.

> **MICHAEL (CONT'D)**
> Is that make-up, too?

> **DAVID**
> Yes, I ... I had a little foundation,
> maybe.

> **MICHAEL**
> You look pox-ridden.

> **MICHAEL (CONT'D)**
> Why do you do that thing with your
> mouth?

> **DAVID**
> What thing?

> **MICHAEL**
> You know, you make it ... sort of
> ... sort of flat. Just like a, like a
> line, straight across your f ... like a
> muppet, you know.

Michael mutters giving his best Muppet impression.

> **DAVID**
> I don't do that.

> **MICHAEL**
> Yeah, I'm looking at twenty different
> photos of you ... I cannot see your
> teeth in one of them.

> **DAVID**
> I can't see your teeth in any of these
> either.

> **MICHAEL**
> Yeah, but I have a twinkle in my eyes.

> **DAVID**
> My eyes twinkle.

> **MICHAEL**
> No, your eyes tire.

> **DAVID**
> Tire?

> **MICHAEL**
> Like a low-impact gorgon.

> **DAVID**
> F ... fuck you.

> **MICHAEL**
> Portals on to a barren ...

                              DAVID
            Ah, Jesus.

                             MICHAEL
            ... parched, arid landscape.

                              DAVID
            I have *said* sorry.

                             MICHAEL
            And I have accepted your apology.

                              DAVID
            Well, it doesn't look like it!

2 INT. JO'S AND LUCY'S HOUSES - DAY   2

                               JO
            Have you rehearsed any of it yet?

                             SIMON
            Yes, of course.

                               JO
            How much of it?

                             SIMON
            It's difficult to quantify.

                               JO
            Give me a, a page number.

                             SIMON
            We've been starting from a more
            conceptual place.

                               JO
            What does that mean?

                             SIMON
            Well, er, it's part of my process. Um
            ... we've begun with a sort of free-
            wheeling discussion about the play.

                               JO
                         (is unconvinced)

                             SIMON
            Er, its, its themes, its inner workings
            and, and, and, and what it might say to
            a twenty-first century audience.

                               JO
            You haven't done anything, have you?

                             SIMON
            Not a thing.

                               JO
            Right.

                              SIMON
        In my defence, the business with Sam
        threw us a little off the rails.

                                JO
        Well, that was the business you failed
        to handle.

                              SIMON
        David said he would deal with it.

                                JO
        And did he?

                              SIMON
        Not really, no.

                                JO
        No. Did he make it worse?

                              SIMON
        Yes.

                                JO
        Alright. So, where are we?

                              SIMON
        Well, Sam's handled. Um, he doesn't
        wanna have anything to do with us, or
        the play any more.

Jo mutters.

                         SIMON (CONT'D)
        Which is good. Um, David and Michael are
        angry.

                                JO
        With you?

                              SIMON
        Mostly with each other.

                                JO
        Alright, Simon. Er, I know this means a
        lot to you ...

                              SIMON
                  (quickly)
        Yes, it does.

                                JO
        Yeah. It's, it's, it's a really big
        opportunity.

                              SIMON
        Yes, it is.

                                JO
        And you promised me that you were up to
        it. So, are you?

                            SIMON
            Yeah.

                             JO
            Then make some fucking progress! Make
            some fucking progress! Do something,
            will you?! Please! Please!

Beat.

            Alright, sorry. It's just, you know ...
            it's fine, it's fine what you're doing.
            Anybody could do it really. Er, I was
            ... I just expected a little bit more of
            you, that's all.

                            SIMON
            Me too.

                             JO
            Well, you know, there's no need to
            ... I don't need somebody hanging their
            head in shame. I just need somebody to
            do something for me, alright? Otherwise,
            what's the point? What's the point of
            you, really?

                            SIMON
            It's a good question.

                             JO
            Yeah, w ... alright. Alright. Well I
            think this has been constructive, so ...
            Yeah?

                            SIMON
            Yeah.

                             JO
            Yeah.

                            SIMON
            Thanks for your time.

                             JO
            Christ. Janine?!

                        JANINE (O.S.)
            What?!

                             JO
            I'm done here.

She walks off.

                        JANINE (O.S.)
            All sorted?

                          JO (O.S.)
            No. Nightmare. Fucking nightmare.

                        JANINE (O.S.)
            You should have furloughed him.

> **SIMON**
> Jo is gonna drop in on our session this
> afternoon.

> **MICHAEL**
> Why?

> **SIMON**
> Er, check in on progress.

> **MICHAEL**
> There's been progress?

> **SIMON**
> Plenty.

> **MICHAEL**
> We haven't read anything yet.

> **SIMON**
> Well, that's deliberate.

> **DAVID**
> Well, why is that?

> **SIMON**
> We've been, um, operating from a more
> conceptual space.

> **MICHAEL**
> Is Jo worried?

> **SIMON**
> No, I think she just feels left out.

> **MICHAEL**
> Left out?

> **SIMON**
> Yeah. Shall we have a look at page, um
> ... page ten?

Beat.

> **SIMON (CONT'D)**
> From, um ... 'We do not have time for
> insanity.'

> **MICHAEL**
> Sure.

> **DAVID**
> Yeah.

> **SIMON**
> Whenever you're ready, Michael.

> **MICHAEL**
> Er, 'We do not have the time for
> insanity.'

                    DAVID
'Life is crammed with insanity.'

                    MICHAEL
'What the hell do you mean?'

                    DAVID
'Your craft should be considered a
breeding ground for madness rendering
falsity as truth.'

                    MICHAEL
Are you gonna do it like that?

                    DAVID
Like what?

                    MICHAEL
Arch.

                    SIMON
Can we just carry on, actually? Michael,
it's with you. Er, 'A profession of
madmen.'

                    MICHAEL
'You think this is a profession of
madmen?'

                    DAVID
'I think that is your mission. Give life
to fantastic characters.'

                    SIMON
I'll read the stepdaughter. 'Believe
me, we are some of the most interesting
characters.'

                    DAVID
'Yes. And we, who have had the luck to
be born as characters, can laugh even at
death.'

                    MICHAEL
Can I just pause for a second? I've got
a quick question about tone.

                    DAVID
Yeah.

                    SIMON
Yep.

                    MICHAEL
So this dialogue is heightened.

                    DAVID
Yeah.

                    SIMON
Mmm-hmm.

                    MICHAEL
My impulse is to take the heat off it.
Sort of try it as natural as possible.
Try and make it sound real.

                    DAVID
Yeah.

                    SIMON
Yeah.

                    MICHAEL
And David seems to be going in a
different direction.

                    SIMON
Can we just read on?

                    MICHAEL
Sure.

                    SIMON
Yeah, we can just save questions like
that until the end.

                    DAVID
Yeah, I would like that.

                    MICHAEL
Yeah.

                    DAVID
Um, 'Because we have the fortune to
exist in a fantasy which nourishes us
for ever.'

                    MICHAEL
'So what do you want here?'

                    DAVID
'Not just to live, but to be heard.'

Beat.

                    SIMON
Michael, that, that's you.
I'll just do it, shall I?
          (reads)
Um, 'So what do you want here?'

                    DAVID
'Not just to live, but to be heard.'

                    SIMON
'For ever?'

                    DAVID
'For however long I have I wanna be
heard.' Are you done for the day,
Michael, are you?

MICHAEL

For now, yeah.

SIMON

I'll do both sides, shall I?

DAVID

Why is that?

SIMON

'How can I help?'

DAVID

Why is that?

SIMON

You guys can just listen. Er, 'I want to tell our story.'

MICHAEL

I'm having trouble with the words.

DAVID

Well, just try reading them.

MICHAEL

No, your words.

SIMON

No, look, we can discuss all of these questions at the end. That's what it's there for.

DAVID

What's wrong with my words?

MICHAEL

I'm struggling to believe them. There's a lot going on.

DAVID

A lot going on? Okay.

MICHAEL

Er, would you try something for me?

DAVID

Oh, sure. Happy to, yeah.

MICHAEL

Is that okay, Simon?

SIMON

Er, I'd rather we just pushed on, actually.

MICHAEL

It won't take a second. Just give me 'I wanna be heard' again.

DAVID
'I wanna be heard.'

MICHAEL
Simon?

SIMON
I thought that was great.

MICHAEL
You don't think he sounds cartoonish?

DAVID
Cartoonish?

MICHAEL
Yeah, I've thought it for a while now.

SIMON
Absolutely not. No, I don't.

MICHAEL
It's why Georgia hasn't asked you to do
the audio book for her novel.

DAVID
What?

MICHAEL
I'm guessing.

DAVID
She's sold her book?

SIMON
David, it's with you. 'I want to be
heard.'

DAVID
'I want to be heard.'

MICHAEL
'I wanna be heard.'

SIMON
Please, can we carry on?

MICHAEL
'I wanna be heard.'

DAVID
'I wanna be heard.'

MICHAEL
'I wanna be heard.'

DAVID
'I wanna be heard.'

MICHAEL
'I wanna be heard.'

                         DAVID
'I wanna be heard!'

                        MICHAEL
'I wanna be heard.'

                         DAVID
But ... I mean, I wanna be heard, so I'm
trying to be heard.

                        MICHAEL
I just, I just ... It's simple. I wanna
be heard.

                         DAVID
It's gotta have something behind
... I wanna be heard! It's gotta have
something behind it.

                        MICHAEL
No, it's gotta come from somewhere.

                         DAVID
Just because you're mumbling doesn't
make it good.

                        MICHAEL
I speak the same language as you. You
don't have to ...

                         DAVID
But you're barely speaking, though.
You're barely speaking ... You're
basically, you're whispering it.

                        MICHAEL
... from a different country. I wanna be
heard. Let's pretend we're all human
beings ...

                         DAVID
Yeah, who have ears that need to receive
the vibrations.

                        MICHAEL
I mean, it's not a hearing thing. It's a
sort of a feeling thing.

                         DAVID
You know, what I'm doing makes sense and
what you're doing is a sort of weird ...

Beat.

                        MICHAEL
It might sound weird to you because you
won't have been used to hearing that
coming out of yourself.

                    DAVID
It's so affected, if you don't mind me
saying. I wanna be heard.

                    MICHAEL
Isn't it interesting, Simon, that if,
if you spend a career speaking in such
a ...

                    DAVID
Is that interesting?

                    MICHAEL
... stilted sort of artificial way, then
hearing something that's truthful can
sound affected.

                    DAVID
              (mimics Michael)
I wanna be heard. It's ... I mean, yeah,
maybe for Theatr Clwyd. I don't know.

                    MICHAEL
Okay. No, let's do it your way. Let's do
it your way. Let's ... We'll do it all
your way.

                    DAVID
That's it. That's what I'm saying. No,
I'm just copying ... I'm just ... No, no,
I'm just doing it exactly ... I'm just
doing it exactly how you wanna do it.

                    MICHAEL
Ooh, listen to me, I want to be heard.

                    DAVID
Well, at least I can hear that. At least
I can hear that.
Simon. Simon. Simon.

                    MICHAEL
Is that better?

                    DAVID
I mean ...

Simon closes his eyes in frustration.

4 INT. DAVID'S HOUSE - DAY   4

GEORGIA is sitting on the stairs, clutching a 'David Tennant'
mug, talking on her mobile as DAVID slowly approaches from the
background.

                    GEORGIA
              (into mobile phone)
Yes it's all completely normal, you just
need to stay relaxed and keep breathing,
okay? It's all gonna be fine. I promise.

                    DAVID
Georgia?

                    GEORGIA
That's it, in. Out.

                    DAVID
Georgia?

                    GEORGIA
Yeah?

                    DAVID
You busy?

                    GEORGIA
Yeah, a little bit, yeah.

                    DAVID
Do I sound cartoonish to you?

                    GEORGIA
What?

                    DAVID
Cartoonish?

                    GEORGIA
No.

                    DAVID
Sure?

                    GEORGIA
Yeah, I'm sure.
          (into mobile phone)
Yeah. That's it. Deep breath in.

                    DAVID
Michael doesn't think I make it sound
real.

                    GEORGIA
          (into mobile phone)
Deep breath out.
          (to David)
 What?

                    DAVID
The play.

                    GEORGIA
Is he still angry at you?

DAVID sits on the stairs by GEORGIA.
Myrtle the dog appears and stands
motionless in the hall.

                    DAVID
I've apologised.

> GEORGIA

Okay. What did Simon say?

> DAVID

He was busy reading the other parts.

> GEORGIA

Why was he reading the other parts?

> DAVID

Michael and I were having a discussion
about tone.

> GEORGIA
> (into mobile phone)

Yeah, sorry. I'm still here. How far
apart are they now?

> DAVID

We're doing a bit for Jo later.

> GEORGIA
> (into mobile phone)

How long?

David assumes Georgia is talking to him.

> DAVID

Not long I wouldn't have thought. Oh,
you ... you're on the ... sorry
...

> GEORGIA
> (into mobile phone)

Yeah, okay, I'll phone them now.
Alright, hold on one sec.
> (to David)
Babe, can I borrow your phone?

> DAVID

Yeah.

> GEORGIA

When are you talking to Jo?

> DAVID

In about an hour.

> GEORGIA

Okay. Well, you know, she's got taste,
and all the money, so why don't you see
what she says.

She dials a number on David's mobile.

> GEORGIA (CONT'D)

Yeah, hi. I'm, I'm phoning on behalf of
Victoria Kaye. She's gone into labour
and said that you'd be able to take her
to hospital?

                    DAVID
I might do a bit of writing later.

                   GEORGIA
Yeah, that's the one.
        (to David)
That's a great idea.

                    DAVID
I've got a really good idea for this
scene where a Scottish hero takes a shit
on a Welsh twat's head.

                   GEORGIA
That sounds promising.
        (into mobile phone)
Yeah, that's the one.

                    DAVID
Did you sell your novel?

                   GEORGIA
        (into mobile phone)
Two three three. Okay.

                    DAVID
Georgia, did you sell your novel?

                   GEORGIA
Alright. Thank you. Bye-bye.
        (to David)
Yes, yes, I did, yeah.

                    DAVID
Why would you not have told me about
that?

                   GEORGIA
Because I didn't know how you were
gonna react to it.

                    DAVID
I'd have been really fucking nice about
it!

                   GEORGIA
You don't seem to be being really
fucking nice about it. I'd just like to
point out that's exactly why I didn't
tell you. Okay?
Okay, I have to go now.

                    DAVID
Where are you going?

                   GEORGIA
Vicky's gone into labour and I need to
go and help her. And you're gonna have
to stay here.

Georgia hands David his mobile.

                    GEORGIA (CONT'D)
          Are you gonna be okay meeting Jo,
          looking after the kids, cooking them
          dinner and getting them to bed?

                        DAVID
          Yes, I ... I ... can manage all that.

                      GEORGIA
          Yeah?

                        DAVID
          How long, how long you gonna be?

                      GEORGIA
          I won't be back till tomorrow.

                        DAVID
          Oh, fine.

     Beat.

                    DAVID (CONT'D)
          Beep, beep. See, that's Road Runner.

                      GEORGIA
          I know.

                        DAVID
          That's cartoonish.

                      GEORGIA
          I really appreciate it.

                        DAVID
          I can do it when I choose to do it.

                      GEORGIA
          Yeah.

                        DAVID
          Go on.

                      GEORGIA
          Okay.

                        DAVID
          Go and do your good deed, Florence
          fucking Nightingale.

5 EXT. TOWN - DAY   5

     Wild goats wandering through the deserted streets of Llandudno.

6 INT. DAVID'S, JO'S AND MICHAEL'S HOUSES - DAY   6

                        JO
          Simon tells me things have become a
          little bit tense between you?

                        DAVID
          No.

                    MICHAEL
Where is Simon?

                       JO
Um, well I'm hosting the meeting and
I'm, I'm not letting him in.

                     DAVID
Okay. Um, he, he said we were gonna read
some of the play for you today. Is that
...?

                       JO
Do you feel ready to read?

                     DAVID
Sure.

                    MICHAEL
Easy peasy.

                     DAVID
Er, but Simon said we haven't actually
spent a lot of time on the actual text.

                       JO
No.

                     DAVID
Yeah. No, we've been operating from a
more conceptual place.

David drinks from his 'David Tennant' mug.

                       JO
Is that you on that mug?

                     DAVID
No.

He quickly puts it down. Michael reacts.

                       JO
How serious is this?
You don't need to put your hand up.

                     DAVID
Michael's being insufferable.

                    MICHAEL
Ah, ha ha ha ha.

                       JO
Okay. Let's try and be a bit more
constructive ... No, you ... no, you
don't have to put your hand up.

                     DAVID
Well, do you think that I sound
cartoonish?

                              JO

No.

                            DAVID

Right. Well, because Michael's upset,
he started throwing around some very
unhelpful phrases.

                              JO

Well, why is Michael upset?

                            DAVID

Well, Michael is upset, Jo, because
he didn't realise that he was second
choice for the role which ... because
apparently that has never happened in
the history of theatre ever.

                              JO

We, we really don't need to keep raising
our hands, so ...
Michael.

                           MICHAEL

Um, it is true that I have never been
the second choice before.

                            DAVID

Sorry, is that, that's, that's literally
your complete point, is it?

                           MICHAEL

I'd like it noted.

                            DAVID

I mean, do you see what I'm having to
work with?

                              JO

Is that why you're upset, Michael?

                           MICHAEL

No. No, I'm upset because David and
Simon are fucking liars.

                              JO

Alright, I admit, it was handled badly
... Yes, David.

                            DAVID

Yes. I will absolutely hold my hand
up that I did hold some stuff back.
The reason I did that is because of
my experience of Michael I knew that
at this time he would become overly
sensitive.

                           MICHAEL

Oh, fuck! Come on!

DAVID

I didn't wanna hold things up because I
knew that we had limited time!

MICHAEL

No, no. No, let's not play the blame
game! Let's not start doing that!

DAVID

Start doing what?!

MICHAEL

Pointing fucking fingers, you Scottish
... ! That is you on that fucking mug!

David grabs his mug and holds it up.

DAVID

Oh, what? Oh, this mug? This mug here.
This one here? Yeah, look at that. Look
at that, my fucking face!

MICHAEL

Yes! You narcissistic Scottish man, boy,
child.

DAVID

Listen, I'm gonna fill this mug full of
your tears and make you drink them.

JO

Let's just all take a step back.

Yeah. That was impressive.

MICHAEL

Sorry. Look, Jo.

JO

Yeah.

MICHAEL

You know as well as I do that I add
concrete value to any project that I'm a
part of.

David picks up on Michael's pronunciation of 'concrete'.

DAVID

Sorry, you add conCRETE value?

MICHAEL

That's what I said.

DAVID

ConCRETE value? Is that the same as
CONcrete value?

MICHAEL

I said CONcrete.

DAVID

You said conCRETE.

MICHAEL

I know what I said!

DAVID

You said conCRETE! It's funny, cos I thought, I thought you were classically trained. I thought you'd know, you know, where to put the emPHAsis on a word, but apparently not.

MICHAEL

I bring gravitas which is very important ...

DAVID

Well, I bring charm which is more important.

JO

Alright, that's ...
No one, no one is doubting what either of you bring to the party, alright. I just want to get this resolved.
The play is a classic. You are both exceptional. And Simon, he really knows what he's doing. He does. We, we have a chance here to come out of all of this with something really special, if we can just resolve ... can we resolve this, please?
David?

DAVID

Yeah.

JO

Yes? Thank you. Yes. Michael?

MICHAEL

I'm sorry. I just, you know, I just wanna make sure that I don't get over-sensitive.

DAVID

Oh, such bullshit!

MICHAEL

See. See. David needs to calm down, too.

DAVID

Such bullshit! Oh, do ... yeah, do I? Cos when I get over-emotional I start to sound cartoonish, don't I?!

MICHAEL

Oh, I've heard that about you as well, yeah.

DAVID

Fuck it! I wrote a scene today about me taking a shit on your big fucking Welsh hairy head!

MICHAEL

Yeah, well, if ...

Michael's mobile phone chimes.

MICHAEL (CONT'D)

Oh ... sh ... Right, I've gotta go. Sorry. Um, I'll be back. I've just gotta drop some shopping off for my neighbour.

JO

Oh, that's kind.
Isn't it? Isn't it? That's kind of him, David.

DAVID

No. She's blackmailing him.

JO

Right. Why?

DAVID

Because he's a lush.

MICHAEL

She's harmless, okay. And she's alone.

JO

Does she have any family?

MICHAEL

Er, her children are stuck in Cardiff. It's no trouble. I just pick up the shopping, I drop it round at four. I ring the doorbell, out she pops. We say hello and hello, and that's the end of it. I did it yesterday and she made me a bara brith to say thank you.

DAVID

Oh, so it's a symbiotic relationship, then?

JO

What's a bara brith, Michael?

MICHAEL

Um, it's a Welsh fruitcake.

DAVID

Takes one to know one!

MICHAEL

Don't, don't ...

                              JO
          What are you dropping off to her today?

                           MICHAEL
          Um ...

Michael takes out a shopping list and unfolds it.

                       MICHAEL (CONT'D)
          ... mixed fruit, sugar, tea, mixed spice,
          flour and eggs.

                           DAVID
          What's she making you today?

                           MICHAEL
          Er, it's another bara brith, innit.
          Alright, hang on.

He stands and steps away.

                           DAVID
          Simon up to this?

                              JO
          He is terrified of you both.

                           DAVID
          Why?

                              JO
          Cos you're behaving like twats. You're
          twats.

                           DAVID
          Yeah. I mean, it'll be fine. We went
          through half a dozen of these in Good
          Omens.

                              JO
          And how did you resolve it then?

                           DAVID
          Battleships.

                              JO
          Battleships?

                           DAVID
          Mmm.

                              JO
          Like with a pen and ... paper and a grid
          with the ... hit and miss and ...?

                           DAVID
          Mmm-hmm. Yeah. Yeah.

Michael enters.

JO

You're back.

DAVID

Just telling Jo about Battleships.

MICHAEL

Oh, yeah.

DAVID

You alright?

MICHAEL

She didn't answer the door.

7 INT. DAVID'S AND MICHAEL'S HOUSES - DAY   7

MICHAEL and DAVID are playing Battleships. The end credits play over this.

MICHAEL

I think the world would be a much better place if more problems ... were resolved like this.

DAVID

'E' four.

Michael imitates an 'incorrect' buzzer.

MICHAEL

Miss.

DAVID

Well, it's certainly helped us over the years, innit?

MICHAEL

Mmm. Do you think it's game specific?

DAVID

We can try something else if you want?

MICHAEL

Like what?

DAVID

Twister.

MICHAEL

It's too sexual. 'B' two.

DAVID

Is a miss. Chess?

MICHAEL

Nah, it's too complex. Snakes and Ladders?

DAVID

Ah, now you're talking. Yeah. Er, 'D' two.

DAVID'S SHIPS

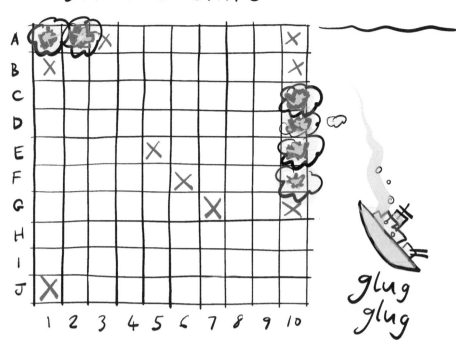

glug
glug

MICHAEL'S SHIPS

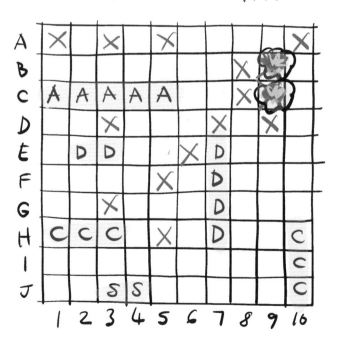

                        MICHAEL
Hit!

                    DAVID/MICHAEL
A very palpable hit!

                        MICHAEL
Er, I'm sorry I let the cat out of the
bag about Georgia's novel.

                        DAVID
It's alright.

                        MICHAEL
'B' three?

                        DAVID
Is a miss.

                        MICHAEL
And that I said you were cartoonish. That
wasn't fair.

                        DAVID
Well, I mean, it's not so bad cos I am,
after all, the voice of Scrooge McDuck.

                        MICHAEL
Er, is that ...

Michael imitates a talking duck.

                        DAVID
What, the voice of Scrooge McDuck?

                        MICHAEL
Yeah.

                        DAVID
No.

                        MICHAEL
Who's that, then?

                        DAVID
I mean, I ... I have no idea. That's like
nothing I've ever heard on Earth. Right.
Um, 'D' three.

                        MICHAEL
I'll do it as Mickey Mouse. 'You've sunk
my battleship.'

                        DAVID
            (imitates Mickey Mouse)
'Victory is mine.'
Does this victory mean we get to re-
explore the conversation about credits?

Beat.

MICHAEL
Ah, you can have it.

Michael is clearly preoccupied.

DAVID
She'll be fine. Michael, she'll be fine.

BLACK SCREEN

Episode Five
Ulysses

EXT/INT. DAVID'S AND MICHAEL'S HOUSES - DAY

> DAVID sitting on his patio. MICHAEL in his living room. Over
> this, the credits: white letters on black.

                    MICHAEL
> I had a dream about you last night.

                    DAVID
> Oh, yeah.

                    MICHAEL
> That, that doesn't seem to worry you?

                    DAVID
> Not uncommon.

                    MICHAEL
> What?

                    DAVID
> Happens all the time.

                    MICHAEL
> Not to me.

                    DAVID
> No?

                    MICHAEL
> No, I can confidently say I haven't, I've
> never dreamt about you before.

                    DAVID
> Never ever?

                    MICHAEL
> No.

                    DAVID
> Missing out.

                    MICHAEL
> Why, do you dream about me?

                    DAVID
> Yeah, all the time.

                    MICHAEL
> So in this dream, um, I was, I was in a
> theatre.

                    DAVID
> Course you were, love.

                    MICHAEL
> I was on the stage.

                    DAVID
> Of course you were.

MICHAEL

Alone. And, um the lights were shining
on my face, so I, I couldn't see the
auditorium, I couldn't, couldn't see
if there was anyone out there. And
suddenly this, this idea occurred to me.
Speak and the room will answer. So I
spoke, but the voice that came out was
diffcrcnt.

DAVID

Whose voice was it?

MICHAEL

Well, no, it was, it was still my voice.
It was, it was just that it had changed.
It was like I'd inhaled helium.

DAVID

And did the room answer?

MICHAEL

They brought the house lights up and the
theatre was empty except for you.
You were watching. Alone.

DAVID

And what did I say?

MICHAEL

'Happy the man, whose wish and care A
few paternal acres bound,
Content to breathe his native air,
In his own ground.'

DAVID

Did I write that?

MICHAEL

No. It ... No, it was in my dream.

DAVID

So, what does it mean, then?

MICHAEL

That I'm pining for a bigger audience.

DAVID

And what about the poem?

MICHAEL

That I should be happy at home.

DAVID

Are you not?

MICHAEL
     (softly)

I'm trying.

ADRIAN LESTER in his living room. SIMON in his living room.

> **ADRIAN**
> I feel fantastic.

> **SIMON**
> That's great.

> **ADRIAN**
> Yeah. I mean, the situation is horrific.

> **SIMON**
> Sure.

> **ADRIAN**
> Globally.

> **SIMON**
> Yeah, I know. I understand.

> **ADRIAN**
> But the time, the time is a gift.

> **SIMON**
> Such a, such a great way of looking at it.

> **ADRIAN**
> Have you read Ulysses?

> **SIMON**
> James Joyce?

> **ADRIAN**
> Yeah.

> **SIMON**
> No.

> **ADRIAN**
> Twice.

> **SIMON**
> You've read Ulysses twice?

> **ADRIAN**
> Yeah. About to go for a third.

Lucy Eaton enters.

> **SIMON**
> That's amazing.

She leans in front of Simon.

> **LUCY**
> (softly)
> Sorry, I just ...

                              SIMON
            Oh, er ... er, Lucy, this is, er, this
            is Adrian Lester.

                              LUCY
            Oh, hi.

                              ADRIAN
            Hi. Hiya.

                              SIMON
            Er, Adrian, this is my sister Lucy.

                              ADRIAN
            Lovely to meet you.

                              LUCY
            Yeah, you too.

                              SIMON
            We were just discussing Ulysses.

                              ADRIAN
            Have you read it, Lucy?

                              LUCY
            Oh God, yeah, twice.

                              ADRIAN
            Oh, me too.

                              LUCY
            Oh, it's sublime.

                              ADRIAN
            Yeah, I'm about to go for a third.

                              LUCY
            Ooh, magical.

                              ADRIAN
            How are you coping through this?

                              LUCY
            Just keeping an eye on this one really.

                              ADRIAN
            Fantastic.

                              LUCY
            Yeah, we're managing alright.

We hear Simon's computer chime.

                              SIMON
            Yeah. Oh, here's Michael.

                              LUCY
            I'll leave you to it.

> **ADRIAN**
> Okay. Er, lovely to meet you.

> **LUCY**
> Yeah, you too.

> **ADRIAN**
> She's lovely.

> **SIMON**
> Oh, she is. Er, happy for me to bring in
> Michael?

> **ADRIAN**
> Yeah, yeah, course.

> **SIMON**
> Oh, er, so they don't know you're here.
> Um, I mean, they'll know who you are,
> obviously, but I think I will just
> introduce you as a new cast member and
> then you can talk me up a bit.

Beat.

> **ADRIAN**
> Er, is there actually a part for me?

> **SIMON**
> Sure.

> **ADRIAN**
> Because the next roles seem to be, um,
> the mother and stepdaughter.

Simon quickly changes the subject.

> **SIMON**
> Er, here's Michael.

Michael's room appears with an empty chair.

> **SIMON (CONT'D)**
> (calls)
> Michael?

> **MICHAEL (O.S.)**
> (shouts)
> I can't find my fucking script!

> **ADRIAN**
> Has it been going well?

> **SIMON**
> Really well. Yeah, seamless.

We see Michael stride past.

> **MICHAEL**
> (shouts)
> Where the fuck is it!

> SIMON

It's an unusual set of circumstances, obviously.

Michael enters and sits.

> MICHAEL

Fuck! I just, I c ... I can't find it anywhere. You'll just have to feed me the lines and I'll try and keep up.

> ADRIAN

Hi, Michael.

> SIMON

Michael, do you know Adrian?

> MICHAEL

Adrian?

> ADRIAN

Er, Adrian. Hi.

> MICHAEL

Adrian! Oh my God, of, of course. I'm so, I'm so sorry.

> ADRIAN

No, not a problem.

> SIMON

I just thought, I thought he could join the cast.

> MICHAEL

Lovely.

> ADRIAN

How are ya?

> MICHAEL

Good. Great. Fine.

A beat.

> MICHAEL (CONT'D)

You?

> ADRIAN

Oh, I'm, I'm, I'm fantastic.

> MICHAEL

Oh, that's great.

> SIMON

Adrian's been reading Ulysses.

> ADRIAN

Er, twice.

> MICHAEL

Well, it's a tough book.

We hear a computer chime.

> SIMON

> Here's David, too.

> MICHAEL

> Oh, bring him in.

> ADRIAN

> Simon says it's been going well, er
> ...

> MICHAEL

> Oh, well, David's a wonderful
> collaborator.

David leans in close to the screen.

> DAVID

> My script has completely vanished.

> MICHAEL

> Very focused.

> DAVID

> I mean, if it was anything of any value,
> I'd just assume the kids had taken it.
> But it's just a shit play.

> MICHAEL

> Yeah, David, do you know Adrian Lester?

We cut in and alternate between them.

> DAVID (O.S.)

> Ah, Jesus, Adrian Lester, fucking hell!

> MICHAEL

> Yeah, no, he's, he's here, he's here now
> on the call with Simon right now.

> DAVID

> Oh, there he is!

> ADRIAN

> Hello, David.

> DAVID

> Hey, Adrian. How you doing?

> ADRIAN

> Um, I'm fantastic.

> SIMON

> I thought Adrian could join our cast.

> DAVID

> Great.

> SIMON

> He and I have worked together before, so
> ...

> DAVID

Brilliant.

> SIMON

Just thought we could flesh this cast out
a little bit.

> DAVID

Yeah, absolutely.

A beat.

> MICHAEL

Er, have you, have you read Ulysses,
David?

> DAVID

No, never.

> MICHAEL

No. Adrian's read it twice.

> DAVID

Wow.
>> (to Adrian)
I imagine it's quite hard to understand
the first time through, isn't it?
>> (to Simon)
Simon, would you just email me the
script again, please?

> SIMON

Er, er, yeah, I have to use the other
computer.

> DAVID

That'd be great, thanks.

Silence.

> SIMON

Be right back.

> ADRIAN

Okay.

Simon stands and walks off.

> ADRIAN (CONT'D)

Oh, I'm really excited to be working
with you both. Simon's great, isn't he?
He's ...

> DAVID

Michael's feeling a bit blue about the
project.

> MICHAEL

Er, I mean, I'd say David was struggling
more.

ADRIAN

Is, is that right?

MICHAEL

Yeah, he's, he's trying to write
something.

DAVID

Yeah, nearly finished, actually.

MICHAEL

Yeah but it's been very tough.

ADRIAN

Oh yeah, the creative process can be
very tricky.

MICHAEL

And Georgia is better at it than he is,
so ...

ADRIAN

You should speak to Simon about it
because ...

DAVID

Michael's neighbour's gone missing.

ADRIAN

Missing?

DAVID

Under suspicious circumstances.

MICHAEL

I ... well I haven't killed her or
anything. I mean she's just not
answering the door.

ADRIAN

That ... that ... must be very
frightening.

MICHAEL

Georgia's birthing a child.

ADRIAN

Oh, you're having another one?

MICHAEL

With another woman.

DAVID

Yeah.

ADRIAN

Well, that's, that's modern.

DAVID

She's helping a friend ...

ADRIAN

So, how are rehearsals going?

DAVID

I mean, Michael's finding it quite hard to
focus. He's started having dark, upsetting
dreams. Really deep, weird, sort of
disturbing dreams.

ADRIAN

Wow, really? Me too.

MICHAEL

Really?

ADRIAN

Yeah. Yeah, most nights.

DAVID

Am I in your dreams?

ADRIAN

No.

DAVID

Hmm.

MICHAEL

David keeps popping up in the collective
subconscious, uninvited, like a sort of
highland whack-a-mole. You just gotta ...

He mimes whacking the mole with a mallet.

ADRIAN

You know, I was in the theatre in mine.

MICHAEL

Me too.

ADRIAN

What, on stage?

MICHAEL

Yes!
          (mutters)
Did we have the same dream?

ADRIAN

Could you speak in yours?

MICHAEL

No, no, I just had a sort of weird high-
pitched sound.

ADRIAN

Yes! Yes! In, in mine I was lying on the
stage and I was, I was trying to scream,
get a sound out, and I, and I couldn't, so
I started twisting and turning and trying
to scream. And then, and then these ropes

ADRIAN (CONT'D)

came out of nowhere and they, and they
were covered in oil, I think, and they
were wrapping around me, wrapped around
me really tight and I couldn't move. Then
the audience, they started shouting,
'Throw him to the bears.'

DAVID

That's vivid.

ADRIAN

Maybe it was honey, maybe it was honey,
not oil on the ropes. Honey. For the
bears.

DAVID

And what did you do?

ADRIAN

Fought them with my hands and my teeth,
just ...
            (groans)

DAVID

Yeah, sure. But I meant more in real life.

ADRIAN

Oh, well, I spoke to my, er, spoke to my
life coach about it.

DAVID

Great. What did he say?

ADRIAN

Well, he told me that it was connected,
er, to a repressed feeling of, of
powerlessness.

MICHAEL

And what did he suggest?

ADRIAN

He told me to just ignore it. Yeah,
just, just breathe it in.
            (inhales)
Breathe it out.
            (exhales)

DAVID

Did it work?

ADRIAN

Yeah. Yeah, it did, actually. It did,
yeah. So now, whenever I feel, you know,
sad, or angry, or powerless, I just, er,
just ignore it.

DAVID

How?

A beat.

                    ADRIAN
          Just ...
                    (exhales)
          ... ignore it.

Michael and David sit in stunned silence.

                ADRIAN (CONT'D)
          Or, or sometimes I go for a little run.

                    DAVID
          When you're down?

                    ADRIAN
          Yeah, that's right.

                    MICHAEL
          How far do you run?

                    ADRIAN
          About twenty miles a day.

                    DAVID
          That, that's a lot.

                    ADRIAN
          It just gives me time to be alone, you
          know, with my thoughts.

                    MICHAEL
          Well, it's nice to have company.

3 INT. LUCY'S HOUSE - DAY   3

  SIMON in the hall. He clutches his mobile phone as he listens at
  a closed door.

                    LUCY
          What are you doing?

                    SIMON
          Sshhh. I'm emailing a script to David.

                    LUCY
          You're snooping.

                    SIMON
          I'm not snooping.

She listens at the closed door.

                    LUCY
          Did you bring Adrian in just to talk you
          up?

                    SIMON
          No, there were other things.

They listen.

Silence.

                              LUCY
            What's he saying?

                              SIMON
            I can't hear if you keep talking.

                              LUCY
            He likes you, doesn't he?

                          LUCY (CONT'D)
            Oh, sshh, sshh.

Simon chuckles softly as they continue to listen.

                              SIMON
                        (softly)
            What do you think he's saying about me?

4 INT. MICHAEL'S, ADRIAN'S AND DAVID'S HOUSES - DAY   4

                              ADRIAN
            And I'm eating well as well, you know.
            Spending more time with my family.
            Reconnecting with my roots.

                              DAVID
            Yeah, I thought I could detect a little
            bit of a hum of an accent in there.

                              ADRIAN
            Oh what, can you, can you actually hear
            it?

                              DAVID
            Yeah.

                              MICHAEL
            Very, very subtle.

                              ADRIAN
            Yeah, it's not a conscious thing.

                              MICHAEL
            No, of course not, no.

                              ADRIAN
            Have either of you two read The Inner
            Voice?

                              DAVID
            No.

                              MICHAEL
            Twice.

                              ADRIAN
            It's about the artifice of acting.

                         DAVID
          Great.

                         ADRIAN
          Yeah, it's about the artifice of acting
          and the, the, the freedom which comes
          from throwing off the mask of an RP
          accent and embracing a true inner voice.

                         DAVID
          That sounds fucking brilliant.

                         ADRIAN
          Mmm, isn't it? Cos Shakespeare, right,
          was from Birmingham.

                         DAVID
          Was he? I mean, bit down the road but
          ...

Adrian adopts his best Birmingham accent.

                         ADRIAN
          'We are such stuff
          As dreams are made on; and our little life
          Is rounded with a sleep.'

A beat.

                         MICHAEL
          And that's Shakespeare.

                         ADRIAN
          Have either of you two thought about,
          you know, leaning into your own true
          voice?

                         MICHAEL
          I didn't think I wasn't.

                         ADRIAN
          Oh well, Mike, if I may.

                         DAVID
          Oh you may, yeah.

                         ADRIAN
          You speak and the sound that emerges,
          it's, oh, it's, it's unfiltered, you
          know, raw! Like, like, like ...
                    (clears throat)
          Watch.

Adrian composes himself and produces his Birmingham accent.

                      ADRIAN (CONT'D)
          'This above all: to thine own self be
          true.'
          Huh? Could you, could you feel ... Have
          a go. Go on, have a go.

Michael quickly passes this on.

> **MICHAEL**
> Dave.

> **DAVID**
> Thanks. Um ...
> 'To thine own self be true.'

A beat.

> **ADRIAN**
> That's great, but a little less RP.

> **DAVID**
> I wasn't doing RP.

> **MICHAEL**
> Just a little less RP, Dave.

> **DAVID**
> I'm from Paisley.

> **ADRIAN**
> Trust me, trust me. Go on.

> **MICHAEL**
> Trust him.

> **DAVID**
> 'To thine own self be true.'

> **ADRIAN**
> Yes.
>> (to Michael)
> Michael.

> **MICHAEL**
> 'To thine own self be true.'

> **ADRIAN**
> Yes, more. More. More.

> **DAVID**
> 'To thine own self be true.'

> **MICHAEL**
> 'To thine own self be true.'

> **ADRIAN**
> 'To thine own self be true.'

> **DAVID**
> 'To thine own self be true, you barm
> pot'

> **ADRIAN**
> Be true.

                    MICHAEL
                (mimics Tom Jones)
          'To thine own self be true.' Think I
          better dance now. Huh!

Michael stands and hurries off.

                    DAVID
                (recites - mimics Sean Connery)
          'To thine own self be true.'

                    ADRIAN
          Is ... is he alright?

                    DAVID
          Yeah, he's fine.

                    ADRIAN
          You know, with the hair and the, and the
          beard, he just looks a bit ...

                    DAVID
          What?

                    ADRIAN
          Wild.

                    DAVID
          Nah, he's fine.

                    ADRIAN
          Okay.

A beat.

          And what about you? Are you alright?
          I mean, you could talk to Simon about
          these things cos he's really ...

                    DAVID
          Thing about Michael is, he feels
          helpless. And it's sobering. Cos, you
          know, you reach the top of the tree and
          then the world changes all around you
          and you find you can't help any more.
          You're just ... you're sat at home
          spelling words backwards in your head.

                    ADRIAN
          What, is he doing that?

                    DAVID
          All the time. Yeah ... You just stop
          feeling useful, don't you? You just
          ... you know, the theatres close, the
          audiences go away, the roles dry up. I
          mean, you've got nothing to offer. You're
          just sat looking at a window, twiddling
          your thumbs, hoping ... it's all gonna
          be alright.

Adrian exhales. Inhales. Exhales.

Silence.

                          ADRIAN
          I'm gonna go for a run.

                          DAVID
          Sure.

A computer chimes as Adrian leaves the call.

Michael enters clutching his script.

                          MICHAEL
          Found my script.

A beat.

                          DAVID
          Where was it?

                          MICHAEL
          I threw it in the bin last night.

                          DAVID
          The bin!

He stands and steps away.

                          MICHAEL
          Where's Adrian?

                          DAVID
          Gone for a run.

A computer chimes as David leaves the call.

                          MICHAEL
          Ah.

                          SIMON
          Where's Adrian?

                          MICHAEL
          Gone for a run.

Silence.

5 INT. DAVID'S HOUSE - DAY   5

GEORGIA TENNANT enters through the front door. She crouches as
Myrtle their dog greets her.

                          GEORGIA
          Hi.

She stands and puts down her handbag. She checks a cupboard and
smells a towel from a folded pile of washing on the worktop.

She passes and stops by the closed bedroom doors.

                          OLIVE (O.S.)
          'The Magic Tree by Olive Tennant.'

She listens as Olive continues, inaudibly. She steps away.

David sitting at the dining table, clutching a large glass of wine.

>   **GEORGIA**
>   Oh, hi.

>   **DAVID**
>   Oh, hello.

>   **GEORGIA**
>   Hello.

Georgia leans in, kisses David and sits.

>   **DAVID**
>   How'd it go?

>   **GEORGIA**
>   Fine, yeah. She had a girl.

>   **DAVID**
>   Nice.

>   **GEORGIA**
>   Helen.

>   **DAVID**
>   Very nice.

>   **GEORGIA**
>   Mmm.

>   **DAVID**
>   You alright?

>   **GEORGIA**
>   Yeah, fine. The, um, the house appears to
>   still be standing.

>   **DAVID**
>   I'm sensing your surprise.

>   **GEORGIA**
>   Well, I'm not trying to hide it.

>   **DAVID**
>   Well, that takes some of the fun away.

>   **GEORGIA**
>   Mmm. I did listen outside the kids'
>   doors. Online lessons?

>   **DAVID**
>   That's right.

>   **GEORGIA**
>   Did you try and teach them at all
>   yourself?

                    DAVID
         I did, yeah.

                    GEORGIA
         Yeah. And how did that go?

                    DAVID
         I realised that I am alarmingly ill-
         informed on every subject under the sun.

                    GEORGIA
         Yeah, well, that is true.

                    DAVID
         I wish I didn't feel so helpless.

                    GEORGIA
         Is the writing not going very well?

A beat.

                    DAVID
         Actually, I finished the screenplay.

                    GEORGIA
         Ooh.

                    DAVID
         So, yeah.

                    GEORGIA
         Can I read it?

                    DAVID
         No, you can't.

                    GEORGIA
         Oh, why not?

                    DAVID
         Because it might be shit.

                    GEORGIA
         Well, I'm sure that I could help.

A beat.

                    DAVID
         It's already in your inbox. I sent it
         like an hour ago.

                    GEORGIA
         Oh, exciting.
                (reads on her mobile)
         Oh, Behind Windows.

                    DAVID
         You like it?

                    GEORGIA
         Mmm, bit wanky.

                              DAVID
                Oh, come on. You can't say that.

                              GEORGIA
                Oh, I can.

                              DAVID
                You don't even know what's in it yet.

                              GEORGIA
                What's in it, then?

A beat.

                              DAVID
                You know, lots of things.

Another beat.

                              GEORGIA
                Well, it sounds excellent.

                              DAVID
                Oh, fuck off back to the hospital.

                              GEORGIA
                Okay, maybe I will.

                              DAVID
                But read my screenplay first.

                              GEORGIA
                Yeah, sure. I will but I'm gonna phone
                Anna first. Okay? Oh, and also ... take
                that.

Georgia takes David's glass of red wine and turns his laptop to
face her.

                              DAVID
                Oh, lovely. Well, I'm glad you got your
                priorities right.

                              GEORGIA
                Okay.

David stands and walks off.

                              DAVID
                Okay. See you later.

                              GEORGIA
                See you.

6 INT. DAVID'S AND MICHAEL'S HOUSES - EVENING   6

ANNA and GEORGIA on their computers.

                              ANNA
                Hi. Sorry. I'm just gonna minimise you
                while I look something up, okay?

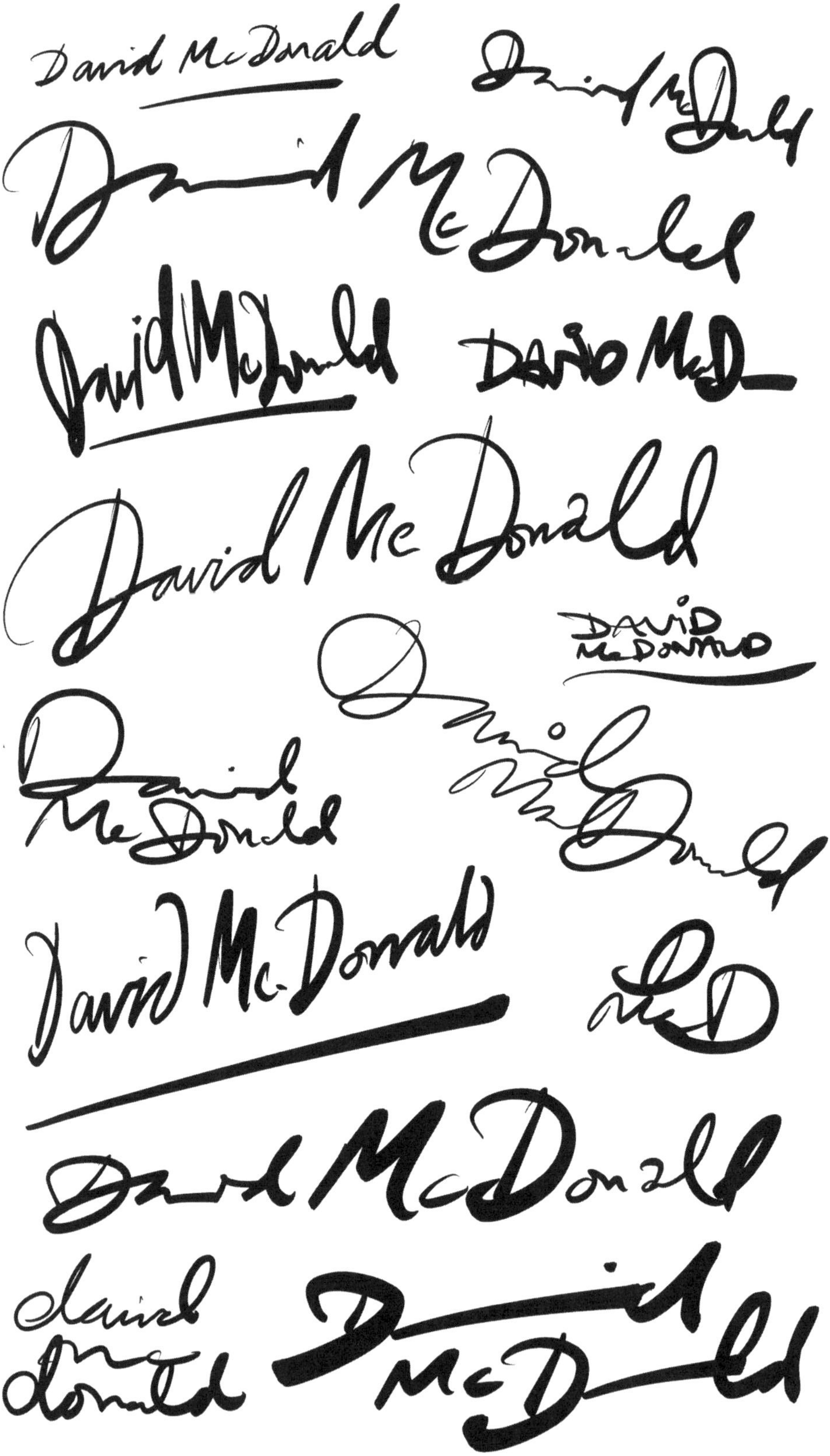
David McDonald
David McDonald
DAVID McDONALD
David McDonald
David McDonald

INT. STONE COTTAGE - PORT TALBOT, WALES - DUSK

Dust motes hang in the dead air of a place long forgotten.
The last rays of sun whisper through cracks in the oak door.
A shadow moves past, eclipsing the sun for a handsome second.

BOOM. The door splits. CHRISTOPHER enters. Even in silhouette
he's impossibly good-looking: sharp jaw, wise eyes. Scottish.
Behind, protected, his daughter SARAH and her baby sister.

                    CHRISTOPHER
              (shouting attractively)
          Matthew! MATTHEW!

There is no answer. His voice echoes off award-less shelves.

                    CHRISTOPHER (CONT'D)
          The war has come. Civilization is
          over and I'm out of fuel. I drove
          here for you. Welsh marauders will
          be here soon. I can protect you.

Still no answer. The empty house of an empty life.

                    SARAH
          Can you smell something?

He sniffs the air. An experienced tracker. His eyes narrow.

INT. PANTRY - CONTINUOUS

Christopher pushes the door open slowly. The burning body of
the bearded man who **was** Matthew is on the floor. Faint flames
lick at the vestiges of a red hoodie. Sarah peers past.

                    SARAH
          Is it him?

                    CHRISTOPHER
          It's him. We were too late.

                    SARAH
          Do you think he tried to run? He
          used to play football, didn't he?

                    CHRISTOPHER
          He used to. Now he's fat and slow.

Christopher takes a cigar from his pocket. Lights it on one
of the flames. Puffs on it and weeps. It's moving, but manly.

                    CHRISTOPHER (CONT'D)
          You son-of-a-bitch.

> GEORGIA

Okay. You alright?

> ANNA

Yeah, just one minute.

Silence as Georgia glances around. Anna quickly stands and hurries off. Georgia waits.

Michael enters and sits. He stares at the screen.

> GEORGIA

Hi, Michael.

> MICHAEL

Jesus Christ. Um ... Georgia.

> GEORGIA

Hi.

> MICHAEL

Oh, sorry. I didn't know you were, er, in there, you know.

> GEORGIA

You alright?

> MICHAEL

Yeah. Just a sec.

> GEORGIA

I ... I was just calling to say that I've just got back from the hospital.

> ANNA

(passes the screen and pauses)
Oh, how did it go?

> GEORGIA

Yeah, really well. She, um ...

Anna walks off.

> GEORGIA (CONT'D)

... she had a girl. Called her Helen.

Silence.

It's weird in hospitals at the moment cos, you know ... but they gave me gloves and masks and stuff, so it was ...

Beat.

Should I call back later?

> ANNA

No. Sorry.

Anna enters and sits.

An ambulance just turned up at our neighbour's. An hour or so ago.

                    GEORGIA
God.

                     ANNA
Yeah. I mean, we didn't see what was
happening but Michael tried to go out
and ask and the paramedics just told him
to go back inside.

                    GEORGIA
And did you see her?

                     ANNA
No.
          (sighs)
But ... we saw a stretcher being carried
in.

                    GEORGIA
Okay, I'll get David.

                     ANNA
          (softly)
Yeah.

Georgia stands and hurries off.

                 MICHAEL (O.S.)
Yeah, yeah, I'm still here, yeah. Thank
you.

Michael enters, speaking into his mobile phone.

          Um, er, sh ... er, I don't know, she's
          about five foot two, um, grey hair,
          glasses, um ... er, I'd say she's in her
          late seventies, early eighties maybe.
          Er, no, sorry, I, I don't know her
          surname. Her first name is, um, Hannah.
          H-A-double N-A-H. My name? Er, Michael
          Sheen. No, Michael.

Georgia and David sit.

                MICHAEL (CONT'D)
S-H-E-E-N.
          (chuckles)
Yeah. Well, we all love Neil Gaiman.
Um, I know, but could, could you please
just, um, ask and, and see if you can
find out, let us know. Um, I mean,
someone must have ordered the ambulance.
So we, we just wanna know where she is
and what's happening. Yes, yes, I'll
hold.

Sorry.

                     DAVID
Do you know where they've taken her?

                              ANNA
          No, we don't know. But Michael's trying
          to find out.

                            MICHAEL
          Oh, this is like a bad dream.

                              ANNA
          No, it'll be fine.

                             DAVID
          It will be fine.

                            MICHAEL
          Hello. Yes. No. Sorry, I explained. I, I
          don't know her surname. Her first name's
          Hannah. Er, she's ... old, um, and on
          her own.

                       MICHAEL (CONT'D)
          Her family's in Cardiff. No, I don't
          know where. And she runs an illegal
          Neighbourhood Watch from the CCTV camera
          mounted on her garage. She likes, um,
          inter-racial soft core pornographic
          literature. Um, she's an angry, shitty,
          blackmailing, little ... Well, she makes
          a very bad bara brith and, um ... she's
          kind.

     A pause. His voice breaks.

                       MICHAEL (CONT'D)
          Sorry.
          Yeah. Yeah, okay. Thank you.

7 INT. MICHAEL'S AND DAVID'S HOUSES - DAY   7

     MICHAEL is clutching his mobile phone to his chest as he stares
     away through an off-screen window. DAVID watches him anxiously.
     The end credits play over this.

                             DAVID
          Yeah. I know this isn't the best time.
          I just, I feel like the last time
          we talked about it, we were playing
          Battleships that time. We did decide
          that ... um, I'd have my name first on
          the poster. Tennant and then Sheen. I
          think it's what we said that we would
          have. Um ... sorry, I know it's ...
          this, this isn't great timing, but,
          um ...

     Michael glances at his mobile.

                         DAVID (CONT'D)
          ... I've just been sent a draft of the
          poster. You'll have ... they'll have
          sent it to you, too. But you won't ... I
          mean, you won't have had time to look

probably but, um, the, they want to
announce ... so they need approval on
the, er, thing. I ... unfortunately, on
the one they've mocked up your name is
actually first. So, um ...

... sorry, this is really bad timing but
they need changes by the end of play
today. So ...

... do you mind if I just go back to
them and tell them just to swap those
names round? Just on the ... so they're
the right way round on the poster?

Michael glances at his mobile.

DAVID (CONT'D)
Um, I, I'm happy to do that on, on
both our behalves quickly, if that's
okay? Or ...

Beat.

... we could leave it as it is and
just ...

Beat.

... let's just leave it.

Michael reacts as his mobile phone vibrates. David watches as
Michael stands and hurries off.

We'll just leave it. We'll leave it.
Don't worry about it.

BLACK SCREEN

Episode Six
The Cookie Jar

1 INT. DAVID'S AND MICHAEL'S HOUSES   1

DAVID and MICHAEL sitting in their respective houses.

Titles begin over this scene. White lettering on a black
background.

                        MICHAEL
           Has it occurred to you ...

           ... that she's read it and hasn't got
           the heart to tell you it's no good?

                        DAVID
           Of course it has.

                        MICHAEL
           Right.

                        DAVID
           Why would that not have occurred to me?

                        MICHAEL
           Just thought I'd check.

                        DAVID
           I mean, that is the single thing that
           is occurring to me, repeatedly over and
           over again, of course.

                        MICHAEL
           Course. Course. What do you miss?

                        DAVID
           About the real world?

                        MICHAEL
           Yeah.

                        DAVID
           Feedback from my wife.
           Um ... oh, rehearsals, mmm, I suppose.
           Film sets.

                        MICHAEL
           Oh, people bringing you coffee every ten
           minutes.

                        DAVID
           They have to be nice to you.

                        MICHAEL
           Yeah.

                        DAVID
           It's like their job to make sure you're
           okay.

                        MICHAEL
           Yeah.

                        DAVID
                    (mimics)
          Would you like some thermals for today?
          You can slip a few on under your
          costume. Nobody'll know.

                        MICHAEL
                    (mimics)
          Yes, I'm a bit cold.

                        DAVID
                    (mimics)
          Yes, I know you are. Don't worry. I'll
          put some heat pads in your shoes.

                        MICHAEL
                    (mimics)
          I need little warm hands and feet like a
          hedgehog.

                        DAVID
                    (mimics)
          Can we pop you over to make-up?

                     DAVID (CONT'D)
          Can we pop you over to make-up?

                        MICHAEL
          And then you go into make-up and it's
          ...

Michael imitates loud dance music.

                     MICHAEL (CONT'D)
          ... fucking disco.

                        DAVID
                    (mimics)
          Alright!

                        MICHAEL
                    (mimics)
          Oh, is the music too loud? No, it's fine.
          It's fine.

                        DAVID
                    (mimics)
          Are you sure? I can't hear you. What did
          you say? Is it too loud?

                        MICHAEL
                    (mimics - chuckles)
          What?

                        DAVID
                    (mimics)
          Please, can I have a professional to
          sort this fucking hair out?
                    (chuckles)

                    DAVID (CONT'D)
          Oh God.
          Michael, I think I'm gonna stop.

                    MICHAEL
          Er, yeah, I should get going as well.

                    DAVID
          I mean, stop doing the play. I'm gonna
          stop doing the play.

2   INT. LUCY'S AND JO'S HOUSES - DAY   2

    SIMON sitting in the living room. JO sitting in her kitchen.

                    JO
          Why do you think that?

                    SIMON
          It's just a vibe, really.

                    JO
          With you?

A beat.

                    SIMON
          With each other and me. Everything,
          really.

Another beat.

                    JO
          Worse than the argument?

                    SIMON
          At least with the argument it felt
          like they cared. Now they're just not
          interested.

Jo sighs deeply.

                    JO
          Is one worse than the other?

                    SIMON
          They're both pretty low.

                    JO
          But you think if one goes the other
          one's just gonna follow?

                    SIMON
          Yeah, I think so.

Jo has an idea.

                    JO
          Can we hook them back in?

                    SIMON
          Yes, yes. How?

                              JO
          A whole new approach to rehearsals.

                            SIMON
          We haven't done anything yet.

                              JO
          Okay. Well, a fresh start. Kick off from
          page one.

                            SIMON
          I suggested that, actually, to them,
          yesterday.

                              JO
          Great. What did they say?

                            SIMON
          Er, Michael called me, um ...

Simon checks his notes.

                        SIMON (CONT'D)
          ... pusillanimous.

A beat.

                              JO
                  (groans)
          What does that mean?

                            SIMON
          I don't know. It's not good, is it?

                              JO
                  (sighs)
          What did David say?

                            SIMON
          David nodded.

                              JO
          To starting over?

                            SIMON
          Or at pusillanimous.

                              JO
                  (calls)
          Janine, get my phone!

                        JANINE (O.S.)
                  (shouts)
          Do you want your old phone, your new
          phone, or your secret phone?!

                              JO
                  (to Simon)
          Right, there's, there's just one thing
          ...

Jo reacts to Janine's reply.

                    SIMON
          Yeah, what, what's the thing? What's the
          thing?

                    JO
                (shouts)
          You can drop that tone, Janine!

                    SIMON
          Is she alright?

                    JO
          She missed her daughter's birthday.

                    SIMON
          Why?

                    JO
          Fixing your mess.

                    SIMON
          What did she have to do?

                    JO
          Well, I had her driving flowers and wine
          and, and ... cards to David and Michael.

                    SIMON
          Michael's in Wales.

                    JO
          Yes, I know he is!

                    SIMON
          Is that even allowed?

                    JO
          You sound just like her.

We hear a door open.

                    JANINE (O.S.)
          Here's your secret phone.

Jo drops her mobile phone as Janine tosses it at her.

                    JO
                (sarcastic)
          Thank you.

                    SIMON
          Sorry, Janine.

                    JANINE (O.S.)
          Pusillanimous prick.

Jo sighs deeply as we hear the door close.

JO

Right, this is a long shot, but there's
an actor that I know who owes me a
favour.

Jo raises her mobile phone to her ear and chuckles.

SIMON

Who? Who is it?

JO

Oh, let's just hope she honours her
debts.
   (sighs)

A beat.

JO (CONT'D)

   (into mobile phone)
Wagwan.
   (laughs)
Hello, trouble. How are you?
   (to Simon)
Go away.
   (into mobile phone)
No, darling, not you.

Simon leaves the call.

JO (CONT'D)

   (into mobile phone)
Listen. Cast your mind back, 2015, Saint
Petersburg.

Jo stands.

JO (CONT'D)

   (into mobile phone)
Good God, do you kiss your grandson with
that mouth?

3 INT. DAVID'S AND MICHAEL'S HOUSES - DAY   3

DAVID sitting in a bedroom. MICHAEL sitting in his living room.
They are waiting for a call from 'someone'.

DAVID

Do you know what this is about?

MICHAEL

I do not.

DAVID

Well, Jo's message was very mysterious.

MICHAEL

It was.

A beat.

                        DAVID
          Did you get the flowers she sent?

                      MICHAEL
          And the wine.

                        DAVID
          What wine?

                      MICHAEL
          Did I say wine? No, flowers. Yes, that's
          right.

                        DAVID
          Yeah, yeah. Very kind.

                      MICHAEL
          Yeah, lovely. The woman who delivered
          mine was a little short with me.

                        DAVID
          Yes. And her car was full of happy first
          birthday balloons.

                      MICHAEL
          Probably does multiple deliveries in a
          day.

A pause.

                        DAVID
          I'm sure she's very efficient.

                      MICHAEL
          Can I tell you something that I
          shouldn't tell you?

                        DAVID
          I don't know. Should you?

                      MICHAEL
          I don't know. Can I?

                        DAVID
          Well, I don't know now, do I?

                      MICHAEL
          Georgia sent me your script.

                        DAVID
          Really?

                      MICHAEL
          Yeah, she wanted to get another opinion
          on it before she spoke to you, but, er,
          she thinks it's incredible.

Beat.

                        DAVID
          And what do you think?

A computer chimes as Judi Dench joins the call and appears
between them. They react.

> ### DAVID (CONT'D)
> Oh, fuck!
> > (to Judi)
>
> Sorry.

Judi gestures.

> ### MICHAEL
> Sorry.

> ### JUDI
> Stop bleating, please.

> ### DAVID
> Sorry. Hello.

> ### JUDI
> I'll be with you in a second.

> ### JUDI'S ASSISTANT (O.S.)
> Jo says flowers question mark.

> ### JUDI
> Yes, yes, that's fine.

> ### JUDI'S ASSISTANT (V.O.)
> Champagne.

> ### JUDI
> That's fine.

> ### JUDI (CONT'D)
> > (to Michael/David)
>
> Oh, I hate this bloody machine. Why
> can't we go back to cups and strings?

A beat.

> ### JUDI (CONT'D)
> I'm asking you, why can't we go back to
> cups and strings?

> ### DAVID
> Yes.

> ### MICHAEL
> Whatever you want.

> ### JUDI
> David?

> ### DAVID
> It's alright. I didn't realise you were
> joining us.

> ### JUDI
> Well, it would have somehow lessened the
> impact, wouldn't it?

                                   DAVID
                Yes, absolutely.

                                    JUDI
                You've grown your hair.

A beat.

                                   DAVID
                Er, extensions, actually.

                                    JUDI
                Oh.

Beat.

                              JUDI (CONT'D)
                Michael.

                                  MICHAEL
                Judi.

                                    JUDI
                Are those extensions, too?

                                  MICHAEL
                Er, no, no, this, er ... this is all me.

                                    JUDI
                Mmm-hmm.

                Well I've been talking to your director.

                                   DAVID
                Simon?

                                    JUDI
                Yes. He's a lovely boy.

                                   DAVID
                He's lovely, yeah.

                                    JUDI
                He's a tad ineffectual.

                                  MICHAEL
                Ineffectual, yes.

                                    JUDI
                And ambitious.

                                   DAVID
                Ooh, absolutely.

                                    JUDI
                A bit like a well-meaning moth
                that keeps bumping into the
                wrong lightbulb.

A beat.

JUDI (CONT'D)

He tells me you're not playing nicely.

DAVID
(hesitantly)
Well, it's been a tough few weeks.

JUDI

Is that right?

MICHAEL

Yeah, we've been through a lot.

DAVID

Been rehearsing this play.

JUDI

So I've been told. And you've fallen out
of love with it?

A beat.

DAVID

Well, it's lost its lustre, yeah.

Beat.

JUDI

Is it a comedy?

MICHAEL

No, it's Italian.

JUDI

Oh, Italian. Any of you speak Italian?

DAVID

Yeah, Michael does.

JUDI

Oh, do you, Michael?

MICHAEL

I don't.

JUDI

Well, perhaps you should have said 'no'.

MICHAEL

I suggested that.

DAVID

Yeah, perhaps we should. I, I, I was
torn, too.

JUDI

Yes. Well, it would have saved a lot of
trouble.

DAVID

But you always say that actors shouldn't
say no because then people will stop
asking you.

JUDI

Yes, yes, I do say that.

MICHAEL

What, you don't mean it?

JUDI

Certainly not.

MICHAEL

Oh.

JUDI

Well, do you think people are ever gonna
stop asking me?

MICHAEL

I suppose not.

DAVID

No.

JUDI

No. No matter how often I say no, they
never do. They keep on and on. Do this,
do that. Play a queen, play a spy, play
a cat. Do you know how tiring it is to
be everyone's first choice for every
bloody role?

MICHAEL

I do.

JUDI

No, Michael, you don't!

MICHAEL

No, no.

JUDI

We're told in this industry to expect
rejection. Now some of us are fortunate
enough to reach the level where we have
to mete out the rejection. That's not an
easy responsibility either.

MICHAEL

So, are, are you saying we should have
said no?

JUDI

I'm saying that the responsibility of
saying yes or no lies squarely with you.
As does your behaviour afterwards. You
said yes.

A beat.

                              MICHAEL
                          (reluctantly)
          Yes.

                              DAVID
          Yes.

                              JUDI
          Then stop fucking about. We're actors.
          When we say yes, we do the bloody job.

A computer chimes as Judi leaves the call. Michael exhales. They
sit in silence.

                              DAVID
          You don't speak Italian?

                              MICHAEL
          You think Simon's a lovely boy?

                              DAVID
                          (imitates Michael)
          No, this hair, it's all me.

                              MICHAEL
          Well, it is!

                              DAVID
                          (imitates Michael)
          It's all me.

                              MICHAEL
          You are just jealous of my mane.

                              DAVID
          Trying to seduce the dame.

                              MICHAEL
                          (chuckles)
          Well, can you blame me?

                              DAVID
          You know, she's a national treasure.

                              MICHAEL
          I felt like a rabbit in the headlights.

                              DAVID
          Yeah. There is something ethereal about
          her, isn't there? Something other-
          worldly.

                              MICHAEL
          It's sort of like being ... consumed by
          Angel Delight.

                              DAVID
          Which flavour of Angel Delight are you
          imagining?

> MICHAEL
> Strawberry, of course.

> DAVID
> I'd have said butterscotch ...
>
> She's definitely hung up, hasn't she?

> MICHAEL
> Well I guess we should do the bloody
> job, then.

A beat.

> DAVID
> I think we probably should, yeah.

They sit in silence.

4   INT. DAVID'S HOUSE - DAY   4

GEORGIA sitting at the dining table, clutching a glass of wine
as she reads a novel. David approaches and sits beside her.

> GEORGIA
> Hey.

> DAVID
> Thank you.

They glance at each other and smile. Georgia sips her wine.

5   INT. DAVID'S, MICHAEL'S AND LUCY'S HOUSES - DUSK   5

DAVID and GEORGIA sitting at their dining table, reading a
script. As the scene continues, MICHAEL and ANNA appear right of
screen in their window, also reading from the script, then SIMON
and LUCY appear in a window to the left.

> GEORGIA
> 'I can't believe you found us.'

> DAVID
> 'The family stare at the woman,
> Christopher and his two girls caked in
> mud from days walking. Sarah has a cut
> on her face.'

> GEORGIA
> 'Are you hurt, little girl?'

> ANNA
> 'I'll be fine.'

> GEORGIA
> 'Where have you come from?'

> DAVID
> 'The girls look at Christopher, tears
> begin to pool in his eyes.'

MICHAEL
'Over the mountains.'

ANNA
'You have food?'

GEORGIA
'And water and a place to rest.'

ANNA
'We can rest? Dad, we can rest.'

DAVID
'Her little sister begins to cry.'

LUCY
'Daddy.'

DAVID
'And his knees give in. He sinks to the floor, gathering his daughters in his arms.'

GEORGIA
'Stay as long as you need.'

MICHAEL
'Oh, thank you.'

DAVID
'Somewhere a dog barks.'

SIMON
'Woof.'

ANNA
'How did you find us?'

DAVID
'The man looks up, tears cutting rivers through the dirt on his face.'

MICHAEL
'When I was young, a circus passed through town. My father lifted me up on his shoulders so I could see. I asked him how the elephants found their way and he told me they parade in single file, just holding the tail of the elephant in front, until they get home.'

DAVID
'He looks to the horizon.'

The reading comes to an end.

GEORGIA
Ohh.

MICHAEL
Ohh.

They all applaud David.

> **SIMON**
> Very good.

> **DAVID**
> It's not too pretentious?

> **MICHAEL**
> No.

> **DAVID**
> No? Sure?

> **MICHAEL**
> Well, not in the right hands.

> **DAVID**
> Right.
> Thanks for reading in, Lucy.

> **LUCY**
> Oh, my pleasure.

> **DAVID**
> And Anna and Georgia, of course,
> obviously.

Georgia mutters.

> **MICHAEL**
> And good work with those dogs, Simon.

> **SIMON**
> Thank you.

> **MICHAEL**
> I mean, such variety.

> **SIMON**
> Yeah.

> **DAVID**
> Got any notes?

> **MICHAEL**
> Nothing.

> **DAVID**
> Come on.

> **MICHAEL**
> No.

> **DAVID**
> You must have something.

Michael inhales and exhales deeply as he considers his reply.

                    MICHAEL
Er ... I, I ... I loved how the daughter
rescues the father. Oh!

                     DAVID
That was actually Georgia's idea.

                    MICHAEL
Oh, it's very, it's very moving.

                     LUCY
And, um, I loved the scene with the
deer.

                     SIMON
Oh, yeah.

                     DAVID
Yes, that one was Georgia too, actually.

                      ANNA
Well, the visual language was striking.

                     DAVID
Thank you. I think, yeah, that was me.

A pause.

                    MICHAEL
What do the elephants symbolise?

                     DAVID
           (thinks)
The elephants ...

                    GEORGIA
Memory.

                     DAVID
Memory.

                    GEORGIA
Mmm.

                    MICHAEL
Ah. Did you write any of it, David?

                     DAVID
I responded very well to notes.

                    MICHAEL
From a published novelist.

                     DAVID
From a published novelist, yeah.

                    MICHAEL
Yeah.
Could I be in the film of your book
instead, Georgia?

DAVID

No, no, no, no, no, no, no, no.

MICHAEL

Er, why not?

DAVID

Because if anyone does that, it's gonna
be me.

MICHAEL

Why?

DAVID

Because I'm married to her.

MICHAEL

Er, what would happen to your film, then?
Who'd look after the elephants?

DAVID

Fuck the elephants.

MICHAEL

Ladies and gentlemen, fuck the
elephants.

DAVID

Yeah.

MICHAEL

I miss elephants.

ANNA

You miss elephants?

MICHAEL

Yeah. David asked me earlier, 'What do I
miss?' And I miss elephants.

DAVID

You miss elephants?

MICHAEL

I do.

DAVID

What, on a day-to-day basis?

MICHAEL

No, not on a day-to-day basis, David.
But I thought about it and I would like
to see an elephant.

A pause.

DAVID

I would like to see an elephant, yeah.

GEORGIA

Well, you've both survived this long
without one, so ...

                    DAVID
          That's true.

                  GEORGIA
          Mmm.

Anna studies Michael's unkempt hair.

                    ANNA
          I miss hairdressers.

Michael laughs out loud as he reacts to Anna's statement.

                    DAVID
          What about you, Lucy?

                    LUCY
          Oh God, I miss my own space.

                    DAVID
          Well ... Simon?

                   SIMON
          Er, nothing. I am fine.

                    DAVID
          Really? Cos I ... May I moot an idea?

                   SIMON
          No.

                  MICHAEL
          Oh, please let him moot. Let him moot an
          idea.

                    DAVID
          May I put forth a moot?

                  MICHAEL
          Yes, he moots so beautifully.

                    DAVID
          I do. And I've missed mooting.

                  MICHAEL
          He's a master mooter.

                    DAVID
          Yeah. Master mootivator.

                  MICHAEL
          You really are. You mootivate me.

                    DAVID
          Thank you. If I may moot.

                  MICHAEL
          Two four six eight moot away.

                              DAVID
          I moot that Simon misses well-behaved
          actors.

                              SIMON
          Absolutely not.

                              DAVID
          Not even trying.

The laughter continues.

                              MICHAEL
          Ah, you lie!

David pulls a 'Pinocchio nose'.

                              DAVID
          Oooh-ooh!

                              MICHAEL
          You lie!

Michael reacts to the sound of their doorbell. Silence.

                              DAVID
          What was that?

                              MICHAEL
          Someone at the front door.

                              DAVID
          Who is it?

                              MICHAEL
          I don't know.
          Er, just, just give me a sec.

Michael and Anna stand and walk off.

                              DAVID
          Rude at this hour.

                              GEORGIA
          Mmm.

A beat.

                              LUCY
          What's the plan with the script, David?

                              DAVID
          Well I'm, I'm sort of hoping that
          Michael will do it.

                              LUCY
          Oh, amazing. Yeah.

                              DAVID
          Although, apparently, he's attached to
          Georgia's novel, so ...

                    SIMON
     Who's directing?

                    DAVID
     I thought I might give it a go myself.

                    LUCY
     Mmm.

                    SIMON
     Give it a go yourself?

                    DAVID
     Well, if you can do it, Simon ...

Anna enters and sits.

                    SIMON
     If I can do it, David.

                    DAVID
               (mutters)
     Yeah.

                    GEORGIA
     Who was it?

                    ANNA
     Er, Hannah's son.

A beat.

                    GEORGIA
     What did he say?

                    ANNA
     I don't know. I left Michael with him.

                    LUCY
     Who's Hannah?

                    SIMON
     Er, Michael's neighbour.

Michael enters and sits beside Anna. Silence.

                    MICHAEL
     She's okay.

Georgia gasps.

                    DAVID
     Brilliant.

                    MICHAEL
     I mean, she was sick but, er, the
     hospital did an amazing job. That was
     her son. She wanted me to know that she
     was okay ...
               (upset)
     ... that she was okay. Oh.

                    MICHAEL (CONT'D)
                  (chuckles/clears throat)
          Excuse me. Excuse me.
                    (clears throat)
          Ah!

Michael stands and steps away, visibly upset.

                       GEORGIA
          Okay. We're gonna leave you guys to it.

                        DAVID
          Yeah.

                        SIMON
          Er, yeah, we'll go too.

                        LUCY
          Mmm. Yeah. Lovely to see you all.

                        DAVID
          And you, Lucy.

                       GEORGIA
          You too.

Lucy stands and steps away.

                        DAVID
          Ah, she's lovely.

                        SIMON
          Yeah, she is. Yeah. Um ... are we
          rehearsing tomorrow?

                        DAVID
          I see no reason why not. Michael and I
          are professionals. When we say yes, we
          do the bloody job.

                        SIMON
          Great. Where from?

                        DAVID
          Have we done anything with scene one
          yet?

                        SIMON
          No.

                        DAVID
          Maybe we should just start with scene
          one.

                        SIMON
          Start from scene one. Page one?

                        DAVID
          Very good. See you there.

                        SIMON
          See you there.

Anna waves.

> **ANNA**
> God natt så gott.

> **DAVID**
> Ooh, what's that?

> **ANNA**
> Goodnight and sleep well.

> **DAVID**
> In Welsh?

> **ANNA**
> No, in Swedish. In Welsh it's ... 'Nos
> da a chysgu'n dda.'

> **DAVID**
> Oh God, you're impressive.

Georgia mutters.

A computer chimes as Anna leaves.

> **DAVID (CONT'D)**
> Mmm, that was alright.

> **GEORGIA**
> Mmm.
> You know what I miss?

> **DAVID**
> No. What do you miss?

> **GEORGIA**
> You wearing a different top.

> **DAVID**
> Oh, sorry.

> **GEORGIA**
> And sleep. I'm going to bed.

> **DAVID**
> (mumbles)
> Goodnight, my darling.

> **GEORGIA**
> Night night.

She lifts her glass of wine from the table as she stands and
exits.

David's computer chimes as Michael calls.

> **DAVID**
> Alright?

A pause.

GT's Carrot Cake

Prep time: Should take 35 mins but will be dependent on accompanied wine consumption.

What you need for the cake:

- 4 eggs (Though maybe start with the full 6 pack so you've got your breakage excess factored in from the start. The outcome of this is also beverage dependent.)

- 100g of natural yogurt (Keep rest in fridge. Great for thrush.)

- 1.5tsp of vanilla extract

- $1/_2$ orange, zested (Note: do not grate fingers. It hurts and adds no enhancement to the flavour.)

- 265g gluten-free (or regular, you animal) self-raising flour

- 335g light muscovado sugar (This isn't easy to procure so start your search 4 days prior to planned bake. You'll need 2 days to visit all your local supermarkets ending in inevitable failure and still be left with a further 48 hours for the disappointing trundle over to Amazon Prime.)

- 2.5tsp ground cinnamon (No need to grind this yourself but if you happen to have a pestle and mortar to hand please do try, film it and pop on Instagram, tagging @georgiatennantofficial. The drunker the better.)

- 3 grated carrots (Easy to find as long as someone you live with hasn't used them in some culinary disaster involving an Easter egg.)

- 100g of raisins (Can also use sultanas. I'm not entirely sure what the difference is.)

What you need for the icing:

- 100g salted butter (Take it out of the fridge before to soften but not so long before that your family use it all and you have to scream at them because you needed that to make a cake and them using it without asking just shows how underappreciated you are and they all look at you like you've lost it but you said the word cake so on some level they realise they need to appear sympathetic so they actually get a slice. Then pop to Co-op to get more.)

- 300g icing sugar. (That shit is skittish, don't breathe too heavily in its vicinity.)

- 100g soft cheese. (Sounds gross and under any other circumstances, is.)

Right, now you've either managed to get all that together and are raring to go or have drunk so much wine that you've passed out and are now dribbling into a cushion with Michael Sheen's face on it (don't pretend we don't all own one, right?) Anyway if you are still here then excellent and welcome to:

THE NEXT STAGE(D)

1. Turn on your oven to 180°C. (Which the internet tells me is also 356°F or gas mark 4.)

2. Get all the cake ingredients above and chuck (literally chuck, you'll find it very satisfying) in a big bowl. Then wash your hands, remove all jewellery, stick hands in bowl and go all Demi Moore in *Ghost* on its ass. Once at the stage where it's lump-free or your hands are so covered in batter you can no longer safely pick up your wine glass (whichever comes first), stop mixing and divide the mix into two cake tins. Pop into oven and bake for 30 mins.

3. Now top up your glass (as if you need reminding). NOW FOR THE ICING.

4. Take the butter, icing and soft (yuk) cheese and mix together. (pretty easy this part so long as you aren't totally rat arsed. Though if you are and are still going with this recipe, you are my hero and soon you'll have a cake so pretty you can instagram and tweet the fuck out of it and all your friends will think you are so together and cool and not at all the drunken mess of a sugarholic you really are.)

5. Once the cake is out of the oven and cooled you can sandwich together the two rounds with the icing and plop the rest on top. At this point some people like to ruin it by adding crushed walnuts but let's not be one of those dickheads.

6. TA-DA! You made a cake!

7. Hopefully it's delicious and you can show it off to all your family and friends whilst telling them all about this great new baker you've discovered in this great new book you've bought OR you could take some 'you' time and grab a fork, run yourself a nice hot bath and be the motherfucking legend we all know you are. Also the plus side to this option is that if you eat it all yourself no one will ever know if this recipe is nonsense and your cake tastes like shit!

8. You're welcome x

MICHAEL

Are you alone?

DAVID

Yeah.

MICHAEL

I have so many notes on your script.

DAVID

Oh, fuck off!

Michael laughs as David rudely gestures.

6 INT. DAVID'S, JUDI'S AND MICHAEL'S HOUSES - DAY   6

DAVID, JUDI and MICHAEL sitting in their respective houses.

JUDI

Well, what was it to begin with?

DAVID

David Tennant, Michael Sheen.

JUDI

Well that's absurd.

MICHAEL

That's what I said.

JUDI

I mean, when in doubt, it's alphabetical
order.

DAVID

(shouts)
That is not a fucking rule!

JUDI

David John Tennant, you're going the
right way for a smacked bottom.

MICHAEL

He's been like this all the way through,
Judi.

DAVID

No, Judi, it says here ... your name
came before Steve Coogan's on Philomena.

JUDI

Yes.

DAVID

Before Billy Connolly on Mrs Brown.

JUDI

Yes.

DAVID

Well, they all come before you
alphabetically.

JUDI

They do.

DAVID

So why does your name come first?

JUDI

I'm Judi Dench.

MICHAEL

Um, what is the significance of 'and'?

DAVID

What do you mean?

Michael studies his mobile phone.

MICHAEL

Gwyneth Paltrow, Joseph Fiennes, Geoffrey
Rush 'and' Judi Dench.

JUDI

Well, there is something to be said for
magnanimity.

MICHAEL

David Tennant 'and' Michael Sheen.

DAVID

Michael Sheen 'with' David Tennant.

MICHAEL

David Tennant 'minus' Michael Sheen.

DAVID

Michael Sheen 'nevertheless' David
Tennant.

MICHAEL

David Tennant 'notwithstanding' Michael
Sheen.

DAVID

David Tennant and 'Martin' Sheen.

JUDI

How about Judi Dench introduces Michael
Sheen and David Tennant?

DAVID

That sounds right, yeah.

MICHAEL

Yeah.

JUDI

Mmm.

End titles begin throughout the ensuing action.

JUDI (CONT'D)

I remember being in a scrap about
billing once.

MICHAEL

How did you resolve it?

JUDI

We had to recite 'The Quality of Mercy'
from The Merchant of Venice backwards.
The first one to get a word wrong took
an item of clothing off. At the end, the
person left with no clothes on at all
got second billing.

MICHAEL

And, and who won?

JUDI

Well, I did, of course. But, um
... it was a close thing.

MICHAEL

Oh, I bet.

JUDI

Have you tried that?

A beat.

MICHAEL

Er, well David only ever wears that
bloody hoodie, so, you know, it's not
really fair.

JUDI

Well, somebody should take something off
...
Anyway, your name will be twice on the
poster, David, cos you wrote it.

DAVID

Well, yes, and I'm directing it,
actually. Any tips?

JUDI

Well, you could try a good warm-up game.

DAVID

Really?

JUDI

Mmm. It always goes well.

You know, 'Who stole the cookie from the
cookie jar'?

Silence as David and Michael react. Beat. Then together.

MICHAEL

David stole the cookie from the cookie
jar!

DAVID

Michael stole the cookie from the cookie
jar!

BLACK SCREEN

Staged

Series Two

STAGED SERIES TWO CAST

In order of appearance

David Tennant	David Tennant
Michael Sheen	Michael Sheen
Romesh Ranganathan	Romesh Ranganathan
Sir Michael Palin	Sir Michael Palin
Georgia Tennant	Georgia Tennant
Anna Lundberg	Anna Lundberg
Lucy Eaton	Lucy Eaton
Whoopi Goldberg	Mary
Nina Sosanya	Nina Sosanya
Simon Evans	Simon Evans
Simon Pegg	Simon Pegg
Nick Frost	Nick Frost
Ben Schwartz	Tom
Christoph Waltz	Christoph Waltz
Ewan McGregor	Ewan McGregor
Hugh Bonneville	Hugh Bonneville
Ken Jeong	Ken Jeong
Jim Parsons	Jim Parsons
Josh Gad	Josh Gad
Cate Blanchett	Cate Blanchett
Phoebe Waller-Bridge	Phoebe Waller-Bridge
Phin Glynn	Michael's Best Friend

Episode One
Saddle Up Sheen!

> **DAVID**
> Michael?
> Michael?

> **MICHAEL**
> David.

> **DAVID**
> You alright?

> **MICHAEL**
> Give me a minute.

> **DAVID**
> What you doing now?

> **MICHAEL**
> I'm worried that I'm in a Hitchcock film.

> **DAVID**
> What do you mean?

> **MICHAEL**
> The birds are coming back to Port
> Talbot.

> **DAVID**
> That's nice.

> **MICHAEL**
> And that large blue finch is the leader,
> it seems.

> **DAVID**
> You alright?

> **MICHAEL**
> Just adjusting. You alright?

2 OPENING TITLE 'ROMESH RANGANATHAN'S 6 MONTHS IN LOCKDOWN'   2

3 INT. ROMESH'S, DAVID'S AND MICHAEL'S HOUSES - DAY   3

> **ROMESH**
> Cachu hwch.

> **MICHAEL**
> Cachu hwch.

They all repeat 'cachu hwch'.

> **DAVID**
> Total bloomin' disaster.

> **ROMESH**
> Er, well look, for those of you just
> joining us, er, welcome to my house.

                    ROMESH (CONT'D)
          Er, welcome to my kitchen. I've been
          imprisoned here for half a year. Er, I'm
          done with Zoom, if I'm being honest with
          you.

Michael laughs.

          But I'm here now with two people who
          actually made it work.
          Michael Sheen and David Tennant. Or
          should that be David Tennant and Michael
          Sheen?

                         MICHAEL
          Ah!

                          ROMESH
          Er, this is, er, Romesh Ranganathan's
          Six Months In Lockdown. A celebration of
          the wonderful things that have basically
          got us through this challenging period.
          Michael and David are here to talk to us
          about their BBC show Staged.

                         MICHAEL
          Thank you for having us.

                          DAVID
          Lovely to be here.

                          ROMESH
          And still with us, of course, er, Sir
          Michael Palin, who waited for Godot,
          er, in an online reading of the Beckett
          classic. I meant to ask, Sir Michael,
          er, did Godot ever arrive?

Sir Michael Palin joins them from his living room.

                       SIR MICHAEL
          No, no.
          We're still waiting.

                          ROMESH
          Okay. Well, while you wait.
          Er, David and Michael, massive
          congratulations on the show.
          I know I have to say that contractually.

                         MICHAEL
          Thank you.

                          ROMESH
          But genuinely, I mean it. Very funny.

                          DAVID
          Thanks very much. Cheers.

ROMESH

First question, um, I guess is what's real and what's not? Like, is Simon that much of an idiot?

DAVID

No. Um ...

MICHAEL

No.

Michael nods profusely.

DAVID

Michael does shout at birds.

ROMESH

Right.

MICHAEL

Yeah, well, I have a bird's nest for hair, so it helps to be courteous.

DAVID

Yeah. Yeah.

ROMESH

But it, it was a television show?

MICHAEL

It was a television show, yes.

ROMESH

So what, no screenplay? No novel?

DAVID

No carrots. No pineapples. None of it.

ROMESH

It did feel real.

MICHAEL

Well, thank you very much.

ROMESH

How much of it was actually improvised?

DAVID

All of it.

MICHAEL

Well, that, er, that does come up a lot.

ROMESH

Was there actually a script then?

DAVID
(hesitantly)
There were ... ideas and then, you know, we, we would play around with it quite a lot.

MICHAEL

Not, not everything made it into the cut
though.

DAVID

No. There are hours of footage somewhere
of us, of us not being particularly
funny.

ROMESH

So what gold did we, er, lose to the
cutting room floor?

MICHAEL

Well, um, there was one moment where,
er, quite memorably, David accused me of
being a cut-price Mike Yarwood.

ROMESH

Well, is that funny?

MICHAEL

Well, no.

ROMESH

I don't think I actually know who Mike
Yarwood is.

MICHAEL

Ahh, you see! I told you, didn't I? I
told you. No ...

DAVID

I don't believe you. I don't believe ...
He's, he's a comedy titan.

MICHAEL

So, Romesh, most of David's
contributions were based on these sort
of bizarre, obscure references.

DAVID

Yeah, yeah. Well that's why they're cut.
But I'm, I'm a little too intellectual,
er, for prime time.

MICHAEL

And not funny.

DAVID

Well, at least I didn't resort to lazy
muppet impressions, did I?

David imitates Michael's muppet impression.

MICHAEL

There was nothing lazy about my muppet
... I was exhausted at the end of it.

ROMESH

Er, do, do you know who Mike Yarwood is,
Sir Michael?

SIR MICHAEL

Yeah, I actually know Mike Yarwood.

DAVID

Really? I didn't realise he, he was
still, um, working.

ROMESH

Well, let's have another clip.

MICHAEL

Great.

DAVID

Lovely.

Generic title clip for Romesh show plays.

ROMESH

And we're off.

DAVID

Okay. Which one is it?

ROMESH

It's, um, 'Cookie Jar'.

DAVID
(muttering)
We've seen them all quite a lot now.

ROMESH

Yeah, I'm sure. I mean, I imagine Sir
Michael's a step ahead there.

MICHAEL

Yes.

DAVID

Yeah.

ROMESH

Er, Sir Michael, how many dead parrots
do you reckon you've seen in your time?

SIR MICHAEL

Oh, a few.

MICHAEL

What is the collective noun for dead
parrots?

DAVID

A Norwegian blue.

MICHAEL

A sunken fjord.

                    DAVID
A macaw.

                    ROMESH
Er, Sir Michael, any ideas? Collective
noun for dead parrots.

                  SIR MICHAEL
A humiliation?

                    ROMESH
Er, have you seen Staged, Sir Michael?

                  SIR MICHAEL
Yeah. Yeah, I've watched a couple.

                    DAVID
Have you? Which ones?

                  SIR MICHAEL
The first one.

                    MICHAEL
Did you like it?

                  SIR MICHAEL
Loved it.

                    MICHAEL
Yeah, great!

                    DAVID
Thank goodness for that.

                  SIR MICHAEL
For what it was, you know.

Beat.

                    ROMESH
And we're back.

Generic show title appears.

                ROMESH (CONT'D)
Er, that was BBC One's lockdown comedy
Staged.
Er, David and Michael, er, you said the
story is fictional, er, but what about
your characters?

                    DAVID
Total fabrication.

                    MICHAEL
Oh ... nothing like us at all.

                    DAVID
Not a ... not a scintilla. No, I mean
I don't think we're very funny in real
life.

MICHAEL
Well, I don't think you're funny. I'm
funny.

DAVID
Sure, obviously. I just mean we're not,
we're not comedians.

SIR MICHAEL
Ah, you're still young.

Michael laughs.

ROMESH
Er, and what's next for you guys?

DAVID
I'm back to proper work, actually. Um,
a, a show that I was working on before
lockdown, er, is revving back up, so I'm
off out to South Africa.

ROMESH
Very nice.

DAVID
We've had a couple of false starts but I
think this is finally it and I am flying
tomorrow.

ROMESH
Great.
And, er, Michael?

MICHAEL
Er, I don't do proper work any more, so
I'm off to New York to see family and
friends.

ROMESH
Right, travel allowing, I imagine.

MICHAEL
Oh, no, it'll be fine. I believe it will
be fine.

ROMESH
Yeah, of course, of course.
Er, and Sir Michael, do, do you reckon
you would have done Staged if they'd
asked you?

SIR MICHAEL
Oh, no, I, I couldn't have kept up.

MICHAEL
Oh ...

ROMESH
What, no, no improvisation in Monty
Python?

SIR MICHAEL

No, we were quite disciplined.

ROMESH

That wasn't the, er, Staged approach.

SIR MICHAEL

No.

Michael leaps to their defence.

MICHAEL

Although, I, I mean I do think some, some quite brave stuff has come out of that more ... sort of improvisatory approach.

SIR MICHAEL

Do you?

ROMESH

Er, Michael, David, we've got another clip, but first, one more question. Er, I think you know what I'm gonna ask. Er, any chance of another series?

DAVID

I mean, it was so specific to that moment, wasn't it?

MICHAEL

Yeah.

DAVID

It was so about being locked in your house and, and ...

MICHAEL

I mean, hopefully we're not gonna go into another lockdown.

DAVID

Well, exactly.

MICHAEL

But ...

DAVID

But having said that, if we, if, if there was a way of doing it, if that's for me it would definitely be a yes.

MICHAEL

I mean, it was a joy to do, so, um ...

DAVID

It was such good fun, yeah.

ROMESH

Okay. So I'm gonna take that as a really waffly yes.

                              DAVID
           Yeah, I suppose so.

                              MICHAEL
           It's a great big Welsh waffly yes from
           me.

                              ROMESH
           Well, on that, er, here's a clip of
           some other strange and wonderful things
           people have made through all of this.

Generic title clip for Romesh show appears here.

                        ROMESH (CONT'D)
           Okay, we're out. This one's, er, a
           little bit longer, so I'm just gonna nip
           to the toilet, guys, alright?

                              DAVID
           Sure.

                              ROMESH
           Great stuff. See you in a sec.

Romesh exits.

                              MICHAEL
           I hope you don't think I was, um,
           dismissing the, the Python approach?

                            SIR MICHAEL
           Oh God, no. No, not at all.

                              MICHAEL
           Good. Cos it ... I mean, it was so
           important to me when I was growing up.
           I'm such a fan.

Beat.

                            SIR MICHAEL
           I didn't really like Staged.

                              MICHAEL
           Okay.

                            SIR MICHAEL
           I don't really like improvisation. All
           these people sort of rolling the comedy
           dice and hoping something sticks.

Romesh re-enters and washes his hands in the kitchen sink.

                              MICHAEL
           Right. No, I understand.

                            SIR MICHAEL
           We worked hard in our day.

                              MICHAEL
           'Waking up before I went to bed.'

                    SIR MICHAEL
Yeah, yeah, that's one of, one of Eric's
great lines.

                      DAVID
Er, I think we ... it's not ... you
know, it's not that we didn't. We worked
hard too.

                    SIR MICHAEL
Oh, I'm sure you did.
You squatted down, you pushed very hard
and you squeezed something out.

                    MICHAEL
Well, I mean, people do like it.

                      DAVID
          (aside)
Fuck you.

                    SIR MICHAEL
You have this well-practised self-
congratulatory back and forth because
people want to celebrate your used
toilet paper again.

                    MICHAEL
I'm ... I'm, I'm a fan of yours.

                    SIR MICHAEL
It was like a thirty-minute Celtic reach
around.

                      DAVID

Whoa!

                    MICHAEL
No, David.

                      DAVID
The episodes are only fifteen minutes.

Romesh leans in close to the camera.

                    ROMESH
Alright?

                    SIR MICHAEL
Yeah.

                      DAVID
Yeah.

                    SIR MICHAEL
Fine.

                    ROMESH
Cool. We've got about another minute.

                              SIR MICHAEL
            Okay. We'll be ready.

                              ROMESH
            Wicked. Alright, see you in a sec.

Romesh leans out.

                              DAVID
            I think you're being a bit unkind,
            actually.

                              SIR MICHAEL
            We made Python fifty years ago.

                              DAVID
            Yeah, and it's a bit dated.

                              MICHAEL
            Oh, David.

                              SIR MICHAEL
            They still talk about us now.

                              DAVID
            I know.

                              SIR MICHAEL
            But they won't talk about you.

                              DAVID
            Why not?

                              SIR MICHAEL
            Because you're not funny.

Romesh sits in.

                              ROMESH
            Oh God. Sorry about that, guys.
            David, Michael, all PR aside, are you
            gonna do a second series, you reckon?

                              MICHAEL
            Unlikely.

                              DAVID
            Wouldn't have thought so.

                              MICHAEL
            No.

                              ROMESH
            Honestly? Why not?

                              DAVID
            Well, we're not funny, are we?

                              SIR MICHAEL
            Yeah. That's a shame.

ROMESH
And we're back.

4   BLACK SCREEN - OPENING TITLES BEGIN   4

5   INT. SIMON'S HOUSE — LIVING ROOM - DAY   5

SIMON
(into mobile phone)
What's going on? ... Yeah, I've got a
suitcase here.

6   INT. MICHAEL'S AND DAVID'S HOUSES - DAY   6

They are not actually talking to each other, but to an unknown
person.

DAVID
This is interesting.

MICHAEL
... this is interesting.

DAVID
But, okay, let me just get ... just so
I understand, it's not ... we're not
talking about a second series, we're
talking about a remake?

MICHAEL
For American television.

DAVID
American Staged?

MICHAEL
But isn't it a bit ... unnecessary?

DAVID
Why don't they just show the episodes we
have already made?

MICHAEL
When do we need to decide?

DAVID
When do they need an answer?

MICHAEL
But I'm flying to New York tomorrow.

DAVID
I'm literally about to leave for the
airport.

Beat.

DAVID (CONT'D)
I need to talk to Michael.

MICHAEL
I need to talk to David.

DAVID and GEORGIA are sitting on a pile of suitcases in the
hall. GEORGIA is scrolling through her phone.

> **DAVID**
> I have news.

> **GEORGIA**
> Yeah, me too.

> **DAVID**
> What's your news?

> **GEORGIA**
> What's your news?

> **DAVID**
> You're not pregnant, are you?

> **GEORGIA**
> What?! No!

> **DAVID**
> I mean, it's not an unreasonable
> question.

> **GEORGIA**
> What's your news?

> **DAVID**
> They want to do an American remake of
> Staged.

> **GEORGIA**
> Oh.

> **DAVID**
> What's your news?

> **GEORGIA**
> Flights to South Africa have been
> cancelled.

> **DAVID**
> Oh, you're kidding.

> **GEORGIA**
> No.

> **DAVID**
> Oh, cock-a-doodle bum tits. Not again?

> **GEORGIA**
> Yeah.

> **DAVID**
> What's the plan?

> **GEORGIA**
> Er, watch this space.

                              DAVID
          Fucking hate this space.

                             GEORGIA
          I know.

                              DAVID
          I just wanna work.

                             GEORGIA
          I know.

                              DAVID
          Do you think I'm funny?

                             GEORGIA
          I think you do and say funny things.

                              DAVID
          That is wilfully opaque.
          I just wanna do new things.

                             GEORGIA
          Have you spoken to Michael?

                              DAVID
                        (mouths)
          No.

8 INT. MICHAEL'S AND DAVID'S HOUSES - DAY   8

                              DAVID
          Alright. So pros and cons. Yeah, pros: I
          really wanna work.

                             MICHAEL
          Con: Michael Palin doesn't think we're
          funny.

                              DAVID
          Can we ask another Python?

                             MICHAEL
          Which one?

                              DAVID
          Eric Idle? He seems nice.

                             MICHAEL
          Michael Palin seemed nice.

                              DAVID
          I like the landscape of America.

                             MICHAEL
          Mmm, me too.

                              DAVID
          I've always really fancied myself in a
          cowboy film.

                    MICHAEL
        Oh yes! What, what would your horse be
        called?

                    DAVID
        Sheen.

                    MICHAEL
        Aww.

Anna Lundberg passes behind Michael.

                    DAVID
        Oh, hey, Anna.

                    ANNA
        Oh, hi, David.

        Aren't you supposed to be flying?

                    DAVID
        Oh, not today.

                    ANNA
        Oh, no.

                    DAVID
        You ready for New York?

                    ANNA
        Yeah, just packing. But can you talk to
        Michael about his legs?

                    DAVID
        I would love to.

                    ANNA
        He says they're too chunky.

                    DAVID
        Chunky.

                    ANNA
        Mmm. So he refuses to pack shorts.

                    DAVID
        I see. Right. Right.

                    ANNA
        Do you wear shorts?

                    DAVID
        Almost exclusively.

                    MICHAEL
        Do you think I'm funny?

                    ANNA
        What, in shorts?

MICHAEL

No! Am I a funny person?

ANNA

Yes.

She exits.

DAVID

Michael, come on.

MICHAEL

No.

DAVID

Wear shorts.

MICHAEL

No.

DAVID

Why not?

MICHAEL

They make my crotch ... too free.

DAVID

Oh, fuck it. Shall we just go to
America?

MICHAEL

Yeah?

DAVID

Yeah. I mean, I do and say funny things.
You have comedically chunky legs. That's
enough.

MICHAEL

We are funny.

DAVID

Oh, we're fucking hilarious!

MICHAEL

Back to work.

DAVID

Staged America!

MICHAEL

Staged America!

DAVID

Come on, Sheen!

MICHAEL

Er, no.
Hey, no. You're ...

                          DAVID
          I'm gonna ride you all the way to
          America, boy.

                          MICHAEL
          You are not riding me anywhere, matey.

                          DAVID
          Saddle up, Sheenie!

                          MICHAEL
          I have put the last saddle on my back
          for you, mate.

                          DAVID
          I love it. We made a thing, let's go to
          America and do it again.

                          MICHAEL
          Yeah. And do you, do you know what? One
          day we will bump into Michael Palin at
          some glitzy fancy dress party, and he
          will say ...
          ... 'I utterly misjudged you, you clown
          gods.'

                          DAVID
          Yes, we'll be invaluable again.

                          MICHAEL
          Because, you know what, you and I are
          masters of our destinies.

                          DAVID
          Kings of the hills!

                          MICHAEL
          Tops of the morning!

                          DAVID
          Docks of the bay!

                          MICHAEL
          Yes!

                          DAVID
          They're gonna fucking love us!

   Beat.

9 INT. MICHAEL'S HOUSE AND MARY'S OFFICE - DAY   9

                          MARY
          They don't want you.

   Michael stares at the screen intently.

                          MICHAEL
          What?

MARY

Either of you.

MICHAEL

Right.

MARY

Now they love the show, but they wanna
recast for the American market.

MICHAEL

That is, er, bad news.

MARY

Oh, I know.

MICHAEL

When did you know this?

MARY

Well the email just arrived.

MICHAEL

So, who is doing it then?

MARY

Well it's only rumours.

MICHAEL

Who?

MARY

Colin Firth and Hugh Grant.

MICHAEL

Colin Firth and Hugh Grant?

MARY

That's just what I'm hearing.

MICHAEL

They're not American.

MARY

Doesn't matter.

MICHAEL

And they're more British than we are.

MARY

Yes, but they're known in America.

MICHAEL

I'm known in America.

MARY

They're known better.

MICHAEL

What, what else does the email say?

                              MARY
          It says they have a lot of respect for
          you both and they want leads with more
          US recognition ... and a pair who are
          more believable as friends.

                            MICHAEL
          Sorry. We, we are actually friends.

                              MARY
          Yes, but nobody's buying it. And they
          also want people with more comedic
          experience.

                            MICHAEL
          I'm funny.

                              MARY
          I know.

                            MICHAEL
          I mean, Colin Firth is not funny. I'm
          fun ... Knock knock.

                              MARY
          You're still on as Executive Producers.

                            MICHAEL
          Knock knock.

                              MARY
          With Simon.

                            MICHAEL
          Simon?

                              MARY
          Yes, he's still involved.

                            MICHAEL
          Doing what?!

                              MARY
          Rewrites. Listen, I didn't think you
          were in a rush to get back to work.

                            MICHAEL
          I'm not. It's just David got me all
          excited about this.

                              MARY
          I thought you were David.

                            MICHAEL
          No, I'm Michael.

Mary's screen goes black.

                        MICHAEL (CONT'D)
          Hugh Grant.

The end credits play over this.

> **DAVID**
> Okay. Choose a card.

> **MICHAEL**
> People don't think we're believable as friends.

> **DAVID**
> I know. I heard.

> **MICHAEL**
> The Palin thing hurt. But that is a gut punch. Why ... why is that?

> **DAVID**
> I suppose they've only ever heard us speak other people's lines, haven't they?

> **MICHAEL**
> Anna keeps telling me I'm dropping into character.

> **DAVID**
> Yes! Georgia says exactly the same to me about me. She ...

> **MICHAEL**
> Right. Yeah.

> **DAVID**
> And I keep saying to her, 'No ... you ... that doesn't that doesn't ...

Beat.

> **DAVID (CONT'D)**
> you can't say that because that's ... I am that person.'

> **MICHAEL**
> It's ... that's ... that's who I am. That's me.

> **DAVID**
> Exactly. I ... Yeah. 'You can't say I'm dropping into character when I'm the character.'

> **MICHAEL**
> I can't be anything else. Say, say something now. Say something that's authentically you.

                    MICHAEL (CONT'D)
And my flights to New York are
cancelled.

                         DAVID
Ah, the world starts, the world stops.
It's arbitrary, isn't it?

                        MICHAEL
'As flies to wanton boys are we to the
gods.'

                         DAVID
Can we not?

                        MICHAEL
Quite right. Okay.

                         DAVID
Yeah, got it. Okay, hold it up.

                        MICHAEL
Yeah.

                         DAVID
I don't wanna see it. But hold it up,
back facing to me.

Michael holds up a playing card. David waggles his fingers as he
tries to summon his psychic powers.

                        MICHAEL
Gonna be like this for a while yet,
aren't we?

                         DAVID
How do you mean?

                        MICHAEL
Staring at the screen, hoping for a
miracle.

                         DAVID
Oh, yeah.

                        MICHAEL
Maybe we can start a magic act ... The
amazing Michael Sheen and the Scottish
David Tennant.

                         DAVID
Three of Diamonds.

                        MICHAEL
No.

                         DAVID
Fuck.

Four of Diamonds.

Michael holds it up again, turns it around.

MICHAEL

It was close. It was the two of
Diamonds.

DAVID

Ah, you see, I was so close.

MICHAEL

I mean ... close enough for jazz. Not
close enough for magic.

BLACK SCREEN

Episode Two
Long Time,
No See

DAVID TENNANT sitting in his kitchen. MICHAEL SHEEN in his sitting room. Over this the credits: white letters on black.

> **DAVID**
> I'm embracing this.

> **MICHAEL**
> How do you mean?

> **DAVID**
> My shoot dates have changed again and location.

> **MICHAEL**
> What, no South Africa?

> **DAVID**
> No. Italy now.

> **MICHAEL**
> Still nice.

> **DAVID**
> So, I'm embracing the fact that I have no control over events, and I am going to welcome the role that chaos needs to play in my life.

> **MICHAEL**
> Right. How, how are you doing that?

> **DAVID**
> The game is happening. But it's being played far away by unknowable strangers.

> **MICHAEL**
> Out of sight, out of mind.

> **DAVID**
> We should quit.

> **MICHAEL**
> What?

> **DAVID**
> It's a young man's game, innit.

> **MICHAEL**
> I'm only fifty.

Beat.

> **DAVID**
> We can do other things.

> **MICHAEL**
> You have zero discernible skills beyond pretending.

                    DAVID
Is there something else you were gonna
do, if you hadn't ended up doing this?

                  MICHAEL
I was gonna be a footballer.

I was.

                    DAVID
Yeah. I could have been a Minister of
the Church.

                  MICHAEL
Yeah. No, no problem with the cassock?

                    DAVID
Not having kilted.

                  MICHAEL
Of course.

                    DAVID
When one has welcomed the breeze to dust
one's lower branches, there's ...

Michael chuckles.

                DAVID (CONT'D)
... there's no going back.

                  MICHAEL
No. Well, you need to do something to
keep the flies off your haggis.

                    DAVID
Exactly, yeah.

                  MICHAEL
The priest and the footballer.

                    DAVID
Yeah. You might struggle a bit at first.

                  MICHAEL
Why?

                    DAVID
Well, you know, you're not in the
... you're not ... you don't ... you're
not in the ... absolute kind of op ...
optimum state of physical peak.

                  MICHAEL
I will have you know, I am a fucking
paragon of human fitness, mate.

                    DAVID
Are you?

MICHAEL
What about you? You would need a total
spiritual overhaul.

                                     DAVID
Has this ever happened to you before?

Michael reflects.

                                    MICHAEL
Once.

                                     DAVID
You got recast?

                                    MICHAEL
I did.

                                     DAVID
Who by?

                                    MICHAEL
Don't wanna say.

                                     DAVID
But you know?

                                    MICHAEL
I know.

                                     DAVID
Oh, come on.

                                    MICHAEL
No, can't.

                                     DAVID
Why not?

                                    MICHAEL
Because I'm doing something about it.

                                     DAVID
What?

                                    MICHAEL
Can you keep a secret?

                                     DAVID
Evidently.

                                    MICHAEL
I am befriending him slowly and
methodically, engineering ways for us
to work together ... insinuating my way
into his life, the better to exact my
slow and decisive revenge.

                          SIMON
        Hi, Nina.

                          NINA
        Hello.

                          SIMON
        Hello. Hi. Oh God, it's lovely to see
        you.

                          NINA
        Yeah, it's lovely to see you, too.
        Ah, this is exciting.

                          SIMON
        It's really exciting.

                          NINA
        More Staged.

                          SIMON
        More Staged.

                          NINA
        Yay.

                          SIMON
        Oh.

                          NINA
        Oh, my word. How have you been?

                          SIMON
        Yeah, good, I think. Yeah, great. And
        you?

                          NINA
        I'm fine. Strange, you know.

                          SIMON
        Yeah. I suppose it is.

                          NINA
        Um, I was offered a play.

                          SIMON
        Oh, great.

                          NINA
        Um, yeah, we weren't allowed to do the
        play. It's difficult.

                          SIMON
        Right. Sure. No, I understand.

                          NINA
        Yeah. And I, I, I feel like sometimes,
        you know, I wanna kill someone ... but I
        won't.

                    SIMON
No, best not.

                    NINA
No. Because I should have been an
astronaut.

                    SIMON
Was that an option?

                    NINA
No.

Beat.

How are you?

                    SIMON
Good.

                    NINA
Actually, where are you?

                    SIMON
Oh, er, ha ha ... I'm in Los Angeles.

                    NINA
Oh, what are you doing there?

                    SIMON
Um ... getting ready to film.

                    NINA
Ah, exciting. What?

A beat.

                    SIMON
What have you been told?

                    NINA
Well, er, actually, not much. Doing more
Staged. They want you for Jo again. Can
you talk to Simon?

                    SIMON
Er ... right, okay. So there's a couple
of things that you should have been told
but it seems you haven't been told.

                    NINA
And what are they?

                    SIMON
Er, well, so it's not a sequel, it's a
sort of remake.

                    NINA
Oh, okay.

SIMON
For the American market. And the most
crucial thing, and I'm sort of really
sorry that I've got to be the one to
tell you this, but we're gonna be doing
it without, er, David or, and, er,
Michael.

A beat.

NINA
Why?

SIMON
Er, so, er, the producers don't think
that they are quite big enough names for
the American market.

NINA
But I am?

SIMON
Well, you're not the lead. That's ...

NTNA
True.

SIMON
It's, it's not quite what I, what I sort
of meant. I sort of meant when you sort
of are the lead of the sort of ...

NINA
Um, but you've managed to keep yourself
involved?

SIMON
Er, well, cos I sort of created it last
time and sort of directed that, that
sort of version of it, so ...

NINA
And you're directing this time?

SIMON
Er, no. No, I'm not.

NINA
Why not?

SIMON
Er, because people don't think I
actually did anything ... last time. So
...

NINA
I mean, I thought David and Michael
improvised most of it, didn't they?

SIMON
No. No. No, they didn't, did they? They

SIMON (CONT'D)

didn't do that. They didn't improvise
it, did they? I, I, I wrote it, didn't
I? I typed the whole thing ... No, no,
I've got pieces of ... blue card. I
wrote ... I write the thing and then I
put them on the wall. And then I write,
write, write, write, write, and we don't
say that they wrote it or improvised it.
But they didn't, did they? We don't say
that, do they, cos they didn't.

A beat as a rewrite drops from the board and falls to the floor.

NINA

Do David and Michael know?

Beat. They clearly don't.

NINA (CONT'D)

Wow.

Beat.

3 INT. DAVID'S HOUSE - DAY   3

A pair of suitcases stand in the hall. GEORGIA TENNANT enters
through a doorway and stumbles into them.

GEORGIA

Ah, shit.
Can you move this suitcase?

David enters.

DAVID

Yeah, yeah, yeah. Yeah, absolutely.

GEORGIA

Cos I don't think the hallway should be
used as an obstacle course.

DAVID

No. I've just been feeding the goldfish.
We never got another one.

GEORGIA

No, you didn't.

DAVID

We had two, and now we've got one.

GEORGIA

Agreed.

DAVID

That's how death works.

GEORGIA

And maths.

DAVID

I am worried that the one that's left
behind's getting a wee bit depressed.

GEORGIA

Oh, I don't have time for this.

DAVID

What do you mean?

GEORGIA

Well, it's just I sense that you are
segueing into some tangent about short-
term memory and I just ... I haven't got
time to play.

DAVID

You love my tangents.

GEORGIA

Yeah, sure. It's just that Lissa's
coming.

DAVID

Today?

GEORGIA

Yeah.

DAVID

What, right now?

GEORGIA

Yeah, for a charity thing.

DAVID

Like in the flesh? Like Zoom doesn't cut
it any more?

GEORGIA

Yeah. Normality beckons, babe.

DAVID

Is that safe?

GEORGIA

Yeah, I think so. As long as we stay a
certain distance apart and use our own
mugs and don't stick our hands in the
cookie jar at the same time. And, oh,
also, more importantly, we don't crack
our heads open by tripping over your
fucking suitcase.

DAVID

Yeah. I'll move it. I'll move it.

GEORGIA

Yeah, that'll be great, thank you.

                                DAVID
                What would you have done if you weren't
                doing this?

Beat.

                                GEORGIA
                What is it you think I do?

                                DAVID
                Come on.

                What's ... what, what's, what's the,
                what's the dream?

                                GEORGIA
                Um ... archaeologist.

                                DAVID
                I never knew that.

                                GEORGIA
                Oh God, I've done it again.

                                DAVID
                What?

                                GEORGIA
                You've sucked me in. You're like a black
                hole.

                                DAVID
                Don't be mean to me.

                                GEORGIA
                Oh, Michael is your procrastination
                buddy and I am your wife. And I've got
                stuff to do, and you really need to not
                be here when that happens.

                                DAVID
                I've just got a lot of stuff to process,
                and feelings and ...

                                GEORGIA
                Yeah. It's just the rest of us just have
                to get on with it, so ...

                                DAVID
                I'm just a bit worried that the goldfish
                that's left behind will do anything to
                have its little buddy to play around the
                castle with.

                                GEORGIA
                Okay. I think that the goldfish left
                behind forgot about the other goldfish
                within seconds.

Sound of mobile phone vibrating. David takes out his mobile phone.

> GEORGIA (CONT'D)
>
> Who is it?

> DAVID
>
> It's Nina.

> GEORGIA
>
> Oh. Hi, Nina.

> DAVID
>
> Hi, Nina.

4   INT. DAVID'S AND MICHAEL'S HOUSES   4

DAVID and MICHAEL are sitting in their respective living rooms.

> MICHAEL
>
> He'll be with us in a couple of minutes.

> DAVID
>
> Okay. Good.

A beat.

> MICHAEL
>
> You alright?

> DAVID
>
> It's everyone else.

> MICHAEL
>
> I understand.

> DAVID
>
> Adrian, Nina, Lucy.

> MICHAEL
>
> Sam?

> DAVID
>
> Yeah.

> MICHAEL
>
> Dame Judi?

> DAVID
>
> Of course.

> MICHAEL
>
> And Simon?

> DAVID
>
> And Simon. Yeah.

> MICHAEL
>
> Anna ... thinks that we should, um,
> should try and stay calm with him.

> DAVID
>   (incredulous)
> Why?

                    MICHAEL
     Because he's on one side of the line and
     we're, we're on the other.

                    DAVID
     Michael, we drew the fucking line!

                    MICHAEL
     I know. Anna said it better.

                MICHAEL (CONT'D)
                   (calls)
     Anna!

                    ANNA (O.S.)
     Yeah.

                    MICHAEL
     Er, what was that Viking saying?

                    ANNA (O.S.)
     What?

                    MICHAEL
     You know, the Viking phrase.

                    DAVID
     The Viking phrase ...?

Anna Lundberg enters and stops beside Michael.

                    ANNA
     Oh ... 'The, the thrall alone takes
     instant vengeance.'

                    DAVID
     What the fuck does that mean?

                    MICHAEL
     Yeah, what does that mean?

                    ANNA
     Actions are too often ruled by emotions.

A beat.

                    DAVID
     That seems a little bit hypocritical
     coming from the Vikings.

                    MICHAEL
     Yeah, what ... she, she's saying
     ... we should remain civil.

                    DAVID
     Fuck that!

                    ANNA
     Don't burn your bridges.

                              DAVID
          No, we won't. We won't.

                              ANNA
          It's the only way to get close enough to
          do some real damage.

                              DAVID
          What would the Vikings recommend?

                              ANNA
          Something with an axe.

Anna leans back and exits.

An awkward silence. Computer chimes.

                              MICHAEL
          Er, right, okay. Now remember the
          Vikings, okay? Just ca ... just calm.
          Deep breaths. Just calm.
          Just ... calm. Sshh. Let ... embrace
          chaos.

                              DAVID
          I'm gonna be fine.

                              MICHAEL
          Great.

                              DAVID
          I'm gonna be really calm and nice.

                              MICHAEL
          Okay. Here we go. Just deep breaths,
          deep ...

                              DAVID
          Yeah.

Simon suddenly appears between them, sitting out on his sunny
hotel terrace.

                        DAVID (CONT'D)
                        (shouts)
          Ah, so that's where you've been hiding,
          you cu ... !

Michael looks exasperated as we realise Simon cannot hear what
they are saying.

                        DAVID (CONT'D)
                        (shouts)
          I said, that's where you've been hiding,
          you fu ... !
                        (mutters)
          Fu ...

                              MICHAEL
          He can't hear you. He can't hear you.
          Thank fuck ...

                    DAVID
        Great!

                    MICHAEL
        ... he can't hear you. Okay. David,
        please.

Simon is busy adjusting his headphones.

                    DAVID
        ... even just seeing his punchable
        little face, I'm finding it very hard.

                    MICHAEL
        I know. I know. I know. You know he's a
        twat, I know he's a twat.

                    DAVID
        Oh, mate ...

                    MICHAEL
        But let's just pretend for this
        conversation ...
                (to Simon)
        It's alright, take your time, take your
        time, Simon. Yeah. No, don't worry,
        don't worry.

                    DAVID
        Yeah, take all the t ... Oh, we got all
        the time in the world. Oh, it's so nice
        to see you, Simon.

                    MICHAEL
                (to David)
        Just pl ... just please, just ... let's
        just give it a try.

                    DAVID
        I'm, I'm on my best behaviour.

                    MICHAEL
        Okay. Thank you.

Michael and David switch into polite mode as it's clear Simon
can now hear them.

                    SIMON
        Hi. Sorry.

                    MICHAEL
        Hey, Simon!

                    DAVID
        Hey!

They chuckle.

                    SIMON
        Hey, sorry about that.
                (mumbles)

MICHAEL

How are you, mate?

SIMON

Yeah, no, good. Sorry. Er, yeah,
Michael, hello, hi. Er, David, goodness.
Long time, no see. How are you?

DAVID

Yeah, Nina phoned me. Yeah.

SIMON

Yeah? Okay, right!

MICHAEL

Um, er, let's just have a little catch-
up first, shall we?

SIMON

Yeah, that'd be lovely.

MICHAEL

How are you?

SIMON

Good. Hey look. I'm in Los Angeles!

DAVID

(laughs)

MICHAEL

So it's happening, Staged America?

SIMON

Yeah, looks like it.

MICHAEL

That is exciting.

SIMON

Yeah. Yeah, it really is. And look, I
know I owe you guys a lot of thanks for
that. Um ... I know we haven't really had
a chance to talk about it all, but ...

MICHAEL

Oh, don't be silly.

SIMON

Well, it's been mad.

MICHAEL

Yes, I bet. So, what, lots of, lots of
new opportunities?

SIMON

I've been run off my feet. There's just
so much work to do.

Beat.

I couldn't have imagined any of this.

DAVID

No. Well, I mean, you couldn't have
imagined anything at all without us,
could you?

MICHAEL

Er, what I ... what David means I, I
think is that we feel, um, you know,
quite a lot of love, er, even ownership
of the project too.

SIMON

Yeah, I mean, I did write it.

MICHAEL

See now David is gonna get a wee bit
ticked off ... with that kind of
territorial attitude, Simon. He thinks
that we both brought a lot to the
project too. We thought we were a team.

SIMON

Oh, me too.

MICHAEL

So we were a little bit hurt when we
heard that we weren't needed.

A beat.

SIMON

Of course.

MICHAEL

But we got past that. But then ... when
we heard from Nina ...

DAVID

Yeah. My friend Nina. Nina, who
... my friend Nina called me up.

MICHAEL

... that literally every other member of
the cast ...

DAVID

Every other member.

MICHAEL

... was coming back except us ...

DAVID

Yeah.

SIMON

Yes.

MICHAEL

I mean, even you ... managed to hold on
to your role.

                         SIMON
          Well, I am Simon.

                         DAVID
          Oh, well who am I, then, fucking
          Spartacus?!

                         MICHAEL
          But ... but you're, you're not an actor.

                         SIMON
          No, but I, but I wrote it.

                         DAVID
          Ah, f ...

                         MICHAEL
          David. David, Vikings. Vikings, David.
          Vikings. Vikings.

David stands and walks off.

                         SIMON
          Vikings? Vikings?

                         MICHAEL
          Okay. Okay. Okay. Whoa, let's ... let's,
          let's just ... let's just talk about
          something else for a minute. Okay, let's
          just shake it up. Um ... Simon, what, what
          were you gonna be when you were young?

                         SIMON
          A director.

                         MICHAEL
          No, I meant ... I meant if, er, that
          didn't work out.

David enters and turns to the screen.

                         SIMON
          I wanted to be a magician.

David laughs and walks off.

                         MICHAEL
          Whoa, David. David's, um, trying to
          learn some tricks.

David steps in.

                         SIMON
          Right.

                         MICHAEL
          Were you, were you any good?

                         SIMON
          I was, actually. I was, I was, I was
          very good.

David grabs a playing card from a deck in his hand and holds it
out.

> DAVID
>> Yeah, what's that card?

> SIMON
>> The seven of Diamonds.

He cannot believe Simon has guessed correctly.

> DAVID
>> Oh, fuck you!

He walks off in disgust.

> MICHAEL
>> Alright, alright. Is, is there anything
>> we can do to help you, Simon?

A beat.

> SIMON
>> Excuse me?

> MICHAEL
>> Help.

> SIMON
>> No. No, I don't think so.

David enters and sits on his sofa.

> MICHAEL
>> No, no, it's not a trick. It's ... we,
>> we just wanna help. We, we, we just,
>> what can we do? What can we do? Come on.
>> What can we do?

> SIMON
>> I wouldn't say this if you hadn't
>> just ... Two of the actors that we're
>> considering for David and ... and
>> Michael, they've actually reached out
>> to, to see if you might make some time
>> to ... talk to them.

> DAVID
>> About what?

> SIMON
>> Er, just to offer some thoughts on your
>> ... experience making the show.

> MICHAEL
>> (slowly)
>> We would be very happy to.

A beat.

                              SIMON
          Really?

                              MICHAEL
          I mean, we're all on the same side.

                              SIMON
          Well then I'll, I'll set it up.

                              MICHAEL
          Great.

                              SIMON
          I really appreciate it.

                              MICHAEL
          No. No, thank you. That's what we
          ... what we needed just to, you know, a
          little, little bit of collaboration.

                              SIMON
          Hey, maybe you could ... give a couple
          of notes on the roles, too.

Michael's anger suddenly erupts.

                              MICHAEL
                    (shouts)
          Fuck you!

He stands and walks off as David leaps from his sofa.

                              DAVID
                    (shouts)
          I mean, I will ... I will put an axe
          into your face and I will nail your
          skull on to the mast of my Viking
          longship before I give any actor another
          bunch of notes about how to play David
          Tennant, you fucking patronising
          mollusc!

Michael paces back and forth, clutching his face. He groans.

A beat.

                              SIMON
          I think we should just let our agents
          talk from here, shouldn't we?

Simon ends the call and disappears as Michael lunges towards
the screen.

                              MICHAEL
                    (shouts)
          Don't you fucking ... !

He sits and breathes heavily. A beat.

                         MICHAEL (CONT'D)
          I didn't even know he had an agent.

DAVID
                    Seven of fucking Diamonds. Unbelievable.

5   INT. DAVID'S AND MICHAEL'S HOUSES - DAY   5

   DAVID is clutching a playing card. The end credits play over
   this.

                              MICHAEL
                    I called Simon back and apologised.

                              DAVID
                    Okay, well done.

                              MICHAEL
                    Told him we'd speak to those other
                    actors tomorrow.

                              DAVID
                    Oh, Jesus. Okay.

                              MICHAEL
                    Why do you think we have never made each
                    other this angry?

                              DAVID
                    Well, because we have a scintilla of
                    respect for each other.

                              MICHAEL
                    Yes.

                              DAVID
                    Yeah. Because we started as colleagues
                    and then we became friends.

                              MICHAEL
                    And then great friends.

                              DAVID
                    Would you say I'm your best friend?

                              MICHAEL
                    No.

                              DAVID
                    No?

                              MICHAEL
                    No, I don't mean it like that.

                              DAVID
                    No, no, no, no. Fine. I just ... well,
                    you know, I thought you might take, take
                    a bit longer to think about it.

   A beat.

                              MICHAEL
                    No, but, but am I yours?

                         DAVID
No.

                        MICHAEL
Well there we are.

                         DAVID
No, you might have been.

                        MICHAEL
If what?

                         DAVID
If you'd said I was yours.

                        MICHAEL
I've got an older friend.

                         DAVID
I'm old.

                        MICHAEL
No, I ... I mean, I've, I've got a
friend who I've known for longer. He
lives in New York.

                         DAVID
Okay. Yeah, I had a friend once.

                        MICHAEL
Who?

                         DAVID
Rather not say.

                        MICHAEL
And you're not friends any more?

                         DAVID
No.

Beat.

So, when you go out to New York you're
gonna see him, are ya?

                        MICHAEL
Well that's why I'm going. He's getting
married.

                         DAVID
Oh, well that's lovely for him.

                        MICHAEL
Well I'm, I'm the best man. It was
supposed to happen earlier this year but
...

                         DAVID
But it all, yeah.

MICHAEL

So, you know, be nice to be there.

DAVID

Well, it'd be nice to be anywhere.

MICHAEL

Yeah.

Beat.

Anna hasn't been to Sweden in ages.
She's really missing her family.

DAVID

Well, I'm sure she is, yeah.

A beat. David gestures with the playing card in his hand.

DAVID (CONT'D)

Hey.

MICHAEL

Um ... four of Diamonds.

He turns the card to reveal Michael is incorrect. Michael
groans. David tosses the card away.

DAVID

We should quit.

MICHAEL

Magic is harder than it looks.

DAVID

Oh God, I hate magic.

MICHAEL

Oh, maybe we could ask Simon to help.

David grins inanely and growls.

BLACK SCREEN

Något med en yxa!

Episode Three
The Dirty Mochyns

1 INT. DAVID'S AND MICHAEL'S HOUSES - DAY   1

   DAVID TENNANT and MICHAEL SHEEN both clutching playing cards,
   deep in thought as they organise them.

   Over this, the credits: white letters on black.

                         DAVID
               Michael.

   Beat.
               Michael, I've got a plan.

                         MICHAEL
               For what?

                         DAVID
               Getting back on the show.

                         MICHAEL
               I thought you'd welcomed chaos into your
               life?

                         DAVID
               I know. We had. But ... we have an
               opportunity.

                         MICHAEL
               What?

                         DAVID
               Reading with the other actors today,
               it's an opportunity.

                         MICHAEL
               Sure.

                         DAVID
               So, have you ever taken part in an act
               of sabotage?

2 INT. SIMON PEGG'S AND NICK FROST'S HOUSES - DAY   2

   SIMON PEGG and NICK FROST in two boxes side by side. The credits
   continue.

                         NICK
               The Welsh must have a good phrase for
               the end of the world.

                         SIMON
               Why do you have to say that?

                         NICK
               Dylan Thomas must have written about it.
               I mean, his poem.

                         SIMON
               Well, yeah, he wrote 'Do Not Go Gentle
               Into That Good Night'.

Dear David,

It's lovely to hear you want to take up magic. Your email mentioned wanting a trick to 'reduce Michael to a fool in the eyes of the world…', I don't know whether the below achieves that, but it might allow you to win a few quid off him.

1. You need a deck of cards. Any kind will do. Shuffle them in front of your audience (or let them shuffle them). Either way, once shuffled, be sure to glimpse the card on the bottom of the deck. For the sake of this explanation, we'll call it the Four of Clubs.

2. Fan the cards and ask your audience to pick one. Once they have looked at it and remembered it, ask them to place it back, face down, on the top of the deck.

3. Now cut the deck (take the top half off and put it under the bottom half). If you've done it right, their card is now the one underneath the Four of Clubs.

4. You have two options. If you're financially stable, just start dealing the cards from the top, turning them face up as you lay them on the table. You could spin some yarn about 'sensing the vibrations of each card'. When the Four of Clubs appears, you know that the next card is going to be theirs. Perhaps you could begin to shudder as if the magical vibrations are having an effect on you. Perhaps you could say, 'I'm getting close.' Then turn over the final card with a suitable ejaculation: 'Ta da.'[1]

5. Option two starts the same but, when you reach the Four of Clubs, deal the next card down (their card) and keep dealing, making sure that their card remains visible. After a few more cards have been dealt, do the same shuddering. Then pause and say: 'I think I've got it. I bet you £5/£10/a People's Choice Award, that the next card I turn over will be your card.' They, still seeing their card visible on the table, will confidently shake on the deal. Put the deck down, remove their card from the table, and turn it face up. Their card was the next card you turned over, and no judge in the land would disagree. Collect your Award, offer an acceptance speech, and move on.[2]

Have fun.
Simon

---

1 On reflection, this seems a little orgasmic. Perhaps shudder less.

2 If you do decide to play for money, a gentle reminder that you owe me £20 from when I bought you lunch and had it taxi-ed to Chiswick.

                    NICK
There you go.

                    SIMON
I did a little bit for the, er, BBC.

                    NICK
Oh, did ya?

                    SIMON
Mmm.
'Rage, rage against the dying of the
light.'
Who wrote that?

Michael appears on screen from his home.

                    MICHAEL
Er, Dylan Thomas.

David also appears from his home so now all four are on screen.

                    SIMON
It was. I ... yeah. I thought it was
Kipling for some reason.

Nick laughs.

                SIMON (CONT'D)
What? Oh, you know loads about poetry,
do you?

                    NICK
I know the fucking classics.

A beat.

                    SIMON
'Rage, rage against the dying of the
light.'
            (to Michael/David)
Any thoughts at the moment?

                    DAVID
No, it sounds good. Um, I wonder if
there's a version where you just go much
more theatrical.

                    SIMON
Theatrical?

                    DAVID
Cos Michael really leaned into it.

                    SIMON
Really?

                    DAVID
Really, yeah.

                              NICK
          Really?

                              DAVID
          Didn't you, Michael?

A beat. Michael considers his part in David's plan.

                              MICHAEL
          Er, really.

A beat.

                              DAVID
          Yeah. Cos I think the arc of the show we
          get to humility down the line, so if,
          if in the early stages you just hammer
          those theatrical stereotypes, I think it
          gives you somewhere to go, to subvert
          it.

                              SIMON
          Alright, so bigger, so ... on the stage
          kind of ...

Simon gives it his all.

                         (recites)
          'Rage, rage against the dying of the
          light!'

                              DAVID
          Honestly, it works. It really works. I
          would blast it.

Simon goes again, with even more gusto.

                              SIMON
                         (recites)
          'Rage, rage against the dying of the
          light!'

                              DAVID
          See, that's brilliant. Fantastic.

                              NICK
          Do you know what it was in the original
          Welsh?

                              SIMON
          Hang on, sorry. How do you mean?

                              NICK
          Before it was translated.

                              SIMON
          Translated?

                              NICK
          What did he originally write?

Beat.

SIMON

Can I just say how grateful we are.

DAVID

It's a pleasure.

SIMON

Just to, you know, have this kind of
access to you is, is ... it's a treat.

DAVID

Listen, we just want the best for it.

SIMON

Well, you know, we're, we're reading it
for the, er, producers tomorrow.

DAVID

Are you? Right.

SIMON

Yeah. And we were a little nervous to,
er, to ask, you know, er, because this
is all a bit ... sort of new, but it's
br ... it's just brilliant to have your
insight.

DAVID

We're just happy to help.

SIMON

I know that we're, you know, supposedly
better known than you.

NICK

Don't say that.

SIMON

Well, I mean, it, you know, let's not
argue the toss. But I'm just saying this
is your show either way.

DAVID

Yeah ... listen, it's ...

SIMON

Yeah. Nick said that you might mislead
us as well.
> (laughs)

NICK

I've got a massage in forty minutes, so
it'd be great if we could crack on.

SIMON

You got it.

DAVID

Sure.

                              SIMON
                         (reads)
                    Cachu hwch.

Silence. Michael smiles politely.

                         SIMON (CONT'D)
                         (reads)
                    Cachu, hwch hwch.

Simon accidentally spits on to his script.

                         SIMON (CONT'D)
                    Spit everywhere.
                         (reads)
                    Cachu hwch.
                         (to Michael/David)
                    Am I saying that right? There's no
                    vowels in this.

                              DAVID
                    Michael, is that ...?

                              MICHAEL
                    Um ...
                         (clears throat)
                    ... sorry, say, say it again.

                              SIMON
                         (reads)
                    Cachu hwch.

A beat. Michael considers his response carefully.

                              MICHAEL
                    Spot on.

                              SIMON
                         (chuckles)
                    I didn't know ...

                              NICK
                    Really?

                              MICHAEL
                    A-absolutely.

                              SIMON
                    So it's cachu hwch.

                              NICK
                    Cos I thought it was cachu hwch.

                              SIMON
                    No, it's cachu hwch.

                              DAVID
                    It is cachu hwch. Yeah.

                              SIMON
                    Hey, is Michael supposed to be Welsh?

                    MICHAEL
          I, I am.

                      NICK
          He is Welsh.

                     SIMON
          Oh, so, er, does that mean I have to do
          a, a Welsh accent?

                     DAVID
          Can you do a Welsh accent?

                     SIMON
                (to Michael)
          What part of Wales are you from,
          Michael?

                    MICHAEL
                (hesitantly)
          The south of Wales. Port Talbot.

                     SIMON
          Yeah, Port Talbot. What, er, Baglan end
          or, or Taibach?

                    MICHAEL
          Er, Baglan end.

                     SIMON
          Baglan, Baglan, Baglan, Baglan.
                (recites - imitates Welsh
                accent)
          'Do not go gentle into that good night.'

A beat.

                     DAVID
                (to Michael)
          Michael?

A beat. Michael considers his answer at length.

                    MICHAEL
                (to Simon)
          It's spot on.

                     SIMON
          Yes, I knew it.

Nick is becoming impatient.

                      NICK
          Don't do this again, man.

                     SIMON
          Why are you talking to me like that?

                      NICK
          Fuck you. Like what?

                         SIMON
          Like I'm a fucking irritant.

                          NICK
          You're not an irritant.

                         SIMON
          Thank you.

                          NICK
          You're a black hole.

                         SIMON
          Oh, fuck you, man.

                          NICK
                    (to Michael/David)
          He refuses to do any kind of
          preparation.

                         SIMON
          Why are you being like this?

                          NICK
          You don't know the poem. You don't know
          the Welsh. You didn't even know that
          Michael was fucking one of the Welsh.

                         SIMON
          I do now.

                          NICK
          Had you even read this before you came
          on the call, Simon?

David's attention perks up as Simon grabs a Star Trek mug.

                         SIMON
          I had read bits, bits of it.

                         DAVID
          That a Star Trek mug?

                         SIMON
          Yeah.

                         DAVID
          Nice.

                          NICK
          Fucking hell.
                    (to Michael/David)
          Scottie does this every fucking time.
                    (to Simon)
          Don't you, Scottie?

                         SIMON
          Oh ...

NICK

So we don't have a chance to switch it
round and try it the other way on the
day.

MICHAEL

The other way?

SIMON

They want us to do it this way, mate.

NICK

They were happy for us to do it both
ways.

SIMON

They want me to play Michael because
Michael and I have the same face.

NICK
(Welsh accent)
I want them to hear me read Michael.

DAVID

You don't wanna read David?

SIMON

Can I speak candidly?

DAVID

Yeah.

SIMON

We feel that David is just a little
tepid.

DAVID

Tepid?

SIMON

Yeah, well, you know, cos he just sort
of floats about, you know.
And he's ... I ... he's sort of
... inert is the word I was looking for.

NICK

Inert, yeah.

DAVID

Inert?

SIMON

Yeah. Michael is surprising, you know.
Michael's fascinating.
Michael, may I ask you a question?

MICHAEL

Yes.

NICK

Don't let him distract you, Michael.

                    SIMON
        Tell me the story about the birds.

A beat.

                    MICHAEL
        What?

                    SIMON
        In Episode One you are really pre ...
        pre-occupied because of birds, and it's
        gorgeous. What you're doing is so ...
        it's subtle but it's lovely.

                    DAVID
        Yeah, but there weren't any birds.

                    NICK
        There were no fucking birds.

                    SIMON
        I mean, in the character's head.
              (to Michael)
        Let's talk about that. I just wanna know
        where that fear came from cos it was
        real.

                    MICHAEL
        Mmm. Um, okay. Well, er ... well, er,
        they were, they were working in teams.

                    SIMON
        Right, and you, but ... and you fought
        back.

                    MICHAEL
        I did fight, yes.

                    SIMON
        You're like a paragon of human physical
        fitness.

                    MICHAEL
        Yeah, well, I was gonna be a footballer,
        you know.

                              SIMON
        That doesn't surprise me one bit.

                              DAVID
        But he very much is not a footballer.
        Er, he is a coward with a Hitchcock
        fetish is what he is.

Simon throws out his best impersonation of Michael.

                              SIMON
        I see you, you little feathered shit.

                             MICHAEL
                    (laughs)

                              NICK
                    (imitates Michael)
        I see you, you little feathered shit.

                              SIMON
                    (imitates Michael)
        I see you, you little feathered shit.

                             MICHAEL
        Ooh. I see you, you little feathered
        shit.

                              SIMON
                    (imitates Michael)
        I see ...
                    (to David/Nick)
        He's doing it.

David is completely unimpressed as the others laugh and joke
around.

                         SIMON (CONT'D)
        He's doing it. He's doing it.

                              NICK
                    (imitates Michael)
        Shit. Shit.

                             MICHAEL
        I see you, you little feathered shit.

                              SIMON
        Oh, my goodness. Why do we even bother?

Silence.

                              DAVID
        But Da ... David is, David is a fighter
        too.

                              NICK
        Against what?

                              DAVID
        Like the ... you know, the apathy.

Simon leans close to his screen.

> **SIMON**
> I don't like you. I find you weaselly.

Beat.

> Michael, what was going on in your head
> when you said that?

> **MICHAEL**
> Oh, um, I mean the truth.

> **NICK**
> Well, how do you mean?

> **MICHAEL**
> Well, you see, Nick, I, I don't actually
> like Simon.

> **SIMON**
> Me?

> **MICHAEL**
> Um, er, no, Simon the writer.

> **SIMON**
> Okay. Okay. Um, but why, why not?

> **MICHAEL**
> Er, have you met him?

> **SIMON**
> No.

> **MICHAEL**
> Meet him.

Beat.

> **DAVID**
> David is a complex character.

> **SIMON**
> He never leaves the house.

> **DAVID**
> Michael doesn't leave the house.

> **NICK**
> He went to the library.

> **MICHAEL**
> Yes, I did actually go to the library.

> **DAVID**
> No, only in the fucking show!

> **SIMON**
> Michael is interesting.

> **NICK**
> Michael is unpredictable.

                              MICHAEL
              Yeah, I am unpredictable.

                               DAVID
              I can be unpredictable.

                               SIMON
              Oh, you ...
              Go on then, do something unpredictable.

A beat.

                               DAVID
              Right now?

                               SIMON

              Yeah.

Silence.

                          SIMON (CONT'D)
              I rest my case. I'm not playing David.

                               NICK
              I'm not playing David.

                              MICHAEL
              I, I could play David.

3 INT. DAVID'S AND MICHAEL'S HOUSES - DAY   3

    GEORGIA TENNANT and ANNA LUNDBERG sitting in their respective
    living rooms.

                              GEORGIA
              We can't.

                               ANNA
              No, you're right. We can't.

                              GEORGIA
              I don't have time.

                               ANNA
              Neither do I.

                              GEORGIA
              And I do not think the boys would
              understand.

                               ANNA
              No, they wouldn't.

                              GEORGIA
              If I'm honest, I don't think I want to.

                               ANNA
              No?

                    GEORGIA
I did have a nice time last time but I
don't think I'd wanna do it again with
someone else.

                    ANNA
I'll let Mary know.

                    GEORGIA
But you can say yes if you want to.

                    ANNA
Oh, no, no. I think it should be both of
us or neither.

                    GEORGIA
Yeah. We're a team, aren't we?

                    ANNA
Mmm.

                    GEORGIA
And presumably they're looking for
people who already have their own
partners, right?

                    ANNA
Mmm, maybe.

                    GEORGIA
That's part of the illusion.

A beat.

                    ANNA
I'll let Mary know.

                    GEORGIA
How is, um, the trip to New York
looking?

                    ANNA
The rules keep changing. And I want us
to go to Sweden first if we can.

                    GEORGIA
Oh, to see family?

                    ANNA
Yeah. I mean, they haven't seen Lyra
in months. But it's a risk. Um, rules
change again, then we're stuck there.

                    GEORGIA
Would that be such a bad thing?

                    ANNA
Michael doesn't like the cold.

                    GEORGIA
David's like that, too.

They both react to a noise off-screen.

> ANNA
>
> What was that?

> GEORGIA
>
> I don't know.

> DAVID (O.S.)
>
> We need bleach.

Georgia stands and exits. Anna waits. Beat.

Georgia re-enters the room and sits on the sofa.

> ANNA
>
> Everything alright?

> GEORGIA
>
> I just found him in the bathroom trying
> to cut his own hair.

> ANNA
>
> Okay.

> GEORGIA
>
> He said he was trying to do something
> unpredictable.

> ANNA
>
> Why?

> GEORGIA
>
> I think he just feels that everyone
> else's lives are going back to normal
> faster than his.

> ANNA
>
> Sure.

> GEORGIA
>
> It's just, um, it's our routine, it's
> how it works. It's, you know, intense
> proximity followed by distance.
> It's, er, you know, it's great. It's
> just that you can't have one without the
> other.

> ANNA
>
> Mmm.

4   INT. DAVID'S AND MICHAEL'S HOUSES - DAY   4

DAVID attempts to cut his own hair with scissors. MICHAEL
enters.

> MICHAEL
>
> Well, that was a good day.

> DAVID
>
> I thought it was a train wreck.

> **MICHAEL**
> Well, it was your plan.

> **DAVID**
> Yeah, the plan was good, but the
> feedback was horrible.

> **MICHAEL**
> Oh, I wouldn't worry about that.

> **DAVID**
> No, you wouldn't worry about it cos
> apparently you're, you're the richest
> character since King Lear.

> **MICHAEL**
> Oh, stop it.

> **DAVID**
> I get a one-word summary in Spark Notes.
> Inert.

Silence. David offers his best Welsh accent.

> **DAVID (CONT'D)**
> (mimics Michael)
> Oh, no, David, you're not inert.

> **MICHAEL**
> No, David, you're not inert.

> **DAVID**
> Absolutely useless.

> **MICHAEL**
> Look, they weren't talking about you,
> they were talking about the character of
> you.

> **DAVID**
> The character is based on me!

> **MICHAEL**
> But there are seismic differences.

A beat.

> **DAVID**
> Name one seismic difference.

An awkward silence is averted as Michael's mobile phone vibrates.

> **MICHAEL**
> Oh, thank fuck.

He looks down at an incoming message.

> **MICHAEL (CONT'D)**
> Oh, ooh, Mary's office.

                         DAVID
     Okay.

                        MICHAEL
     Tom wants to speak to us.

                         DAVID
     Who the fuck's Tom?

                        MICHAEL
     Mary's assistant.

                         DAVID
     Is it?

                        MICHAEL
     Yeah. Right, I'm gonna send him a link.
     Okay?

Going back to their previous conversation.

                    MICHAEL (CONT'D)
     You're taller.

                         DAVID
     I'm taller?

                        MICHAEL
     On the show.

                         DAVID
     Oh, right, so I'm ev ... I'm even less
     impressive in real life?

Tom joins from his office on screen.

                          TOM
     Hi there. Hey.

                         DAVID
     Ah.

                        MICHAEL
     Hey, hey, Tom.

                          TOM
     Michael.

                         DAVID
     Hi, Tom.

                          TOM
     David!

                         DAVID
     How you doing?

                          TOM
     Oh, I'm fucking great. Thank you so much
     for asking. Nobody ever asks me that, so
     thank you.

                    DAVID
Sure.

                    TOM
And you? And you, David?

                    DAVID
Inert and dwarfish.

                    TOM
Oh, well it's a good look for you. I
like that on you.

                    DAVID
Thank you. Thank you.

                    MICHAEL
And I'm, I'm good, too.

                    TOM
I don't have time, Michael.
          (to both)
So, I just wanna keep you guys in the
loop real quick. Mary wanted you to know
that Nick and Simon called and they were
just so grateful for the time that you
spent with them today.

                    DAVID
Great.

                    TOM
Great.

                    MICHAEL
Great.

A beat.

                    TOM
But they are stepping away from the
project. Fuff, I know. I know.

What a shame. What a shame. But fuck it,
okay. The team is already looking for
another pairing.

                    MICHAEL
Another pairing.

                    TOM
She wants to set up a meeting with both
of you tomorrow.

                    MICHAEL
That, that is great. That is great.

                    TOM
David, are you still at the same Gmail
account?

                    DAVID
Course.

                    TOM
Great.
          (to Michael)
And, Michael, I don't have any contact
information. May I send it to your, er,
your band's MySpace account?

Michael cannot believe what he's hearing.

                  MICHAEL
You have no contact ... you're my agent
and you have no contact information for
me?

                    TOM
I do have your MySpace account for a, a
Welsh rock band that you used to be in.

                  MICHAEL
The Dirty Mochyns.

                    TOM
That's right, the Dirty Mochyns. That's
right. Right here. And I'll just DM that
... It's bouncing back. It's, it's just
sent me to a different one of your band
pages on MySpace, Michael. Um ...

                    DAVID
How, how many bands have you been
involved in, Michael?

                  MICHAEL
Um, well, after the D ... so, after the
Dirty Mochyns, it was the Ugly Gussets.

                    DAVID
Can I get these on Spotify? Cos I might
just have to ...

                    TOM
You can. Er, er ... Michael, you know
what I do have ... Is this you? Er, the
real, therealdavidfrost@aol.com?

                  MICHAEL
That is not me.

                    TOM
Yeah, he talks just like you when he ...
I can read one of his emails back.
'Hey hey, ho ho, it's me Michael, you
know how I roll. Er, I would love to do
this thing with Duracell. Batteries are
my jam.'
          (to Michael)
Is that not you?

                    DAVID
          That does sound like you, Michael. That
          does sound very like you.

                    TOM
          I'm gonna scroll through it. Tenet. Did
          you get the Tenet audition?

Michael mishears Tom.

                    MICHAEL
          The Tennant audition?

                    TOM
          Yeah. No, Tenet. Tenet. Christopher Nolan
          did a movie called Tenet. The Joker? Did
          you get that? You got a straight offer
          for Joker? Did you get that?

                    MICHAEL
          No. No. No, I didn't get any of them.

                    DAVID
          A lot of his stuff goes to Martin Sheen.
          That's usually who people really want.

                    TOM
          Okay. Alright. So I'll forward your
          stuff to Martin Sheen, does that sound
          good?

                    DAVID
          Just do that, Tom. Just do that.

                    TOM
          Okay thank you guys. Okay I'll send this
          link to you guys.

                    MICHAEL
          This is about the new pairing?

                    TOM
          No, no, no, no. No, she actually wants
          to just talk through the session that
          you had with Simon and Nick today.

          Who knows what that means. Er, great.
          Okay. Talk soon.

Tom leaves.

                    MICHAEL
          Sh-she wants to run through the session
          we had with Simon and Nick today.

                    DAVID
          Oh, fuck, yeah.

                    MICHAEL
          Oh ... that is worrying.

SIMON and NICK play a game on their mobile phones. The end
credits play over this.

> **SIMON**
> Hey, I'm ...
> ... I'm sorry we fell out again, man.

> **NICK**
> And me.

> **SIMON**
> It's just an ugly side of me, you know.

> **NICK**
> Yeah. Me too.
>
> Yeah!

> **SIMON**
> Ah, you fiend!

Beat.

> God dammit.
> When did we start playing games to, to
> resolve our arguments?

> **NICK**
> I don't know. What was the alien one?

> **SIMON**
> Do you remember any of the titles?

> **NICK**
> Not really.
> It was an argument, though, right, about
> billing? I remember that.

> **SIMON**
> Yes. Yes. How childish is that. If and
> when we work together again ...

> **NICK**
> Mmm-hmm.

> **SIMON**
> ... you go first.

> **NICK**
> No.

> **SIMON**
> Yeah, I insist.

> **NICK**
> No, absolutely not. I don't want to.

> **SIMON**
> When in doubt, alphabetical order.

NICK

Yeah, I know the rule. We all know the
rule.

SIMON

Well, Frost comes before Pegg.

NICK

There are exceptions.

SIMON

And Nick comes before Simon, so ...

NICK

Alright, well, so what's your middle
name?

SIMON

John.

NICK

Ah-ha! My middle name is John.

SIMON

Is it?

NICK

Yeah.

SIMON

Did I know that?

NICK

Well, apparently not.

SIMON

Hey.

NICK

But you're first.

SIMON

No, you're first.

NICK

I owe you everything.

SIMON

You're, you're, you're funnier.

NICK

I know.

SIMON

You're more handsome.

NICK

I know.

SIMON

You're the best.

                              NICK
          Yes, I know.

                             SIMON
          Oh, man. I miss you, bud.

                              NICK
          Ah, man, I miss you. I'm glad we're not
          doing it.

                             SIMON
          Yeah, me too.

                              NICK
          Can you imagine that?

                             SIMON
          What, ending up like them?

                              NICK
          I don't even believe they're friends.

They laugh.

                                              BLACK SCREEN

Episode Four

Woofty Doofty, David

1 INT. DAVID'S AND MICHAEL'S HOUSES - DAY

    DAVID on his sofa, MICHAEL in his sitting room. Over this, the
    credits: white letters on black.

                            DAVID
                Do you never get, like, you're at the
                mercy of your thoughts, like they're
                gonna smother you?

                            MICHAEL
                No.

                            DAVID
                Do you meditate?

                            MICHAEL
                Never needed to. I'm a very tranquil
                person.

                            DAVID
                Never plagued with conscience?

                            MICHAEL
                Nope. Is that troubling?

                            DAVID
                Oh, I don't know. You ever done anything
                bad?

                            MICHAEL
                Fuck, yes. All the time.

                            DAVID
                Well then, yes, it is a little
                troubling. Yeah.

    Beat.

                Any progress on New York?

                            MICHAEL
                Hmm, I'm thinking of asking Mary if she
                can help out with it.

                            DAVID
                Oh, yeah. What could she do?

                            MICHAEL
                She's got connections. How's Italy
                looking?

                            DAVID
                Romania.

                            MICHAEL
                Did I know it was Romania?

                            DAVID
                Oh, I don't know. I mean, you know,
                chuck a dart at a globe, it's just ...

                          MICHAEL
How's Romania looking?

                           DAVID
I don't know. I mean, I usually have
someone who sorts all these things out
for me. Georgia says I could drive.

                          MICHAEL
Can you drive?

                           DAVID
I usually have someone who does that for
me too.

Beat.

You know there's a rumour that Mary
killed one of her clients with their own
Golden Globe.

                          MICHAEL
That's ridiculous.

                           DAVID
You said she's got connections.

                          MICHAEL
In air travel. You are sounding
paranoid.

                           DAVID
I did not sleep.

                          MICHAEL
Then go and have a nap.

                           DAVID
She could fire us.

                          MICHAEL
No.

                           DAVID
No?

                          MICHAEL
Not both of us.

                           DAVID
Oh, are you gonna throw me under the
bus?

A beat.

                          MICHAEL
What?

                           DAVID
Are you ... Answer the question. Are you
gonna throw me under the bus?

MICHAEL

I mean it was your idea.

DAVID

Are you gonna tell her that?

MICHAEL

Er, probably not.

DAVID

What does 'probably not' mean?

MICHAEL

I probably won't tell her that because
she probably won't even be angry.

DAVID

Yes, but if she is angry ...

MICHAEL

Well, it was your idea.

DAVID

She will fire me.

MICHAEL

No, she won't.

DAVID

I can't be agentless. Not right now.

Oh, fuck. Fuck!
Are Nick Frost and Simon Pegg, are they
her clients?

MICHAEL

No.

DAVID

Fuck!

MICHAEL

They're not!

DAVID

She's gonna rip my fucking face off!

MICHAEL

They're not.

DAVID

Are you su ...? You know that?

MICHAEL

Absolutely.

DAVID

I've gotta get back to work.

                              MICHAEL
          We're in this together.

                               DAVID
          You promise?

                              MICHAEL
          I promise.

                               DAVID
          Scout's honour?

                              MICHAEL
          Will a cub do?

                               DAVID
          Yeah, cub's honour.

                              MICHAEL
          Dib dib. Dob dob.

                               DAVID
          It's a solemn tryst you make as a child.
          Do not mock it.

                              MICHAEL
          I make to thee, at this momenth, a
          solemn tryst.

                               DAVID
          Say it in Welsh.

                              MICHAEL
          Ych-a-fi, solemn tryst,
          A gwrog, rhyfelwyn, rhybudd.
          Amen.

                               DAVID
          Was that just a load of old bollocks in
          Welsh?

                              MICHAEL
          Yeah.

2 INT. DAVID'S, MICHAEL'S AND LUCY'S HOUSES - DAY   2

                              GEORGIA
          Simon can't write women.

                               ANNA
          No.

                              GEORGIA
          He just can't.

                               ANNA
          Sorry, Lucy.

                               LUCY
          No, no, he really can't.

GEORGIA

I have never called anyone chiquitas.

ANNA

Does he not understand women?

LUCY

I think he's confused.

ANNA

But he has a girlfriend now?

LUCY

Yeah, I know.

ANNA

Yeah, so maybe he'll improve.

GEORGIA

Yeah, but I need this scene now. So I
can't really afford to wait for him to
mature.

ANNA

Shall we just read it through?

LUCY

Yeah. No, we can fix it as we go. It
can't be that bad.

GEORGIA

'Hey, chiquitas.'

Beat.

LUCY

What did you ask him to do?

GEORGIA

Oh, um, like I'm presenting this, er,
this charity thing and I thought like a
Staged-style skit might be quite a nice
way to open it.

LUCY

Yeah, great.

GEORGIA

So I thought, oh I know, I'll ask the
writer of Staged to write us something.
And this is what he's written, for us,
for me. So, um, I don't think I can get
past 'chiquitas'.

ANNA

Well, there's a 'honey' later. Then
'bitches'. And then 'baby'.

GEORGIA

Okay, nobody calls each other 'baby'.

                    ANNA
Michael says it to Lyra.

                  GEORGIA
Well he should just learn her name.

                    LUCY
Simon just lacks understanding.

                    ANNA
He's your brother.

                    LUCY
It's not genetic. And he's not the
worst.

                  GEORGIA
Oh God, no.

                    ANNA
Mmm-mmm. I read for a character once
who was described as having happy
breasts.

                    LUCY
I had a stage direction once that said
'she covers her startled buttocks'.

                  GEORGIA
How did you do that?

                    LUCY
I offered to draw some sort of big wide
eyes on them with a Sharpie.

                  GEORGIA
And did you?

                    LUCY
No, I did not. It got cut.

                  GEORGIA
Ah.

                    LUCY
Let's carry on reading. It might get
better.

                  GEORGIA
Okay.
'Hey, chiquitas.'

                    ANNA
'Great to see you again, gals.'

                    LUCY
'Hi, bitches.'

They all laugh.

                            GEORGIA
          Fuck me, it's awful.

A beat.

                             LUCY
          Shall I ... shall I make some changes?

                            GEORGIA
          Can't we just do the original? It was
          much better then.

                             LUCY
          Let me have a look.

                            GEORGIA
          Have you got time?

                             LUCY
          I mean, it can't be that difficult.
          Simon does it.

                            GEORGIA
          Mmm.

David enters the room.

                            DAVID
          Hi, baby. Can I have this room in about
          twenty minutes?

                            GEORGIA
          What? No.

                            DAVID
          I need it.

                            GEORGIA
          Why?

                            DAVID
          I think I'm gonna be shouted at.

                             LUCY
          Hi, David.

David sits beside Georgia.

                            DAVID
          Oh, hi, Lucy. Hi, Anna. Alright?

                             ANNA
          Hi. How are you?

                            DAVID
          I'm gonna be shouted at.

David tries again.

                        DAVID (CONT'D)
          Can I have the room?

                         GEORGIA
          Did you book it on the calendar?

                         DAVID
          What calendar?

                         GEORGIA
          The one on the fridge.

     A beat.

                         DAVID
          No.

                         GEORGIA
          No. Well then you can't have the nice
          room.

                         DAVID
          But I need it.

                         GEORGIA
          Why?

                         DAVID
          I need to look valuable.

                         GEORGIA
          Use the den.

                         DAVID
          I didn't know there was a calendar on
          the fridge.

                         GEORGIA
          Well, it's new. And you missed
          orientation, so ...

                         DAVID
          Well, that's really unfair.

     David leaves.

3   INT. MICHAEL'S HOUSE - DAY   3

     MICHAEL's chair is empty. DAVID is sitting in his den.

                      MICHAEL (O.S.)
          Won't be a sec.

                         DAVID
          Alright.

                      MICHAEL (O.S.)
          How long have we got?

                         DAVID
          Couple of minutes.

                      MICHAEL (O.S.)
          Great.

                         DAVID
              Definitely in this together, yeah?

Michael enters, wearing a smart shirt.

                         MICHAEL
              Yes. As ever.

                         DAVID
              What the fuck's that?

                         MICHAEL
              What?

                         DAVID
              Why are you wearing a shirt?

                         MICHAEL
              I just put it on.

                         DAVID
              As long as I have known you, I have
              never seen you wearing a shirt.

                         MICHAEL
              I have historically worn a shirt.

                         DAVID
              Why are you wearing a shirt?

                         MICHAEL
              Well, just because you've fused with a
              hoodie.

                         DAVID
              Are you trying to impress Mary? Are ya?

                         MICHAEL
              No!

A beat.

                         DAVID
                   (softly)
              Fucking wanker.

David stands and hurries off. Michael pulls a partially-tied tie
over his head and quickly fastens it.

David leans in as he buttons a patterned shirt.

Michael pulls on his jacket and watches as David clears his
mantelpiece and carefully positions awards trophies.

                         MICHAEL
              What ... what are they?

                         DAVID
              Just a little design choice.

                         MICHAEL
              Are you set dressing?

DAVID

You know, a bit of visual furniture.

MICHAEL

Jesus, you are shameless.

DAVID

I just think the, the frame was a bit
empty, I think.
Better.

Michael hurries off.

DAVID (CONT'D)

Where are you going?

MICHAEL (O.S.)

Just getting some books.

A beat.

DAVID

What books?

MICHAEL (O.S.)

Just, you know, books from my library.

DAVID

Is it the fucking Twilight books?

Michael leans in close to the camera.

MICHAEL

Three billion dollars worldwide, chum.

DAVID

Wanker!

David stands and hurries off.

MICHAEL

Right, no, no. Don't, don't you bring
Harry Potter in ... do not bring Ha ...
Right!

Michael hurries off as David enters, clutching his stack of
Harry Potter books and sits. He watches as Michael slowly wheels
pushchair into frame.

DAVID

Is that Lyra?

MICHAEL

Could you be quiet, please? She's
sleeping.

DAVID

You're using your daughter as leverage?

MICHAEL

I am being an attentive father.

                              DAVID
          How?

                             MICHAEL
          I'm helping her sleep.

                              DAVID
          She was asleep already.

Tom's image from his office appears between Michael and David.

                               TOM
          Hi there!

                             MICHAEL
          Hey, hey.

                              DAVID
          Hey, Tom.

                               TOM
          Hey.
          Whoa, Michael, did you make your own
          suit?

Michael quickly thinks up an excuse.

                             MICHAEL
          Er, I, I was just doing a, an awards
          thing. I won ...

                               TOM
          You won an award?

                              DAVID
          What, what did you win?

                               TOM
          Oh, talking about awards. Woofty doofty,
          David, what are those behind you?

                              DAVID
          Oh, these guys. Just, you know ...

                               TOM
          Oh my goodness, we have a little Doctor
          Who. What else have we got back there? I
          mean, what can't you do?

                              DAVID
          It's just a few. Er, you know, most of
          them are over there.

                             MICHAEL
          Sorry, could ... sorry, sorry, er, guys,
          could you just keep it down a little
          bit? The, the baby's sleeping.

                              DAVID
          Is, is she actually in there?

MICHAEL

Yes. Could you please keep it quiet?

TOM

Could we see her? Could we see her then?

DAVID

Could we see her?

MICHAEL

I don't wanna wake her up. I don't wanna disturb her.

TOM

I'll be so quiet, Michael.

MICHAEL

Do you, do you have children, Tom?

TOM

No, I'm infertile.

MICHAEL

Right. Right.

TOM

So I got Mary for both you guys, if you want.

DAVID

Yeah. Tom ... before you put her on ... this story about Mary and the Golden Globe, that's not ... I mean, that's just stupid, isn't it?

TOM

What are you talking about?

DAVID

The, there was a client with a Golden Globe and there was a ...

TOM

(quickly)

Yeah, that was never proven, right, it was a story. There's so many rumours going around Hollywood ... There's ... a ... literally there's no way. I don't even know why we're talking about this. There's no way to prove anything.

A beat.

DAVID

And what's her mood like today?

TOM

Oh, she's great.

DAVID

Good great or bad great?

                              TOM
Oh, she's as per, as per.

                            DAVID
Is 'as per' like positive or negative?

                              TOM
                    (laughs)
Michael, did you hear him?
                    (mimics David)
Is 'as per' like positive or negative?
                    (laughs)

                         TOM (CONT'D)
Or is it as per? David.
                    (laughs)

                            DAVID
Okay.

                           MICHAEL
He's ridiculous.

                             TOM
She's Mary, David.

                            DAVID
Yeah.

                             TOM
Oh, man, I needed that. I was hoping
you'd slam dunk a laugh in my face, and
you did today.
                    (to Michael)
Oh, Michael, you should try learning
jokes. I think it would help you.

                           MICHAEL
Tom ...

                             TOM
It would get rid of, like, the visual
stuff.

                           MICHAEL
T-Tom, does, does Mary like children? Is
she a big children fan?

                             TOM
I'm sorry, Michael, you're making
literally no sense.

                           MICHAEL
If I, if I held the baby here ...

                             TOM
Are you Lion Kinging her, are you
cradling ...? Tell me the position the
baby is.

MICHAEL

I could, I could dandle her. Do you know dandling?

TOM

Yeah, it's a Michael Jackson 'over the thing' thing. You don't wanna do that.

DAVID

I can also get my baby, if you think it'll help.

TOM

How old is your baby, David? Tell me everything.

DAVID

The same. She's, she's also one.

TOM

Oh my, that is so ...

MICHAEL

David's got so many of them, though. They mean much less to him than my one means to me. It's spread out over his.

TOM

I'm gonna head out, okay.
(to Michael)
And enjoy whatever bar mitzvah you're going to after this, Michael. That's why I assume you're wearing that.

MICHAEL

Thank you.

TOM

Talk soon.

MICHAEL

Bye.

TOM

Here comes Mary!

Tom's computer chimes as he ends his call.

Mary's computer chimes as she appears between David and Michael.

MARY

How's the baby, David?

It is apparent that Mary has their names mixed up.

DAVID

Me?

                    MARY
No.
               (to Michael)
You.

                  MICHAEL
Michael.

                    MARY
Michael. I thought you were David.

                  MICHAEL
No.
               (chuckles softly)

                    MARY
How's the baby?

   Michael takes a quick glance into the pushchair.

                  MICHAEL
Um ... she's, she's asleep.

                    MARY
Then why is she on the call?

                  MICHAEL
I'm being attentive.

                   DAVID
Do you have any children, Mary?

                    MARY
I have clients.

   David and Michael chuckle politely.

                MARY (CONT'D)
Simon and Nick are out.

                  MICHAEL
Ah, we heard. Yeah.

                   DAVID
Yeah.

                    MARY
Which one of you wants to tell me what
happened?

   Silence.

                   DAVID
Er ...

                  MICHAEL
What did they say?

                    MARY
They said you were dickheads.

                    DAVID
Did they?

                  MICHAEL
They said that?

                   MARY
I'm summarising.

                  MICHAEL
From what?

                   MARY
A quote.

                  MICHAEL
Right.

                   MARY
So what did you do?

Another silence.

               MARY (CONT'D)
Guys, you did something. What did you
do?

                  MICHAEL
It was David's idea.

                    DAVID
Seriously?

                   MARY
What did you do?

                    DAVID
Look, Simon and Nick reached out to us.

                  MICHAEL
Through David.

                    DAVID
To both of us.

                  MICHAEL
You know, mainly David.

                    DAVID
Can I tell the story?

                   MARY
Are you sweating?

                  MICHAEL
Yeah, you do look a bit shiny, David?

                    DAVID
Am I shiny?

                    MARY
          Are you sick?

                    MICHAEL
          I told him he should have a nap.

                    MARY
          Just keep going, okay.

David decides it's best to answer truthfully.

                    DAVID
          Well, Simon and Nick reached out, to
          both of us, and they actually asked if
          we would jump on a call so that they
          could ask us some questions.

                    MICHAEL
          And then David suggested ...

                    DAVID
          No, I didn't s ... no, it wasn't a
          suggestion, it was, it was a joke.

                    MICHAEL
          Oh, it wasn't a joke.

                    DAVID
          It was a joke.

                    MICHAEL
          No, it was a plot.

                    DAVID
          No, it was, it was a joke that Michael
          took too seriously.

                    MICHAEL
          No, it was a plot to sabotage them.

                    MARY
          Sabotage them?

                    MICHAEL
          Yes.

                    MARY
          Why?

                    DAVID
          Listen, Mary, can I moot an idea?

                    MARY
          The fuck is a moot?

                    DAVID
          Might it be that actually we have done
          the production, and indeed you, a bit of
          a favour here?

A beat.

MARY

Explain how.

DAVID

Well look, Michael and I are still
available. Yeah?
Simon and Nick, if we're all honest
about it, were never really right for
this. Well, it's a tired old bit of
shtick that they do, it's all a bit ...
      (groans)
... you know, it's, it's, it's, it's,
it's niche. Um, and now they've stepped
away, we can step back in. We're the
originators and your clients.

MARY

Simon and Nick are also my clients.

DAVID

      (softly)
Fuck.
      (to Mary)
Okay. Are they? Right.

MARY

And they're exceptional actors.

DAVID

No, no, sure, sure. It's just that
Michael said that ...

MARY

Yeah. But, you know, their value
... far exceeds yours on every level.

MICHAEL

So ... is ... er, M ... is that both of
us though?

MARY

Yeah.

MICHAEL

One not more than the other?

MARY

No, both.

DAVID

I am talented.

MARY

But they're box office gold.

DAVID

Well ... Harry Potter made nearly ten
billion.

MICHAEL

You were in one film!

                    DAVID
          That is not helpful.

                    MICHAEL
          And only one scene!

                    DAVID
          And, and also a flashback.

                    MICHAEL
          I was actually, actually in four of the
          Twilight films.

                    DAVID
          I'm Doctor Who!

                    MICHAEL
          Not any more, baby!

David quickly holds up a large glass award.

                    DAVID
          Well I've still got the People's Choice
          Award. And this turned sideways, I turn
          it like that, I ram it up your tight
          Welsh rectum!

                    MICHAEL
          And that is exactly where that award
          should go, right up there with the rest
          of my excrement!

Mary sits in silence as Michael and David finish their tirade.

                    MARY
          And on a personal note, you managed to
          embarrass me.

                    MICHAEL
          How?

                    MARY
          Simon and Nick, they talk to people.

                    MICHAEL
          Well we can, we can fix that. We can talk
          to people.

                    DAVID
          Yeah.

                    MARY
          Who could you talk to?
                    (laughs)

                    MICHAEL
          Um ...

                    MARY
          The werewolves in Twilight? Harry
          Potter?

                    MARY (CONT'D)
(to Michael)
Your sleeping baby?
        (to both)
You can't talk to anybody.

                        DAVID
Sorry, Mary.

                      MICHAEL
Sorry, Mary.

                        MARY
So here's what we're gonna do. I'm gonna
offer you both up to read again with
whoever they wanna see next. And you're
gonna do it politely and you're gonna do
it competently and you're gonna fucking
do it for free. Okay?

                        DAVID
Of cour ... absolutely. Makes sense,
yeah.

                      MICHAEL
Yeah. Yeah.

                        MARY
I can mend some relationships but you
motherfuckers show people that you can
play well with others. Do you understand
me?

                        DAVID
Yeah. Got it.

                      MICHAEL
Yeah, and, and is there absolutely no
chance that we can play ourselves in
this?

   Mary's screen goes black.

4 INT. DAVID'S AND MICHAEL'S HOUSES - DAY   4

                        DAVID
I was in more scenes.

                      MICHAEL
What, in Harry Potter?

                        DAVID
Originally, yeah.

                      MICHAEL
They cut them?

                        DAVID
Well, they rewrote them.

                         MICHAEL
          Without you?

                          DAVID
          Without my character, yeah.

                         MICHAEL
          So they were cut.

                          DAVID
          They were changed.

Beat.

          We're valuable.

                         MICHAEL
          Hugely.

                          DAVID
          We are.

Beat.

          What are we gonna do now?

                         MICHAEL
          Play nicely.

                          DAVID
          You ever had a scene cut?

                         MICHAEL
          Once.

                          DAVID
          Oh yeah, what in?

                         MICHAEL
          In GoldenEye.

                          DAVID
          GoldenEye? What were you gonna do in
          GoldenEye?

                         MICHAEL
          You know the scene when he says, 'Bond.
          James Bond'?

                          DAVID
          Of course.

                         MICHAEL
          Well, it was Pierce Brosnan's first time,
          so they wanted the character to say that
          twice.

                          DAVID
          Right. So what did you have to do?

                         MICHAEL
          I had to say, 'Say it again.'

And ...

                    MICHAEL

He said it again.

                    DAVID

Right.

David in his best James Bond impersonation.

'Bond. James Bond.'

                    MICHAEL

Say it again.

                    DAVID

'Bond. James Bond.'

                    MICHAEL

And scene.

                    DAVID

They cut that?

                    MICHAEL

They did.

                    DAVID

Wankers. No credit? Nothing?

                    MICHAEL

Nothin'. And I can't play Bond now.

                    DAVID

Really?

                    MICHAEL

Yeah, that's the rule. That's why they
couldn't offer it to me last time.

                    DAVID

Was that why?

                    MICHAEL

Mmm-hmm.

                    DAVID

Right. Yes, I was rumoured to be in the
running to play James Bond once.

                    MICHAEL

You were rumoured?

                    DAVID

Ex-Doctor Who could be stepping out of
the Tardis and into a dinner jacket,
that kind of stuff. Yeah. No, there
was ... they did that thing where they
Photoshopped my head.

                    MICHAEL
With your head put on like a Pools
winner.

                    DAVID
Well, yeah, I mean, it, it wasn't
the greatest Photoshop ever, but the
principle was there.

Beat.

Have you never been in the running for
Doctor Who?

                    MICHAEL
I came close.

                    DAVID
Did you?

                    MICHAEL
Mmm. I was offered it.

                    DAVID
No?! What happened?

                    MICHAEL
I don't know. They just suddenly changed
their mind. Said they decided to go in a
different direction.

                                    BLACK SCREEN

Episode Five

The Warthog and
the Mongoose, Part 1

DAVID TENNANT sitting on his patio. MICHAEL SHEEN in his living
room.

Over this, the credits: white letters on black.

> MICHAEL
> You're not.

> DAVID
> Maybe I am.

> MICHAEL
> Why?

> DAVID
> Cos I move through time like a dust mote
> ... floating. I'm present ... but I'm
> not really there.

> MICHAEL
> When did these conversations become so
> poetic?

> DAVID
> I'm just afraid of becoming invisible.

> MICHAEL
> Yeah, I'm afraid of glass and
> electricity.

> DAVID
> Okay.

> MICHAEL
> So obviously lightbulbs are a ... no-no.

> DAVID
> Right.

> MICHAEL
> And dying.

> DAVID
> Sure. Oh, this quiet is not good for me.

> MICHAEL
> You should see a therapist.

> DAVID
> I've got you.

> MICHAEL
> I have been struck off.

> DAVID
> Have you? Why?

                    MICHAEL
Gross incompetence.

                    DAVID
Well, not before time.

                    MICHAEL
Yeah. You know, you have seemed a little
bit more ... oh, introspective recently.

                    DAVID
Have I?

                    MICHAEL
I mean, don't get me wrong. You have
always thoroughly enjoyed talking about
yourself.

                    DAVID
Well, there's a lot to say.

                    MICHAEL
But you've started ...
... seeming a bit ...

                    DAVID
What?

                    MICHAEL
... a little ...

                    DAVID
Yeah?

                    MICHAEL
... boring.

                    DAVID
Boring?

                    MICHAEL
Tedious.

                    DAVID
Oh, now you're just throwing around
hurtful comments.

                    MICHAEL
Needy.

                    DAVID
Just cos you won't listen.

                    MICHAEL
I do nothing but listen. That is
literally all I do every minute
... of every day.

                    DAVID
My thoughts are interesting.

                         MICHAEL
          To you.

                          DAVID
          I am a public intellectual.

                         MICHAEL
          By what standard?

                          DAVID
          I was Dictionary Corner on Countdown. On
          two occasions.

Beat.

          I'm just going through something.

                         MICHAEL
          Oh ... I have gotta go.

                          DAVID
          What, already?

                         MICHAEL
          Yeah ... oh, sorry, time's up.

                          DAVID
          I've only had forty minutes.

                         MICHAEL
          Yeah, well, I've got another call.

                          DAVID
          With who?

                         MICHAEL
          New York.

                          DAVID
          Ohh, wedding stuff, is it?

                         MICHAEL
          Wedding stuff.

                          DAVID
          I've never been a best man.

                         MICHAEL
          Oh, Jesus.

Michael stands and walks off.

2 INT/EXT. MICHAEL'S AND DAVID'S HOUSES, SIMON'S LA APARTMENT - DAY   2

                          SIMON
          So I know that we joke about it and
          about how much of it was improvised and
          I enjoy that as much as everybody else.
          It's a funny joke.

                          DAVID
          Would you say thirty per cent?

                    SIMON
        Thirty?

                    MICHAEL
        At least.

                    SIMON
        Ten. At most.

                    DAVID
        I mean, twenty-five.

                    SIMON
        It's not a negotiation.

                    DAVID
        And the Hamlet stuff, that was definitely
        me.

                    MICHAEL
        Two, four, six, eight, moot away.

                    DAVID
        Yeah, the ... having the mug in shot,
        that was all me.

                    MICHAEL
        Fucking disco!

Michael imitates dance music.

                    DAVID
        Well, that whole bit, wasn't it, that
        was all a bit, the whole being on set
        bit.

                    MICHAEL
        I mean, I, I find it difficult to remember
        anything that was scripted. It's the im
        ... I mean, regardless of the percentage,
        it's the improv that zings.

                    DAVID

Cos all the bits that people talk
about ...

                    MICHAEL

Muppet dance.
          (mutters)

                    DAVID

Yeah, we could have done without the
muppet dance.

                    MICHAEL

People love that. There are memes of
that everywhere.

                    DAVID

So irrespective of the percentage...
          (mutters)

                    MICHAEL

Ten per cent.

                    DAVID

... we contributed a significant amount.

Simon leaps to his defence.

                    SIMON

But, but I wrote it. I wrote it. I sat
down, at a computer, this one, and I
typed the whole thing out. It took
weeks.

                    MICHAEL

Yeah, and we improved it ...
          (clicks his fingers)
... immediately.

                    DAVID

Bang.

Silence.

                    SIMON

So, the other Davids and Michaels have
been reading the script, um, and they're
requesting changes.
They've got notes ...

                    DAVID

Okay.

                    SIMON

... but I'm not allowed to be a part of
those conversations because people don't
think that I had anything to do with it.

                    DAVID

Why not?

SIMON

Because that's what you told them. You
told them I didn't write it.
You said that.

MICHAEL

When?

SIMON

All the time. In all the interviews.

MICHAEL

We gave you full credit in those
interviews.

SIMON

Full credit?

MICHAEL

Credit.

SIMON

So I know you're reading with the other
Davids and Michaels today.

DAVID

We are, yeah. I'm reading with the
Michaels.

MICHAEL

And I am reading with the Davids.

DAVID

Yeah, I'm sorry that will be boring for
you, Michael.

MICHAEL

Well, I'll get through it somehow.

SIMON

So could I ask a favour? Could you try
and find out what their notes are, what
their thoughts are?

                         DAVID
              I suppose.

                         SIMON
              Thank you. And maybe even just ... talk
              me up a bit.

A beat.

                         DAVID
              Talk you up?

                         SIMON
              Mmm-hmm.

                         DAVID
              I mean, we're doing this under
              sufferance. This is, you know, this is a
              punishment for us.

                        MICHAEL
              Yeah, this is our Community Service.

                         SIMON
              I'm not asking you to lie for me.

                        MICHAEL
              Oh. Oh, you're not asking us to lie. So
              ... so what are you asking from us then,
              Simon?

A beat.

                         SIMON
              Just ... tell 'em I wrote it.

3 INT. DAVID'S AND CHRISTOPH'S HOUSES — DAY   3

                        CHRISTOPH
              I don't like it.

                         DAVID
              Well, Simon Evans wrote it.

                        CHRISTOPH
              I don't think I wanna do it.

                         DAVID
              Right.

                        CHRISTOPH
              I, I'll read it, but I have my concerns.

                         DAVID
              Like what?

                        CHRISTOPH
              Feels cruel.

                         DAVID
          Cruel?

We cut away as Christoph searches for a descriptive word.

                        CHRISTOPH
          Unbarmherzig.

                         DAVID
          What does that mean, exactly?

                        CHRISTOPH
          Merciless.

                         DAVID
          Sure.

                        CHRISTOPH
          Remorseless.

                         DAVID
          Yeah.

                        CHRISTOPH
          Pitiless.

                         DAVID
          Well, it's supposed to be funny.

                        CHRISTOPH
          It's not.

                         DAVID
          No. Okay.

                        CHRISTOPH
          It's acrid.

Silence.

                         DAVID
          Shall we read a bit?

CHRISTOPH

Sure.

DAVID

Okay.

CHRISTOPH
(mumbles)
Okay.

DAVID

Um, so it's the scene where we're, we're
looking down at a series of photographs
and we're gonna choose one and I'm
calling out the numbers. Er, I'll go
from the top of the page.

DAVID (CONT'D)
'What about 2145?'

CHRISTOPH
'Is that make-up?'

DAVID
'I put on a little foundation.'

CHRISTOPH
'You look pox-ridden.'

DAVID
'I do not.'

CHRISTOPH
'Why do you always do that thing with
your mouth?'

DAVID
'What thing?'

CHRISTOPH
'It's just a straight line across your
face. You look like a muppet.'

DAVID
'Well, your smile is a straight line,
too.'

CHRISTOPH
'But I got a twinkle in my eye.'

DAVID
'I have a twinkle in my eyes.'

CHRISTOPH
'Your eyes tire.'

DAVID
'Tire?'

CHRISTOPH
'Like a low-impact gorgon.'

DAVID

'Oh, fuck you.'

CHRISTOPH
(to David)

See what I mean?

A beat.

4 INT. MICHAEL'S AND EWAN MCGREGOR'S HOUSES - DAY   4

MICHAEL

'I mean, I just wanna make sure I don't
get over-sensitive.'

EWAN

'Ah, this is bullshit!'

MICHAEL

'You should calm down!'

EWAN

'Oh, why? Because when I get emotional I
sound cartoonish?!'

MICHAEL

'Oh, I've heard that, too.'

EWAN

'Look, I wrote a scene today where I
took a shit from a high height on your
big stupid Welsh hairy head!'

MICHAEL
(to Ewan)

Okay. Good. Good.
I mean ... I got nothing to say. You,
you got any questions, or anything I can
help with, or ...?

                              EWAN
            The, the writer.

                            MICHAEL
            The writer is Simon Evans.

                              EWAN
            Is he, like, anti-Scottish?

                            MICHAEL
            I don't think so.

                              EWAN
            David is just always whining.

                            MICHAEL
            I don't think it was meant as like a
            cultural comment.

                              EWAN
            He can't be, he can't be like that,
            though, David, in real life, can he?

    Beat.

5   INT. DAVID'S AND CHRISTOPH'S HOUSES - DAY   5

                             DAVID
            He calls me cartoonish later.

                           CHRISTOPH
            Michael's a cartoonish character.

                             DAVID
                      (softly)
            Yeah.

                           CHRISTOPH
            He should have a shark tank in his
            basement. A castle in a volcano. I've
            done enough of both of them.
            Yeah, trust me.

    A beat.
            Listen to me.

                             DAVID
            Yeah.

                           CHRISTOPH
            Whatever they say, Michael's a paper
            doll. He's a, he's a lazy stereotype.
            David's the real person.

                             DAVID
            Yes. Yes, actually, David is the real
            person.

                           CHRISTOPH
            With real struggles. He's trying to
            connect ...

                    DAVID
Yes, he is trying to connect.

                  CHRISTOPH
... across distance, strange technology,
just trying to speak and be heard.

                    DAVID
Yeah. Michael just keeps shutting him
down.

                  CHRISTOPH
It's sociopathic.

                    DAVID
Yeah. I'd never thought about that
before.

6 INT. MICHAEL'S AND EWAN'S HOUSES - DAY   6

                    EWAN
Do you think I sound cartoonish?

                  MICHAEL
Have, have you ever tried a thing called
actioning?

                    EWAN
No, I don't ... no, I don't think so.
No.

                  MICHAEL
You work out what your character's
action is on every line, like what he or
she is doing.

                    EWAN
If it can bring this more alive, then
let's try.

MICHAEL

Okay. Um, so just, um ... let's try the
... have you got the scene, um, that
begins with David putting his hand up?
Do you know that one?

EWAN

Yeah, yeah, yeah. Got it.

MICHAEL

I'll be ... I'm Jo. So, um ...

EWAN

Okay.

MICHAEL

Er, David.

EWAN

'Michael's being insufferable.'

MICHAEL

Right, great. So, so what's, er, what's
David trying to do there?

EWAN

Whine.

MICHAEL

It's, it's sort of better if you think
of it in terms of what he's trying to do
to the other character.

EWAN

Okay. Oh, right.

MICHAEL

So what's he trying to do to Michael?

A beat.

EWAN

To whine at him.

MICHAEL

Okay. Um ... yeah, okay, let's, let's
just ... Do you wanna do another bit?
What, what have you got? Have you got
something else there?

EWAN

Yeah.

'Please, please, please, please.'

MICHAEL

So what's he trying to do there?

                    Desecrate the memory of Robert the
                    fucking Bruce.

  Michael chuckles softly.

7 INT. DAVID'S, LUCY'S AND MICHAEL'S HOUSES - DAY   7

  GEORGIA TENNANT, LUCY EATON and ANNA LUNDBERG sitting in their
  respective houses.

                                    LUCY
                    When are we filming?

                                  GEORGIA
                    It has to be ready a fortnight today.

                                    LUCY
                    I'm available!

                                    ANNA
                    Me too.

                                  GEORGIA
                    It's just an online thing.

                                    LUCY
                    Great.

                                  GEORGIA
                    Just like, um, some sketches and a
                    celebrity auction.

                                    LUCY
                    I have so much time.

  Georgia gives Lucy a thumbs up.

                              LUCY (CONT'D)
                    So much time.

                    GEORGIA
          I snapped at David earlier.

                     LUCY
          Why? How come?

                    GEORGIA
          He did a, a thing.

                     ANNA
          Yeah, Michael's struggling, too.

                    GEORGIA
          In what way?

                     ANNA
          Well, he's not sleeping very well.

                    GEORGIA
          Oh. David's grinding his teeth.

                     ANNA
          Michael's getting headaches.

                     LUCY
          Do you have any idea why?

                     ANNA
          He wants to feel mobile. He wants to go
          to New York with me. He wants to hug
          people. Raise a glass. Lift Lyra up and
          show her off.

                     LUCY
          Does he talk to anyone?

                     ANNA
          A therapist?

                     LUCY
          Yeah, maybe.

                     ANNA
          Talks to David.

                     LUCY
          I suppose it's good that they have each
          other, isn't it?

     Beat.

8   INT. DAVID'S AND HUGH'S HOUSES - DAY   8

     DAVID sitting in his kitchen. HUGH BONNEVILLE sitting in his
     living room.

                     HUGH
          Well, David is a little two-
          dimensional.

                    DAVID
          That's ... he's fine. It's the Michael
          character really.

                         HUGH
          Really? You think?

                    DAVID
          Yeah, yeah, yeah, yeah, yeah, that's
          what we found.

                         HUGH
          No, he strikes me as quite rich, sort of
          quite textured ...

A beat.

                         HUGH (CONT'D)
          ... really.

                    DAVID
          You know, improvisation's key.

                         HUGH
          Um ...

                    DAVID
          It's just listening.

                         HUGH
          Right, okay.

                    DAVID
          Listening and responding.

                         HUGH
          But you expect me to be funny?

                    DAVID
          Ideally, yeah.

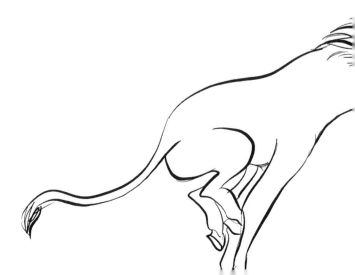

HUGH

Do you know what, I'm, I'm just, I'm
just more comfortable with a script.

DAVID

Well, it's just that that's the way we
made it work before.

HUGH

Well, sure, but, you know, Simon, er, Ev
... Simon Evans has sent me a script, so
...

DAVID

Yeah. Yeah, but, you know ... what he's
written down is just like a skeleton
that we then build on.

HUGH

Right.

DAVID

Nuance is key.

HUGH

You said improvisation was key.

DAVID

Different keys.

A beat.

HUGH

Okay.

DAVID

Is that a banister?

HUGH

Yeah.

DAVID

You're sitting at the bottom of the
stairs?

HUGH

Yeah, it's just easier cos ... there's
lights down here. It's just, just ...
you know, it's fine.

DAVID

I've never seen inside your house. I
thought it'd be classier.

HUGH

Yeah, yeah, it's just quite old, David.

DAVID

What is it made of?

                        HUGH
              It's actually plastic.

                        DAVID
              Is it? Ooh.

                        HUGH
              Um ... I'm ready when you are.

                        DAVID
              Wouldn't get away with that in Downton,
              would ya?

     Beat.
              Shall we read some?

9 INT. MICHAEL'S AND KEN'S HOUSES - DAY   9

     KEN claps his hands together for synchronisation purposes.

                        KEN
              Ken Jeong. You have my CV and, er ...
                   (sniffs)

     Michael waits patiently.

                        KEN (CONT'D)
              I am David. I am an asshole.

     Pause.
              Michael's being insufferable.

     Michael lowers his head on to the table.

10 INT. DAVID'S AND HUGH'S HOUSES - DAY   10

     DAVID and HUGH in their respective houses.

                        HUGH
              'You look pox-ridden.'

DAVID

Can you try ... a different flavour?

HUGH

Yeah, yeah.

DAVID

Find something kinder.

HUGH

Yeah, so it goes like, like, just like a, a kinder tone in the line.

DAVID

No, no, no. Put something in this, kinder.

A beat.

DAVID (CONT'D)

Let's start again. I'll take it from the top.

HUGH

Okay.

DAVID

'What about 2145?'

HUGH

'Is that make-up?'

DAVID

'I put on a little foundation.'

HUGH

'You look really handsome.'

DAVID

That's great. That's much better.

11 INT. MICHAEL'S AND KEN'S HOUSES - DAY   11

KEN

This must be really hard for you.

MICHAEL

Er, how do you mean?

KEN

You know, reading these same things over and over again. Just seeing a parade of people ...
... just playing versions of your best friend.

MICHAEL

He's not my best friend.

KEN

Oh, I'm sorry. I, I thought it ...

                    MICHAEL
I have a friend in New York.

A beat.

                         KEN
Still ... strange, with all due respect.
I mean, if I were you, I, I'd be acting
out. You know, I'd be snapping. You
know, just shouting at birds.

                    MICHAEL
No one does that.

                         KEN
Screaming about my deepest fears with
this dude. He just doesn't get it. You
know, I, I, I watched this and you're
the angel, and he is just ... doesn't
see your brightness. It's just, like,
you know, he's like ...
          (Ken mimics David)
... Michael, you know, I'm jealous of
your greatness. You know, how can I
be as great as you? You know, I don't
have your range, innit. I'm just not as
great.
          (Ken mimics Michael)
Well don't compare yourself. It's not a
competition. You know, it's, it's not,
it's not Britain's Got Talent, innit.
          (Ken mimics David)
I didn't say it's Britain's Got Talent.
It's just I want, you know, I just want
what you have. I want you. I want what
you have, you know. You know, give me
what I want, innit.
          (Ken mimics Michael)
It's like ... it's not like that. It's
just, you know, acting is, is energy.

                    KEN (CONT'D)
It's like a ball of energy.
You're just playing, you're just tossing
it back and forth, back and forth,
innit.
          (Ken mimics David)
It's not about that. It's about having
the biggest ball ...
          (shouts)
... and the brightest energy! Fuck you!
          (mimics Michael - shouts)
Fuck you!
          (mimics David — shouts)
Fuck you, innit!
          (mimics Michael — shouts)
Fuck you, innit!

12 INT. DAVID'S AND HUGH'S HOUSES - DAY   12

                    HUGH
I've, I've gotta say, it just feels like
we're going against the spirit of the
scene.

                    DAVID
No, no. Come on, come on, come on, this
is good, this is much better. Focus in.
Don't, don't, don't, don't lose it.

                    HUGH
Okay.

                    DAVID
Pick it up. I'll pick it up.

                    HUGH
Okay.

                    DAVID
I'm feeling inert.

                    HUGH
You're not feeling inert.

                    DAVID
Well, maybe I am.

                    HUGH
Well, if you're feeling inert, then
... Why?

                    DAVID
I move through time like a dust mote
floating. Present but entirely without
impact.

Silence.

                         KEN
          I can see that you're grieving.

                       MICHAEL
          I'm fine.

                         KEN
          You're not fine.

                       MICHAEL
          Yeah, I'm fine.

                         KEN
          You're not fine.

                       MICHAEL
                   (upset)
          No.

                         KEN
          Michael, you're going through something
          profound. That we all identify ourselves
          in our reflections, how people see us.
          And your other person isn't seeing you.

                       MICHAEL
          You are so right. I miss ... people
          getting too close to me.

                         KEN
          I miss buffets.

          Using that.

Ken slowly sits back.

                     KEN (CONT'D)
          Michael's being insufferable.

Michael stands and walks off.

                     MICHAEL (O.S.)
          Fuck.

                                        BLACK SCREEN

Episode Six

The Warthog and
the Mongoose, Part 2

DAVID's empty chair and sofa. MICHAEL's empty chair.

We hear footsteps as GEORGIA TENNANT passes. She stops, leans to
the screen.

Over this the credits: white letters on black.

> **GEORGIA**
> Hello.

Beat.

> Hello.

Anna Lundberg enters, looks at the screen.

> **ANNA**
> Hi.

> **GEORGIA**
> Hi.
> What's going on?

> **ANNA**
> What, didn't you call me?

> **GEORGIA**
> Er, no.

> **ANNA**
> (calls)
> Michael.

> **MICHAEL (O.S.)**
> Yeah.

> **ANNA**
> Did you call David?

> **MICHAEL (O.S.)**
> Er, er, yes, well I did try to call but
> then I changed my mind.

> **ANNA**
> Why?

> **MICHAEL (O.S.)**
> Well, it occurred to me, if I wanted to
> endure a deluge of vacuous crap ... I
> can just put my head in the toilet.

> **ANNA**
> He said, er ...

> **GEORGIA**
> Yeah, I heard him, yeah.

> **ANNA**
> He just needs to vent to someone.

> MICHAEL (O.S.)
> Oh, and you can tell him that, if you
> like, er, the toilet thing.

Georgia senses it's time to change the subject.

> GEORGIA
> Right.
> Okay, if you could go anywhere in the
> world, where would you go?

> ANNA
> Oh.

> GEORGIA
> Mmm.

> ANNA
> Um ...

Anna sits.

> ... Cambodia.

> GEORGIA
> Yes.

> ANNA
> The food, the culture.

> GEORGIA
> Yeah, yeah.

> ANNA
> It's so unfamiliar. There's a temple in
> the hills and it's the quietest place I
> have ever been.

> DAVID (O.S.)
> Who are you talking to?

A beat.

> GEORGIA
> Anna.

> DAVID (O.S.)
> Oh. Tell her to tell him he's a twat!

Another beat.

> ANNA
> Where would you go?

> GEORGIA
> I think ... I would take a road trip
> around Europe.

> ANNA
> That's intrepid.

GEORGIA

I'd start in Austria.

ANNA

I love Austria.

GEORGIA

Then I'd go to Czechoslovakia.
Then Poland.

ANNA

Yeah, that's the route the Nazis took.

GEORGIA

Right.
That, that isn't why I suggested those
countries.

ANNA

No.

GEORGIA

Maybe I'd go on to Paris.

ANNA

That's just making it worse.

MICHAEL (V.O.)

Did you tell him ...
          (off-screen)
... about the, er, shitty ears?

DAVID (O.S.)

I heard that!

MICHAEL (O.S.)
          (shouts)
What?!

DAVID (O.S.)
          (shouts)
I heard you!

A beat.

GEORGIA

Have you heard of the Bechdel test?

ANNA

No.

GEORGIA

Right. Well, it's the measurement of
whether a scene features at least two
women talking to each other about
something other than a man.

Anna chuckles.

> DAVID (O.S.)
> Tell Michael I never want to speak to
> him ever again as long as I might live.

> MICHAEL (O.S.)
> Tell David that's the best news I've
> heard all day!

2 INT. DAVID'S HOUSE AND JIM PARSONS' APARTMENT - DAY   2

DAVID lying back on his sofa.

JIM sitting in his living area.

> JIM
> Can you hear me from over there?

David gestures with a thumbs up.

> JIM (CONT'D)
> Okay.
> It's just I don't know ... like, it's
> hard ... you're only in the corner of
> mine but maybe it's, maybe I could do
> something, um ... anyway.
> Um, do you wanna, you wanna read it,
> read through it?

> DAVID
> There's not really any point.

> JIM
> Oh.

> DAVID
> They're reworking the Michael character,
> doing rewrites.

> JIM
> Oh. Why?

> DAVID
> Cos he's a psychopath.

A beat. Jim laughs.

Another beat.

> JIM
> Um, wait, I'm sorry, are you not
> kidding? I can't see your face very
> well. Is that a joke? Why, why do you
> say he's a psychopath?

David sits up.

> DAVID
> Well, have you read the script, Jim?

> JIM
> Yes, I've read the script.

                    DAVID
Well there you go, then.

A beat.

                     JIM
I like this a lot.

                    DAVID
Really? Okay.

                     JIM
Okay. See, er, I ... to me, David, the,
the character of Michael just seems very
real.

                    DAVID
He's entirely implausible.

                     JIM
Well no, I ... I mean in like a comedy
way. He's just like heightened, it's
exaggerated for comedy.

                    DAVID
What he is is a fucking arsehole, that's
what he is.

                     JIM
I didn't get that. He's an asshole.

                    DAVID
Yeah.

                     JIM
That's so fascinating to me. It's not
... Where, where do you see the asshole
in this?

David continues his assassination.

                    DAVID
No. No, no, he's not an interesting
arsehole. That doesn't make him
enigmatic and complicated. He's a, he's
... an entirely featureless arsehole.
He's a vanilla arsehole.
He's the most featureless vanilla
arsehole you could ever come across.

                     JIM
I wonder could you be more specific,
like, about what's in here that, that,
that reads asshole to you. I need a toe
hold in here.

                    DAVID
Well, he says I look pox-ridden.

                     JIM
Okay, pox-ridden. Yeah.

Jim makes notes on his script.

>   DAVID
> Er, then he compares me to a muppet.

Jim laughs. David doesn't think this is funny.

>   JIM
> Which is the com ... comedy, but, yeah,
> I mean, it's ... I guess it's harsh.
> Asshole.

>   DAVID
> He says that my eyes tire.

>   JIM
> But I think ... I mean, it's just kind
> of fun playing ... we're just kind of,
> we all put out something that, like, we,
> we, we give something of ourself to the
> process that we allow to be made fun of
> without hurting too much. And, I mean,
> your eyes are a little bloodshot.

David reacts.

>   DAVID
> Oh, right, are they?

>   JIM
> Um, from here, I think.

>   DAVID
> Are they, are they portals to a barren,
> parched, arid landscape?! Are they?

David pulls his eyes open as he leans close to the screen.

> Can you ... what, can you see the
> scorched earth there?
> Have you got that?

>   JIM
> No. I don't see ... I think that's
> definitely something you'll have to add
> later in post and edit.

>   DAVID
>   (disinterested)
> Great.

>   JIM
> I mean, you're not even playing the
> part. I don't ...

>   DAVID
> Well, no, of course.

                         JIM
          Look, here's what I think it is.
          I think what you're responding to in
          Michael is the way he's lashing out.

                              DAVID
          Lashing out?

                         JIM
          Yes. Because ...

                              DAVID
          Mmm.

                         JIM
          ... his feelings are hurt.

                              DAVID
          Right. Jim, have you even read the
          script?

                         JIM
          David, have you?

A beat.

          Cos we're not seeing the same thing at
          all.

                              DAVID
          I've read all of my bits.

                         JIM
          David lied to him.

                              DAVID
          Well, only in the show.

                         JIM
          Yes, you lied to him in the sh ... What,
          what are we talking about?

A beat.

                              DAVID
          Nothing. That's it.

                         JIM
          Okay.

                              DAVID
          Yeah.

                         JIM
          So Michael is hurting ...

                              DAVID
          Yeah.

                         JIM
          ... because he feels disconnected from
          his best friend.

                    DAVID
        Well ...

                    JIM
        Yes. And it's very sweet to me.
        I mean, Michael is defined by David, and
        he doesn't have him right now. And David
        is defined by Michael.
        It's a symbiotic relationship. People
        love this kind of thing. It's symbiotic
        like a, a warthog and a mongoose.

A beat.

                    DAVID
        Which one am I?

                    JIM
        I don't know, David. This didn't go like
        I thought it would. You know what, oh
        my God, I, I, I forgot that my phone is
        ringing.

                    DAVID
        I don't hear your phone.

3   INT. DAVID'S HOUSE AND SIMON'S HOTEL ROOM - DAY   3

    GEORGIA and SIMON EVANS sitting in their respective locations.

                    GEORGIA
        Okay, he's not talking to Michael. Yeah.
        And when he doesn't talk to Michael, he
        talks to me, at me.

Beat.

                    SIMON
        Okay.

Beat.

                    GEORGIA
        Do you like bats, Simon?

                    SIMON
        Bats?

                    GEORGIA
        Bats.

Beat.

                GEORGIA (CONT'D)
        Yeah. He's a bit like a bat. Just sort
        of, um, spraying out white noise, echo
        locating. Triangulating my position with
        his inane bollocks.

SIMON

Do you have a cupboard? Have you tried
hiding?

GEORGIA

Okay. You need to fix this.

SIMON

Why do I need to fix this?

GEORGIA

Because you broke it.

SIMON

How did I break it?

GEORGIA

Because you left them here.

SIMON

Not deliberately.

GEORGIA

No?

SIMON

No!

GEORGIA

No?

Beat.

SIMON

No.

Silence. Georgia composes herself.

GEORGIA

Okay, Simon. There is a, there is a call
that you scheduled today with them.
Yeah. What, what, what's it about?

SIMON

Just notes on the, on the script from
the other actors.

GEORGIA

Okay, so you just need to, need to get
them talking.

SIMON

Right.

GEORGIA

So you'll need to try being bright and
enthusiastic.

Simon pulls the lid from his pen and begins to write.

> **GEORGIA (CONT'D)**
> And ... what are you doing?

> **SIMON**
> I'm writing down bright and
> enthusiastic.

She reacts.

> **GEORGIA**
> Right. Okay, Simon, are you going to be
> able to handle this?

> **SIMON**
> Yes, I can ha ... yes, I can handle
> this.

> **GEORGIA**
> David and Michael, they, they just need,
> they have to start talking.

> **SIMON**
> David called me a mollusc.

> **GEORGIA**
> You've been called worse.

> **SIMON**
> I've not.

> **GEORGIA**
> (shouts)
> You fucking should have been!

She glares at him as he turns away.

4   INT. MICHAEL'S, DAVID'S AND SIMON'S HOUSES - DAY   4

MICHAEL SHEEN and DAVID TENNANT sitting in their respective
houses. SIMON is sitting in his garden in LA.

> **DAVID**
> Um, Michael is a sadist ...

> **MICHAEL**
> And David is a soggy paper bag.

> **DAVID**
> No. I mean, the ... I think the pressing
> note was that Michael comes across as
> ... an impossible character.
> Nobody could be that ludicrously
> revolting.

> **MICHAEL**
> Er, can I, can I just stop you there?

> **DAVID**
> Mmm.

                    MICHAEL
          Because what's interesting is, from the
          people who were reading with me ...

                    SIMON
          Yeah.

                    MICHAEL
          ... they felt that they wanted to see
          the Michael character, um, be more
          punishing of the David character.
          That if he is gonna be that ...

Simon mutters.

                 MICHAEL (CONT'D)
          ... needy and whingey and moany, that
          they wanted to see Michael come in
          harder with him, like to really, like,
          give it to him because he needs, he
          needs to be shaken like a rag doll.

                    SIMON
          Michael, do you want to shake David?

                    MICHAEL
          It's not me. Hey, these are just
          characters. It's got nothing to do with
          me. I am neutral in this.

                    DAVID
          Interesting. Cos the ch ... the people
          I were, were, were reading with had
          the, had very much the directly opposite
          experience. They were ...

                    MICHAEL
          Mmm.

                    DAVID
          ... they found this boorish bully, this
          unpleasant ... who loved the sound of
          his own voice ...

                    SIMON
          Okay.

                    DAVID
          That's their feedback. I'm just giving
          you an honest appraisal.

                    SIMON
          Thank you, David. Thank you.
                    (to Michael)
          And, Michael, thank you to you, too.

A beat.

                    MICHAEL
          Just a vessel. Just giving you what was
          said.

                    SIMON
          Maybe, Michael, would you like to say
          thank you to David? Would you like to
          thank David for his honesty?

                    MICHAEL
                    (insincere)
          Merci beaucoup to you.

                    SIMON
          David, would you like to thank Michael
          for his honesty, too?

                    DAVID
          That didn't feel very sincere, so I
          don't wanna, I don't wanna get involved
          in this. I think it, I think it
          trivialises something quite important.

                    SIMON
          Okay, well there's, um, that's a lot to
          be getting on with.

     Simon fastens the lid on to his pen.

          Er ...
                    (coughs)
          ... I don't have time for a lot of that
          but I can ... it's food for thought,
          isn't it?

5 INT. MICHAEL'S HOUSE AND JOSH'S OFFICE - DAY   5

     MICHAEL is sitting in a small spare room.

     JOSH GAD is sitting at his desk.

                    JOSH
          Where are you?

                    MICHAEL
                    (hesitantly)
          I'm in my house.

     Josh studies his screen.

                    JOSH
          You're not in your kitchen.

                    MICHAEL
          Er, no. I'm, I'm in my spare room. The
          baby's asleep in the kitchen.

     From Josh's reaction, it is obvious this isn't going as he had
     planned.

                          JOSH
                    (sighs softly)
         Shit.
                    (to Michael)
         I mean, I, um ... I sort of need you
         to be in your kitchen. I'd prepared
         it, I prepared it that way. For you to
         be doing it in your kitchen and I'd be
         doing it where I feel most comfortable.

                          MICHAEL
         Well, I, I'm, I'm so sorry, Josh, but,
         um ... er, our baby didn't sleep at all
         last night, and, um, and then she just
         fell asleep in the kitchen.
         So if you can work with it being in the
         spare room, um, rather than the kitchen,
         I would be very appreciative.

                          JOSH
         Alright.

                          MICHAEL
         Okay.

                          JOSH
         Okay. I can act wherever. I don't need
         that. I don't need that ...

                          MICHAEL
         Thank you.

                          JOSH
         Fine. Let's go. Let's go.

                          MICHAEL
         Okay. But, you know, you'd, I don't
         think you needed to learn it.

                          JOSH
         I learn things. That's what I do.

Josh clicks his fingers to get Michael's attention.

                       JOSH (CONT'D)
         Look at me. Look at me.

                          MICHAEL
         Yeah. Yeah.

                          JOSH
         'So, maybe I held some things back. But,
         um, only because I have found in my time
         with Michael that, er ... '

Michael is preoccupied, continually glancing off-screen. This
throws Josh off.

                       JOSH (CONT'D)
         Fuck's sake, man. For fuck's sake.

                              MICHAEL
            What?

                               JOSH
            This is serious.

                              MICHAEL
            Yeah, I'm ... yeah, I'm sorry, I'm, I'm
            being serious.

                               JOSH
            This.

                              MICHAEL
            I'm being serious. I'm sorry.

Josh clicks his fingers.

                               JOSH
            Let's go again. Let's go again. 'I
            wanted to avoid any hold-up.'

                              MICHAEL
            'Let's not play the blame game.'

                               JOSH
                 (softly)
            Stay with me. That's it, stay with me.
            'Er, you know, as our time was so
            limited.'

                              MICHAEL
            'Yeah, let's not start doing that.'

                               JOSH
            Now let's take it somewhere else. Okay?
            'Doing what?'

Michael stares blankly, then glances down at his script.

                              MICHAEL
            'Er, pointing fingers?'

                               JOSH
                 (softly)
            That's it. And I throw you the ball.

Michael rubs his face.

                              MICHAEL
            Um, sorry, what ... what do you want me
            to do? I ...

                               JOSH
            Fucking make it up, okay. Improvisation,
            I believe it's called.

                              MICHAEL
            I'm really tired.
                      (chuckles)
            Sorry.

                         JOSH
          Look at me. Look at me.

                       MICHAEL
                      (shouts)
          I don't want to!

                         JOSH
                   (mimics David)
          Look at me. I'm David.
          I'm David.
                      (mutters)
          I've called you every name under the
          sun. You've taken it. You've taken it
          like a wee bit baby. You've just taken
          it. To call you over-sensitive.

Michael finally explodes and launches at 'David'.

                       MICHAEL
          Do you know what ... do you know what?!
          Do you know what?
          You don't know the meaning of over-
          sensitive. You're like a fucking walking
          nerve end! Everything upsets you! I
          mean, I mean, I wanna be, I wanna be
          there for you, but there's not a day
          goes by that something isn't gnawing
          at your stupid, stupid brain! You know,
          I could cope when it was about the
          big things. You know, when your daily
          existential panic attacks were about a
          fucking plague! But now the summit of
          your concerns seems to be ...
                   (mimics David)
          ... 'Oh, oh, I can't use the dining room
          for my phone call.' Or ... 'Oh, I didn't
          know there was a family calendar.'
          And that's fine. You know, that's fine.
          But don't get on a video call with your
          stupid hangdog eyes and whine and whine
          and wh ... ! Look, if, if it helps you to
          expunge, then fucking God bless and go
          for it. But I don't work that way. I ...
                   (breathes deeply)
          I, I want to be there for ... God knows
          I wanna be there for all my friends, you
          know. I, I don't wanna be here for them,
          I wanna be there for them!

Josh watches intently as Michael continues.

                   MICHAEL (CONT'D)
          Do you know what I'd like? As if you'd
          ever fucking ask. I would like just
          to hug someone, you know, because I'm
          struggling too. And listening to your
          agony aunt spoken word, self-indulgent,
          self-help shit, undergrad beat poem is
          fucking killing me!

Michael finishes.

Silence. Josh applauds him.

> **JOSH**
> That was fucking wild.

6 INT. DAVID'S HOUSE - DAY   6

GEORGIA standing in the hall by the closed toilet door. GEORGIA knocks at a door.

The end credits start over this.

> **GEORGIA**
> I just wondered whether you were ever gonna come out.

> **DAVID (O.S.)**
> Am I a warthog or a mongoose?

> **GEORGIA**
> Oh, I don't know. Er ...
>   (exhales deeply)
> ... I guess you'd be the mongoose.

> **DAVID (O.S.)**
> Oh, fuck you.

> **GEORGIA**
> Alright, fine. Be the warthog. I thought you meant physically.

> **DAVID (O.S.)**
> Well, it's better than being Rafiki.

> **GEORGIA**
> Which one's Rafiki?

> **DAVID (O.S.)**
> He's the baboon.

> **GEORGIA**
> Just call the fucking warthog.

She walks off.

7 INT. MICHAEL'S AND DAVID'S HOUSES - DAY   7

MICHAEL and DAVID sitting in their respective living rooms.

> **DAVID**
> I have become needy.

> **MICHAEL**
> I've stopped listening.

> **DAVID**
> I just wanna get back to normal.

> **MICHAEL**
> I know.

                         DAVID
          Can't go out, can't stay in, can't go to
          work. It's like every shred of normality
          is now smeared in shit.

                        MICHAEL
          I feel trapped.

                         DAVID
          What, in these little digital boxes?

                        MICHAEL
          Yes.

                         DAVID
          I fucking hate them.

                        MICHAEL
          Oh, I hate them. Staring at your face
          all day.

                         DAVID
          Well, yes, I have to stare at my face
          too, grinning like a fucking loon.

They both pull faces as Michael mutters incomprehensibly.

                      DAVID (CONT'D)
          Like a ... You're funny.I find you funny.
          Yes, you're so fucking funny.
          A smile I don't believe in any more.

                        MICHAEL
          Fuck. You know, I haven't smiled
          properly in months. I'm clamping my jaw
          so hard it's giving me headaches.

David grimaces as he clutches his cheeks.

                         DAVID
          My masseter muscles are like fucking
          walnuts.

A beat.

                        MICHAEL
          How long have we been here?

Another beat.

                         DAVID
          What, in this hellscape, pixel-mirror,
          time dungeon?

                        MICHAEL
          Yes.

                         DAVID
          A million years.

                              MICHAEL
          Really?

                               DAVID
          Mmm.

                              MICHAEL
          How do we escape?

Pause.

                               DAVID
                         (softly)
          I don't know.

David exhales deeply as they stare at their screens.

                                             BLACK SCREEN

Episode Seven
The Loo Recluse

DAVID TENNANT is in his sitting room. MICHAEL SHEEN is in his kitchen.

Over this the credits: white letters on black.

> **DAVID**
> So Romania is off, but, Michael, Northampton is a go situation.

> **MICHAEL**
> The gateway to the west, Northampton.

> **DAVID**
> Nothing will stop me getting to Northampton.

> **MICHAEL**
> Oh, do you know, I'm s ... I'm so happy for you. And proud.

> **DAVID**
> Thank you. Thank you very much.

> **MICHAEL**
> Six across. Sword of dot, dot, dot, dot, dot, dot.

> **DAVID**
> Omens.

> **MICHAEL**
> It's eight letters.

> **DAVID**
> Sword of Damocles.

> **MICHAEL**
> (mispronounces)
> Damocles.

> **DAVID**
> Yep!

> **MICHAEL**
> Yes.

> **DAVID**
> We should have a system by now.

> **MICHAEL**
> Like what?

> **DAVID**
> I don't know.

> **MICHAEL**
> I could do cross, you could do down.

Is that a joke?

You'll be the cross one and I'll be the
down one?

Michael realises what he has said.

MICHAEL

Ah-ha-ha. I, I was ... I came up with it
last night.

DAVID

You're a funny old fish, aren't you?
Cos you're not an intentionally funny
person.

MICHAEL

Is that correct?

DAVID

Well, yeah.

MICHAEL

Well, I tell jokes.

DAVID

No, you don't. You s ... you stumble
and topple headlong into funny things,
completely accidentally occasionally.

MICHAEL

Oh, do I? You make me sound like a
wounded gazelle.

DAVID

No, it's endearing.

MICHAEL

Seven across.
          (chuckles)
Oh my God. Lead actor in Staged.

DAVID

Fuck off!

MICHAEL

          (chuckles)
Yes.

DAVID

You're kidding?

MICHAEL

          (chuckles)
Yeah.

Silence as Michael studies the crossword.

                              DAVID
          How many letters?

                             MICHAEL
          Twelve.

They both quickly count on their fingers.

                         MICHAEL (CONT'D)
                    (chuckles)
          Yeah!

Michael reacts.

          What?

                              DAVID
          No?

2   INT. DAVID'S AND MICHAEL'S HOUSES AND MARY'S OFFICE - DAY   2

     DAVID sitting in his kitchen. MICHAEL sitting in his living
     room.

                              MARY
                    So, talk to me about the auditions. You
                    know, the ones where I, I, I asked you
                    clearly to behave ... for the sake of
                    your careers. Your careers.

                             MICHAEL
                    Absolutely.

                              MARY
                    So, did you, or did you not, use these
                    sessions with A-list Hollywood talent as
                    an impromptu therapy thing?

                             MICHAEL
                    Er, well, um, David was feeling
                    vulnerable, er, you know, a bit tender
                    ...
                         (to David)
                    ... weren't you?

                              DAVID
                    Well, some of the improvisations got a
                    wee bit personal.

She reacts.

                              MARY
                    You realise you're a laughing stock,
                    yeah?

Silence.
                    You know this, right?

                              DAVID
                    Can we just have one more chance?

                    MICHAEL
We can be professional, Mary, we really
can.

                    DAVID
Yeah.

                    MARY
I think you're cursed.

                    MICHAEL
Cursed?

                    MARY
Have you ever met a wizard?

                    MICHAEL
          (hesitantly)
No.

                    MARY
Are you sure?
          (chuckles)
Because I think the wizard must have
fucked you in the ass!

Mary's computer chimes as she leaves the call. Silence follows.

                    MICHAEL
I'm pretty sure I would have remembered
that.

                    DAVID
Well, not if you were enchanted.

We hear Tom's computer chime as he joins the call from his office.

                    TOM
Hey, guys.

                    DAVID
Hi.

                    TOM
Hi. How was that?

                    DAVID
Lovely.

                    MICHAEL
Tom, um ... do you think you could get
her to give us another chance?

                    TOM
A chance of what?

                    MICHAEL
Of reading with the actors.

                    TOM
No need, it's done. It's already cast.

What?

                    MICHAEL
What?!

Beat.

          Really? What, they've cast ... us?

                    DAVID
Finished?

Tom panics as he realises he has said too much - again.

                    TOM
          Er, no, I shouldn't have said anything.
          Pretend I didn't say anything. Pretend I
          didn't say anything, for real.

                    MICHAEL
                    (stutters)
          Who, who ... who is it?

                    TOM
          I can't say. Michael, I cannot say.

                    DAVID
          Oh, come on.

                    TOM
          No, I can't, I can't.

                    MICHAEL
          Tom, please, please, come on.

                    DAVID
          We just wanna know who it is. We just
          wanna know who it is.

                    TOM
          No, it's still embargoed, still
          embargoed. Mary would kill me, with
          a trophy that she found she would
          absolutely kill me.

                    DAVID
          Tom.

                    TOM
          Oh, David, don't do that.

                    DAVID
          What?

                    TOM
          Don't first-name me. You remember the
          last time you first-named me? Do you
          remember this?

He laughs and holds up a picture of himself and David at
Disneyland together. Michael and David are clearly shocked.

                    MICHAEL
        When did you go to Disneyland with Tom,
        David?

David is stunned.

                    TOM
        Unbelievable. Oh.

                    MICHAEL
        Well, look ...

                    DAVID
        So, can you help us out?

                    TOM
        Okay. This is, this is what's happening,
        this is what's happening. In the books
        right now there is a call with Simon and
        the other actors about a rewrite.
        Then after that there's gonna be a whole
        big announcement. Then you'll find out at
        the announcement.

                    MICHAEL
        So, so why don't you let us join the
        call?

                    DAVID
        Yes.

                    TOM
        No. No.

                    MICHAEL
        Come on. It would make David so happy if
        you could do that.

                    DAVID
        It would.

                    TOM
        David, would it really make you happy?

                    DAVID
        I'd love it.

                    MICHAEL
        And then, when David comes over to LA
        next ...

David prepares himself for what's coming.

                    DAVID
        Yeah?

                    MICHAEL
        ... you know, if you get us on that
        call, I'm sure David would love to spend
        time with you and hang out, go for
        dinner, take in a show.

                        TOM
        Michael, you said hang out.

                      MICHAEL
        Yeah, yeah, yeah. If you tell us, if ...
        hmm.

Tom rips out his earphones as he stands.

                       DAVID
                    (mouths)
        What the fuck is this?!

                        TOM
                    (mumbles)
        Shit, shit, shit, shit ...

He pushes his chair aside as he paces back and forth. Michael
frantically gestures for David to be nice to Tom.

                      MICHAEL
                    (softly)
        Come on.

He blows kisses.

                  MICHAEL (CONT'D)
        Kiss.

                        TOM
        Yeah, that would be great. That would be
        great. That would be great.

Tom grabs his earphones as he sits.

                    TOM (CONT'D)
        That would be great. That would be
        ...

                      MICHAEL
        Um, yeah ... if you can get us on that
        call, Tom.

                        TOM
        I know exactly where we'd get food. I
        know exactly where we'd get dinner.
        I've already planned the courses and
        everything, and I know exactly what
        we'll be drinking at the time.
        I'm into that. I, I think this is
        amazing.

                      MICHAEL
        And then I could maybe, you know, I'll
        be over soon and we could hang out as
        well.

Tom instantly makes Michael's excuses for him.

                              TOM
                          (inhales)
                    So much traffic, though, right, Michael?
                    So much traffic here.

A beat.

                              DAVID
                    We just wanna know who it is.

                              TOM
                    And we can eat anything we want, and we
                    can talk about anything we want?

                              DAVID
                    You can choose, of course. Listen, you
                    know the city, you can show me round.

Tom becomes nauseous with excitement. A beat.

                         DAVID (CONT'D)
                    What do you say?

                              TOM
                    What do T say?

                              DAVID
                    Yeah.

Michael and David react as Tom vomits into the waste bin.

3 INT. CATE BLANCHETT'S AND PHOEBE WALLER-BRIDGE'S HOUSES - DAY   3

CATE BLANCHETT is on a call with PHOEBE WALLER-BRIDGE. PHOEBE
opens her script.

                              CATE
                    So, d-do you know either of them?

                              PHOEBE
                    I, I used to know David.

                              CATE
                    And what about, um ... Simon, do you
                    know, do you know Simon?

                              PHOEBE
                    Allegedly.

                              CATE
                          (inquisitively)
                    Oh, what does that mean?

Phoebe reacts with a disgusted look.

                              PHOEBE
                    Oh, no. No. No, no, I just have no
                    memory of him whatsoever.

                              CATE
                    Uh-huh.

                    PHOEBE
He sent me an email that said 'Long
time, no see'.

                    CATE
Urghh, God, hate that phrase.

                    PHOEBE
Makes me so nervous.

                    CATE
Oh. Well, did you challenge?

                    PHOEBE
No, I just replied, 'You too. Can't
wait to catch up. Blah blah blah.' I
asked around, but apparently he's quite
forgettable.

Don't tell him I said he was
forgettable.

                    CATE
I won't.

                    PHOEBE
Or that I forgot him.

She drinks. Simon suddenly joins the call.

                    SIMON
Hi.

Phoebe and Cate react.

                SIMON (CONT'D)
Hi.

                    PHOEBE
Hi.

                    CATE
Hello.

                    SIMON
Hello there. Hello. Hi.
Er, Cate, Simon. Lovely to meet you.

                    CATE
Er, Simon, hi.

                    SIMON
Phoebe!

                    PHOEBE
Hey.

                    SIMON
            (chuckles)
Yay.

                    PHOEBE
            (chuckles)
    Long time, no see.

                    SIMON
    Long time ...
            (chuckles)
    ... no see.

                    CATE
    Um, you've worked with Phoebe be ...
    before.

                    SIMON
    Yeah. Yeah, yeah, yeah. Yeah, we go back
    a way.

                    CATE
    Er, when was that? Sorry, Phoebes just
    hasn't had a chance to, to, to, to tell
    me. When was that?

Simon quickly passes the question to Phoebe.

                    SIMON
    Oh well, Phoebe, you ...

                    PHOEBE
            (laughs)
    Um, did I not? I thought I'd, I thought
    I'd ...

                    SIMON
    You tell it. You tell it this time.
            (chuckles)

                    PHOEBE
    I was just talking to Cate about it.
    Um, I can't remember the name of the, um
    ...

                    SIMON
    The play.

                    PHOEBE
    ... the play.

                    SIMON
    Yeah, Like A Fishbone.

                    PHOEBE
    Like A Fishbone. At the Royal Court.

                    SIMON
    At The Bush.

                    PHOEBE
    Yeah, a couple of years ago.

                    SIMON
    Yeah. Well, 2010.

                    PHOEBE
Couple of years ago, yeah.

                    SIMON
Yeah, yeah, happy, happy ...
          (to Cate/Phoebe)
Look, it's lovely to be in your, both
your orbits, to, to sort of read a
little bit of this. It's, er, it's a
sort of scene from, er, Series One
of the UK version and we've sort of
tinkered with it a little bit ...

                    PHOEBE
The Adrian Lester bit. Love it.

                    SIMON
There you go.
          (exhales)
God, thank you.
          (to both)
Er, I'm just gonna go and grab, er, a
notebook quickly.

                    CATE
Okay.

                    PHOEBE
Really nice to see you.

Simon stands and leans close to the screen.

                    SIMON
Oh, it's so lovely to see you.

Phoebe chuckles politely as he leans out.

She leans close to her screen.

                    PHOEBE
          (softly)
Fuck you.

The screen suddenly splits as Michael's screen joins the call.
Phoebe and Cate react to Michael clutching a screaming toy in
his mouth.

                    PHOEBE (CONT'D)
Jesus!

He rips it from his mouth as he sees them.

                    PHOEBE (CONT'D)
Michael.

                    MICHAEL
Phoebe.

                    CATE
Hello!

                    MICHAEL
        Fuck me, it's Cate Blanchett.

                     CATE
        H-hi.

                    MICHAEL
        What are you doing here?

                    PHOEBE
        What are you doing here?

Simon enters and sits in, clutching his script.

                     CATE
        Um, so ... er, Simon, um, we, we, we
        just weren't aware that Michael was
        actually gonna be here.

                     SIMON
        I, I was unaware Michael was going to be
        here.

                    PHOEBE
        Yeah, we were actually specifically told
        that he wouldn't be here.

                    MICHAEL
        Yeah, um, sorry ... we are just supposed
        to be observing, but ...

                    PHOEBE
        What do you mean by 'we'?

                    MICHAEL
        What, what are you doing here?

                     CATE
        Er, we're reading for the show.

                    MICHAEL
        Which show?

                     CATE
        Your show.

                    MICHAEL
        My show?

                     CATE
        Our show.

                    PHOEBE
        David's not coming, is he?

David joins the conversation.

                     DAVID
        Hello.

                    PHOEBE
        Jesus.

                    DAVID
        Sorry I'm late.

Silence as he reacts.

                DAVID (CONT'D)
        Phoebe?

                    PHOEBE
        David.

A beat.

                    DAVID
        Long time, no see.

                    PHOEBE
        Yeah, long time, no see.

                    DAVID
        What are you doing here?

                    PHOEBE
        What are you doing here?

                    MICHAEL
        Stop repeating each other.

                    PHOEBE
        I'm sorry, I just ... I won't be in the
        same room as him.

                    DAVID
        Well, technically we're not in the same
        room.

                    PHOEBE
                (mimics David)
        Oh! Oh, technically we're not in the
        same room.

                    DAVID
        Yeah, technically we're not in the same
        room, that's right.

                    PHOEBE
        Oh, we're not in the same room, are we?

                    DAVID
        We're not actually in the same room, are
        we? We're in different rooms.

                    PHOEBE
        Thank God we're not in the same room.

Michael is exasperated with this.

MICHAEL

Jesus. Simon, Simon, sorry, could you
remind me again, what are they doing here?

Silence.

CATE

Er, we're the new Michael and David.

Michael and David react, stunned.

4 INT. DAVID'S HOUSE AND TOM'S OFFICE - DAY   4

GEORGIA TENNANT and TOM sitting in their respective locations.

TOM

David?

GEORGIA

Er, no.

TOM

Who, who are you? Who are you?

GEORGIA

Who are you?

TOM

Who am I? I'm Tom.

GEORGIA

Who the fuck is Tom?

TOM

Er, David's best friend Tom.

Georgia looks at him blankly.

Okay, your silence is insane. Can you
please get him for me?

GEORGIA

Um, er, n-no.

TOM

Who are you?

Are you his personal assistant? Do you
clean his, his Daleks? Are you like his
pâtissière? Do you make his pastries?
Tell me what you're doing there.

GEORGIA

Well, er, yeah, all those, all those
things, and also his wife.

A beat. Tom reacts.

TOM

Georgia. So you've made love with him?

Georgia gasps at this remark. She glances away for David's support.

> **TOM (CONT'D)**
> Okay. Sorry, can you, can you, can you tell me where he is? Where is he?

> **GEORGIA**
> (clears throat)
> Yeah, he's just on a call.

Tom reacts, rips out his earphones and tosses them to the desk as he stands, steps away.

> **GEORGIA (CONT'D)**
> What?

> **TOM**
> What? What do you mean? Is it with Phoebe and Cate? Georgia, it's with Phoebe and Cate.

> **GEORGIA**
> Who are Phoebe and Cate?

> **TOM**
> I'm gonna be sick. Mary's on her way over here right now.

> **GEORGIA**
> Oh.

> **TOM**
> Did you know that Phoebe hates David?

> **GEORGIA**
> Phoebe?

> **TOM**
> Yeah. Cos I had no idea. Nobody told me.

> **GEORGIA**
> Phoebe as in Waller-Bridge.

> **TOM**
> Yeah, the monologue woman. The monologue woman.

> **GEORGIA**
> Yeah, you're fucked.

Tom sighs deeply.

FADE TO BLACK --

5   INT. MICHAEL'S, DAVID'S, PHOEBE'S, CATE'S AND SIMON'S HOUSES — DAY   5

MICHAEL, DAVID, PHOEBE, SIMON and CATE sitting in their respective houses. In silence.

> **SIMON**
> Right, Michael.

> **SIMON (CONT'D)**
> Who, who, who let you in?

A beat.

> **MICHAEL**
> (hesitantly)
> Er, Tom did.

> **SIMON**
> Who's Tom?

> **DAVID**
> Mary's assistant, Tom.

> **PHOEBE**
> Well, he shouldn't have done that.

> **DAVID**
> Oh, let it go, Phoebe.

> **PHOEBE**
> Er, David, why don't you tell them.

> **DAVID**
> (quickly)
> No.

> **PHOEBE**
> We worked on Broadchurch together.

> **DAVID**
> (clarifies)
> Second series.

> **SIMON**
> Shall we just read instead? Let's read
> the scene.

> **MICHAEL**
> Um, sorry ... Cate, can I ... I'm, I'm
> just gonna get this out the way.
> I am a huge fan.

> **CATE**
> Oh my God. Thank you. I mean, you're
> Michael Sheen, for God's sake.

> **MICHAEL**
> Oh, you're Cate Blanchett.

> **CATE**
> Cate Blanchett's a big fan.

Simon and Phoebe look on as the praise continues.

> **MICHAEL**
> Oh, that's massive.

                              CATE
          I mean ... no, no, seriously, seriously,
          I think you have this way of just losing
          yourself in your roles. It's ...

                            MICHAEL
          I ... well, excuse me, didn't someone
          play Bob Dylan?

Simon tries to divert the conversation.

                             SIMON
          Can we, can we read?

                            PHOEBE
          No, I'd like David to tell the story
          first.

                             DAVID
          I don't think anyone wants to hear the
          story.

Pause.

                            PHOEBE
          Simon wants to hear it ...
                    (to Simon)
          ... don't you?

                             SIMON
          I suppose so.

                            PHOEBE
          No, I remember that, I remember that
          from The Donmar.

                             SIMON
          Er, The Bush.

                            PHOEBE
          Like a Goldfish.

                             SIMON
          Fishbone.

                            PHOEBE
          Well, so we were filming Broadchurch, on
          location, there were long days, and it
          happened that occasionally I would need
          the bathroom. So when I did need to go,
          early on David would find a way of making
          his phone emit a sound.

                            MICHAEL
          A sound?

                            PHOEBE
          Like a text alert.

                              CATE
          A text alert?

DAVID

It's like a ping.

CATE

A ping?

PHOEBE

Well, he was methodical. I'd go and his phone would ping. I didn't notice at first. Weeks passed. Cause and effect swap places, his phone would ping. And it just, it became Pavlovian.

CATE

This, this can't be real.

PHOEBE

It is real! I heard it and I had to go, immediately and involuntarily.

DAVID

It was a joke.

PHOEBE

I was written out of scenes.

DAVID

It was a joke!

PHOEBE

Whole scenes because I had to go to the toilet!

DAVID

That's not what happened.

PHOEBE
(shouts)
That is what happened!

DAVID

I thought it would be funny.

Cate comes to Phoebe's rescue.

CATE

Well, it's not.

DAVID

Yeah, alright. How much comedy have you done?

MICHAEL

She is funny. Have you seen Notes on a Scandal?

DAVID

Yeah. Have you?

PHOEBE

You ruined my career. I stopped being
cast, roles dried up. I was difficult
to work with. No one wanted to hire me
because they called me 'The Loo Recluse'.

DAVID

What about Fleabag?

PHOEBE

I had to fucking create Fleabag!

DAVID

I inspired you.

SIMON

Can we read, please? Can we read?

PHOEBE

I had to carve my way back in.

SIMON

Please can we read?

DAVID

Hang on. If you two are playing us,
who's playing our other halves? Who's
playing Georgia?

CATE

You mean George.

DAVID

George. Is that a joke?

PHOEBE

You wouldn't know a joke if it came on
your face.

CATE

Er, sorry, who are, who are you talking
to about the partners, er, Simon?

SIMON

Oh, er, well, unconfirmed, but fingers
crossed, um ... Martin Freeman.

CATE

Ah.

Michael reacts.

MICHAEL

No. No. No. Fuck you. No. Not Martin
Freeman. Not again.

CATE

Oh, he's lovely.

MICHAEL

No, he is a fucking thief.

Silence.

                         MICHAEL (CONT'D)
             I ... Okay, look, I, I was going to be
             Bilbo Baggins.

                              CATE
             You were supposed to be in The Hobbit?

                            MICHAEL
             The role was mine, I'd accepted it and
             then he stole it from me.

                              CATE
             Oh, no, no, no, no, he's a sweetheart.

                            MICHAEL
             No, he is a monster.

                             SIMON
                         (defeated)
             Can we read, please?

                             DAVID
             Is that when you were recast?

                            MICHAEL
             Yeah.

                             DAVID
             I thought it was me.

A beat.

                            MICHAEL
             Sorry, when would you ever replace me?

                             DAVID
             You do look like a hobbit.

                              CATE
             Er, Peter Jackson, he did ask me about
             you.

                            MICHAEL
             And what did you say?

                              CATE
             Well, I was honest and said I'd never
             heard of you.

David reacts.

                            MICHAEL
             Oh.

Beat.

             Well, did he ask you about Martin?

                        CATE
            Well, yes, and I just ... said I thought
            he was alright in Frost/Nixon.

Michael cannot believe what he's hearing.

                        MICHAEL
            That, that was, that was me.

                        CATE
            That was you?

                        MICHAEL
            That was me!

                        DAVID
            Yeah, that was him, yeah.

                        SIMON
                  (pleadingly)
            Please can we read.

Michael buries his head in his hands.

                        MICHAEL
            Oh, you ruined my career.

                        CATE
            Hey, back off, hairy legs. I didn't know
            that was you.

                        MICHAEL
            'I lose myself in my roles.'

                        CATE
            Well, do it less.

                        MICHAEL
            Sorry, do it less?

                        CATE
            Yes, lose yourself less.

                        MICHAEL
            'Lose myself less.'

                        SIMON
                  (pleads)
            Please can we read? Please. Please.
            Please. Please can we ...

                        PHOEBE
            Fine, fine, fine, fine ...

Simon repeatedly bangs his script against the desk.

                        SIMON
            Can we read? Can we just read? Can we
            read it? Can we just read it once?
                  (shouts)
            Just please read it!

Silence.

                              PHOEBE
                    Fine. Yeah.

                             MICHAEL
                    Yeah, great.

                              SIMON
                    Thank you.

The silence is broken as David's mobile phone chimes.

                              DAVID
                    Oh.

Phoebe reacts.

                              PHOEBE
                         (softly)
                    Fuck you.

She stands and hurries off to the toilet.

6 INT. TOM'S OFFICE - DAY   6

We open on an empty table. TOM enters clutching an empty
cardboard box to clear his desk. He sets it down.

7 INT. MICHAEL'S AND DAVID'S HOUSES - DAY   7

MICHAEL and DAVID in their respective houses as Michael
continues with his crossword.

                             MICHAEL
                    Yes. Yes, the seventh letter of lead
                    actor, in Staged, is the last letter of
                    four across.

                              DAVID
                    And four across is ...

                             MICHAEL
                    For all time.

                              DAVID
                    Right. It's infinite. Last letter is 'E'.
                    D-A-V-I-D T-E-N-N-A-N-T.

                             MICHAEL
                    Or what about immortal.

Michael counts on his fingers.

                         MICHAEL (CONT'D)
                    Last letter is 'L'. M-I-C-H-A-E-L ...
                    S-H-E-E-N.

                              DAVID
                    Er, any other across words?

                    MICHAEL
          Um ... two across. Animated animal. Er,
          it's three letters and it shares a first
          letter with either you or me.

They think.

                    DAVID
          Dog.

                    MICHAEL
          Man.

                    DAVID
          Man?

                    MICHAEL
          Dog?

                    DAVID
          Yeah, there's loads of animated dogs.

                    MICHAEL
          It's ant.

                    DAVID
          Ant?

                    MICHAEL
          Yes. Animated animal, three
          letters. Ant from the movie Antz.

                    DAVID
          Oh, right.

                    MICHAEL
          And it is immortal.

                    DAVID
          That doesn't fit with either of us.

                    MICHAEL
          Because it's Adrian Lester.

Silence. David reacts.

                    DAVID
                (disappointed)
          Ohh. Oh.

Michael throws screwed-up crossword in disgust.
                                        BLACK SCREEN

The Crossword

Created by Geoff Iles. Answers to crossword on p.392.

MICHEAL – THE CROSS ONE

1   Lead actor in *Staged* – allegedly! (12)

9   Working to make the sea blue (7)

10 Challenge we set the Royal Society for spectators (7)

11&15 A lady entitled to put our Boys in their place (4,5)

12 Michael's Psycho-logical fear (5)

13 2-way partner of one (4)

16 I called out in a French accent (7)

17 Avoidable loss of direction gets on one's nerves (7)

18 Welsh swine (7)

21 The Girls re-staged *Staged* for this charity event (7)

23 This *Staged* Recluse returned with time to get a utensil (4)

24 Sub (1-4)

25 Problematically assisting read-throughs at first is what the Boys wanted to achieve in *Staged2* (4)

28 Ep.1 has remedy for this bon vivant (7)

29 A fruit of 22 at last we hear (7)

30 Bad egg bought by this unsightly shopper? (4,8)

DAVID – THE DOWN ONE

1   Dead men made this change (7)

2   Return to York for this garment (4)

3   New territory for *Staged2* (7)

4   Devil in the detail – like David's grey hoodie perhaps? (5,2)

5   Michael loses his aspiration and it's noticed (4)

6   Infinite need to alter points (7)

7   Topic dull, right, but it's what we are talking about (7,6)

8   The two fools, I state, make a killing (13)

14 Pirandello softly puts down these literary works (5)

15 See 11

19 This is a challenge with just 2 carrots and some stale chocolate (7)

20 Drop-down for 24 listing (3-4)

21 First man solves 'animated animal' clue and is resolute (7)

22 Like David & Michael, always found together (2,1,4)

26 Director's sibling is fortunate to lose a kilo (4)

27 Hurry to an online meeting (4)

Episode Eight
Until They Get Home

1 INT. MICHAEL'S AND DAVID'S HOUSES - DAY   1

      MICHAEL SHEEN sitting in his living room. DAVID TENNANT sitting
      in his kitchen.

      Over this the credits: white letters on black.

                              DAVID
                  Right, woll ...
                          (clears throat)

      David pulls on his jacket.

                          DAVID (CONT'D)
                  ... I have to go.

                              MICHAEL
                  Ooh. Off to work?

                              DAVID
                  Off to work.

                              MICHAEL
                  Yeah. Escape.

                              DAVID
                  Escape.

      A beat.

                              MICHAEL
                  What would you do if the world was
                  actually ending?

                              DAVID
                  I'd come visit you.

                              MICHAEL
                  Here?

                              DAVID
                  Yeah, I'd bring the entire family.

                              MICHAEL
                  All seven of you?

                              DAVID
                  And Myrtle.

                              MICHAEL
                  Right ... right.

                              DAVID
                  That's alright, isn't it?

                              MICHAEL
                  I mean, it's a lovely thought. I'm not,
                  I'm not sure it's practical. I mean,
                  we'd have to get a very big shop in.

DAVID

Just make a big omelette, we'll be fine.

MICHAEL

Can I just say, if, if it does end
...

DAVID

Yeah.

MICHAEL

... just hold off for a little bit on
that.

DAVID

It depends how long we've got, though.
It's quite a long drive.

MICHAEL

Yeah, well, I'll tell you what,
hopefully we'd all perish before you
actually arrived, cos it is quite a way,
isn't it?

DAVID

Hopefully?

MICHAEL

But I'd know that you were coming and
that would make me feel good, but then
you wouldn't actually get here because
that would be difficult.

DAVID

So, what would you do?

MICHAEL

Er, do I know the world is ending?

DAVID

Hey, what do you mean?

MICHAEL

Do I know the world's ending? Has it
been announced?

DAVID

I don't fucking know. It's your
hypothetical situation.

I didn't come up with it.

MICHAEL

You gotta give me some details.
Do I know the end is coming?

DAVID

Yes, you do.

MICHAEL

I would have a nap.

>   DAVID
>   And if it, if it was a surprise?

>   MICHAEL
>   Er, well then I wouldn't know it was
>   coming, would I? So, I would just be doing
>   normal things ... more than likely I would
>   be talking to you. Exactly like this.

>   DAVID
>   Yes.

Silence.

2 INT. DAVID'S, LUCY'S AND MICHAEL'S HOUSES - DAY   2

GEORGIA, LUCY and ANNA in their respective houses.

>   GEORGIA
>   Sorry, it's, um, it's chaos here.

>   LUCY
>   Everything alright?

>   GEORGIA
>   The suitcases are back.

Lucy mutters.

>   GEORGIA (CONT'D)
>   Um, so, right, if we can just go through
>   this a couple of times, even just once,
>   we'll be good to go.

>   LUCY
>   Seven-thirty start.

>   GEORGIA
>   Yep. So, our scene's up first live and
>   then they do the auction.

>   ANNA
>   Ooh, getting close.

>   GEORGIA
>   Yeah.

>   LUCY
>   I'm really looking forward to it.

>   GEORGIA
>   Yeah, we just need to, er, get David to
>   leave first.

>   LUCY
>   (softly)
>   Yeah.

>   ANNA
>   Michael's heading to the airport in a
>   couple of hours.

                           LUCY
           Aren't you going with him?

                           ANNA
           Nope, I'm going to Sweden. Tomorrow.

                         GEORGIA
           Sweden?

                           ANNA
           So he can get to New York but he has to
           isolate. We don't want Lyra to isolate.

                           LUCY
           And he has to go to New York?

                           ANNA
           There's a wedding. He's the best man.
           He's written a speech.

                         GEORGIA
           Well, doesn't he have to isolate too,
           though?

                           ANNA
           He's booked a room across the road of
           the ceremony, so he's going to shout his
           speech.

                         GEORGIA
           Are you joking?

Anna shakes her head.

                           ANNA
           Mmm-hmm.

                           LUCY
           Well, you're gonna have a lovely time.

Anna suggests they begin.

                           ANNA
           Shall we?

                           LUCY
           Yeah, sure.

                         GEORGIA
           Sorry, we do actually just need to wait
           for David to leave.

3   INT. MICHAEL'S AND DAVID'S HOUSES - DAY   3

     DAVID and MICHAEL in their respective kitchens.

                         MICHAEL
           The birds are ... flying away.

                           DAVID
           Yeah, they, they do that this time of
           year.

A beat.

> MICHAEL
>
> How do they stay in formation?

> DAVID
>
> You know I'm not an ornithologist?

> MICHAEL
>
> Er, I am aware of that fact.

> DAVID
>
> Yeah.

> MICHAEL
>
> But I was just wondering if you might
> hazard a guess.

> DAVID
>
> I would hazard that they follow the one
> in front ...

> MICHAEL
>
> Ah, probably.

> DAVID
>
> ... until they get home.

> MICHAEL
>
> Like the elephants.

> DAVID
>
> Like the elephants. You alright?

> MICHAEL
>
> Yeah. Anna and Lyra aren't coming to New
> York.

> DAVID
>
> Oh.

> MICHAEL
>
> Am I a bad father?

> DAVID
>
> No.

> MICHAEL
>
> Am I a bad friend?

> DAVID
>
> No.

> MICHAEL
>
> No.

A beat.

> DAVID
>
> Eh, listen though, we did it.

                    MICHAEL
          Yeah, we, we did do it.

                     DAVID
          Yeah. Sanity intact.

                    MICHAEL
          Intact-ish.

                     DAVID
          Just about serviceable.

                    MICHAEL
          Yeah. I mean, enough for jazz.

                     DAVID
          Quite good for jazz.

                    MICHAEL
          Absolutely. And we never ran out of
          things to say.

                     DAVID
          Is that true?

                    MICHAEL
          Well, I did have to do a lot of the
          heavy lifting.

David gives Michael 'the finger'.

                     DAVID
          Oh, fuck you.

                    MICHAEL
          Well, no, only when you ... only when
          you were having your existential crisis.

                     DAVID
          You had one of those too.

                    MICHAEL
          Yes, but mine was smaller because I have
          a smaller existence.

                     DAVID
          Yeah.

                    MICHAEL
          And I had time, therefore, to keep the
          badinage going.

                     DAVID
          Well thank goodness you had all those
          years of experience to fall back on.

                    MICHAEL
          Yes, well, love, I had the, er, the
          craft of improv.

David imitates shooting spider's web.

MICHAEL (CONT'D)
Ooh, Spidey. Improv. Spider webs.

DAVID
Yeah, Spidey.

MICHAEL
Yes. Oh, here comes my zap, pow, bang, wallop.

Michael adopts his kung-fu pose.

DAVID
Come on, serve me one up, serve me one up.

MICHAEL
Here it comes, here it comes, here it comes, here it comes. Oh, and there it is.

Michael fires a blow. David groans and falls.

DAVID
Oh, he's coming back, he's coming back, he's coming back. And ...

David sits up, fires a return at Michael.

MICHAEL
In my face like improv jizz.

DAVID
Oh, yeah.

A beat.

MICHAEL
There must be things that we still haven't talked about.

DAVID
No. I really have to go.

MICHAEL
Books!

DAVID
No.

MICHAEL
We never did books.

DAVID
They are waiting for me outside.

MICHAEL
Come on.

                        DAVID
            I'm going. I have to go. This is me. I'm
            leaving.

Michael tries to reel David in.

                        MICHAEL
            No. No.

David groans loudly.

                        MICHAEL (CONT'D)
            Books. Books.

4   INT. DAVID'S, LUCY'S AND MICHAEL'S HOUSES - DAY   4

    GEORGIA, LUCY and ANNA.

                        GEORGIA
            Their conversations are like gas. It
            just expands to fit whatever vessel they
            put it into.

                        LUCY
            I don't have that kind of relationship
            with anyone.

                        GEORGIA
            I think it's a fear of silence.

                        ANNA
            Oh.

A beat.

                        GEORGIA
            I like silence.

                        ANNA
            I adore it.

                        GEORGIA
            It's cos you have a one-year-old.
                    (to both)
            Silence is like ...

A car horn sounds.

                        GEORGIA (CONT'D)
            Oh, for fuck's sake! David!

She stands and walks off.

5   INT. MICHAEL'S AND DAVID'S HOUSES - DAY   5

    As before.

                        MICHAEL
            We've never talked about love.

                        GEORGIA
        Can you get off that machine and out
        of the house before I bury you in the
        garden with your fucking goldfish!

Michael finds this highly amusing. He reacts as Georgia quickly
leans in close to the screen.

                    GEORGIA (CONT'D)
        Hi, Michael.

                        MICHAEL
        H-hi, Georgia.

                        GEORGIA
        Hi. Could you let him go?

                        MICHAEL
        Happily.

                        GEORGIA
                (softly)
        Okay.

Georgia exits. A beat.

                        DAVID
                (softly)
        Okay.

Michael watches as David stands.

                        MICHAEL
        You on, er, you on set today?

                        DAVID
        Yes, this very evening.

                        MICHAEL
        Yeah. What time do you wrap?

                        DAVID
        Ooh, middle of the night I would have
        thought.

                        MICHAEL
        Yeah, well, Cardiff is lovely in the
        middle of the night.

                        DAVID
        I'm very excited.

Michael chuckles. A beat.

                    DAVID (CONT'D)
        What if I can't remember how to do it?

                        MICHAEL
        Act?

                          DAVID
          Yeah.

                          MICHAEL
          No, it's easy peasy, man.

                          DAVID
          It's just that I have no other
          discernible skills.

                          MICHAEL
          That's true.

                          DAVID
          It's pretending.

                          MICHAEL
          It's just pretending.

                          DAVID
          Right, this is it, I have to go.

                          MICHAEL
          Right you are.

They stare at each other.

                          MICHAEL (CONT'D)
          I'm still not ready.
                    (chuckles)

                          DAVID
          Georgia's really angry.

                          MICHAEL
          Well, I'll miss this.

                          DAVID
          Listen, we've got so much still to talk
          about.

                          MICHAEL
          Yes.

                          DAVID
          Next time.

                          MICHAEL
          Yeah.

They both hesitantly move to end the call.

                          MICHAEL (CONT'D)
          No, no.

David chuckles. Michael shouts. David ends the call. Michael, as
he sits motionless, glances around.

6 EXT. HOTEL/INT. LUCY'S HOUSE - DAY   6

SIMON on a sunny terrace watches as LUCY hurries past.

                            LUCY
          Just a minute.

                            SIMON
          No rush. This is a, this is a bad time,
          is it?

Lucy leans in.

                            LUCY
          No, no, um, I'm just getting ready for,
          er, we're filming the thing for Georgia.

                            SIMON
          Oh yeah, sure. No, sure. Cool.

                            LUCY
          Yeah, so I've just got to ...

She gestures with her mascara and hurries off to apply it.

                            SIMON
          I'm coming home.

                         LUCY (O.S.)
          What?! When?!

Lucy enters.

                            SIMON
          Today. Now. There's a car outside now.

                            LUCY
          But what about the rewrites?

                            SIMON
          Phoebe's gonna do 'em.

                            LUCY
          Right.

                            SIMON
          It is funnier. She's made it funnier.
          That's good.

A beat.

                            LUCY
          Well, you can't write women.

                            SIMON
          Yeah, I don't ... you, you're not
          supposed to say that. You're not ...
          that's not ...

                            LUCY
          But you can't.

SIMON

How much of this have you changed for
this thing that you're doing? How much
of what I wrote have you ... what have
you ch ... what have you changed?

LUCY

Just the pronouns.

She slowly retreats.

7   INT. DAVID'S HOUSE/HOTEL ROOM - EVENING   7

GEORGIA crawls into her seat.

DAVID

Hey. Hi, baby.

David watches from his bathroom.

GEORGIA

Hey, babe.

David chuckles as Georgia takes a sip of her cocktail.

DAVID

How are ya? How did it go?

GEORGIA

Mmm. Yeah, really well, thanks.

DAVID

How was the scene?

GEORGIA

(inhales)
Yeah, it was really, it was really good.

DAVID

Yeah.

GEORGIA

Anna and Lucy were very funny.

DAVID

Right.

GEORGIA

I was hilarious, obviously.

DAVID

Possible spin-off?

GEORGIA

Well, never say never.

DAVID

I don't think you've ever told me what
the scene was.

                              GEORGIA
          Oh, it's, um ... it's like, well it's a
          version of that scene that you did in
          Series One where you're all talking over
          each other, only, um, Anna's Michael,
          Lucy's Simon and I'm you.

                              DAVID
          Ahhh.

                              GEORGIA
          Yeah.

                              DAVID
          People liked it, did they?

                              GEORGIA
          Yeah, it was really interesting.
          Actually, most people said that they
          preferred it to the original.

                              DAVID
          Did they?

Georgia continues with her cocktail.

                              GEORGIA
          Mmm.

                              DAVID
          Most people?

                              GEORGIA
          Across the board, actually.

                              DAVID
          Right ...

                              GEORGIA
          Yeah.

                              DAVID
          And were the, were these people you
          would trust or ... ?

                              GEORGIA
          Oh, with my life.

                              DAVID
          Surprising, but, okay, okay, yeah ...
          And did you hit all your targets?

                              GEORGIA
          We exceeded them.

                              DAVID
          Very good.

Georgia mutters as she continues with her cocktail. A beat.

GEORGIA

Where are you?

DAVID

I'm in the hotel room.

GEORGIA

Are you sat on a loo?

DAVID

This is the only place the wi-fi will
work, promise.

GEORGIA

Sure, yeah. No, sure.

DAVID

No, it felt a bit odd, actually.

GEORGIA

What, on set?

DAVID

Yeah, I felt nervous.

GEORGIA

Nervous?

DAVID

Yeah. I know, that didn't used to
happen.

GEORGIA

No.

A beat.

DAVID

I felt sort of flabby.

GEORGIA

Flabby?

DAVID

Yeah. I mean, you know ...
intellectually flabby.

GEORGIA

Yeah, I mean, not obviously ...
        (mutters)

DAVID

Like I couldn't remember quite how to do
it.

GEORGIA

Ah. Well ... er, that'll get better.

DAVID

Yeah. I bet Michael wouldn't have felt
nervous.

<pre>
                         GEORGIA
          I miss you, baby.

                         DAVID
          I miss you too, baby.

A computer chimes.

                    DAVID (CONT'D)
          Oh, it's Michael.

                         GEORGIA
                    (not surprised)
          Ah, of course it is.

                         DAVID
          Shall I let him in?

David does not wait for her answer.

                    DAVID (CONT'D)
          I'll let him in.

Georgia is clearly disappointed.

                         GEORGIA
                    (softly)
          Okay.

                         DAVID
          Nice to see New York.

Michael joins the conversation from his living room. He is
wearing a dinner jacket and bow-tie and is sipping a glass of
champagne.

                    DAVID (CONT'D)
          Hey, the big cheese in the Big Apple.

                         MICHAEL
                    (theatrically)
          Hello.

                         DAVID
          That's not New York.

                         MICHAEL
                    (to Georgia)
          Oh, d'you know what, I've often said
          that your husband has the observational
          skills of a pewter tankard.

                         GEORGIA
          And I have yet to disagree with you.

                         MICHAEL
          Mmm.

                         DAVID
          You're still at home.
</pre>

                         MICHAEL
          There is no getting past you, is there,
          Sherlock?

Georgia grins as she sips her cocktail.

                         DAVID
          Is Anna still there, too? Oh, there she
          is.
                    (to Anna)
          Anna.

Anna enters from behind Michael wearing an evening dress.

                         ANNA
          Hi there.

                         DAVID
          Ooh, don't you look dandy.

                         ANNA
          Ooh, thank you.

                         MICHAEL
          Yes, it's only you letting the side
          down, college boy.

                         DAVID
          Well, nobody told me there was a fucking
          dress code, did they?

                         MICHAEL
          Are you in a toilet?

                         DAVID
          I am in the toilet because it's the only
          place that the wi-fi works in this crappy
          hotel room.

                         MICHAEL
          Is he always this cranky late at night,
          Georgia?

                         GEORGIA
          Er, yeah, always.

                         DAVID
          Well, what happened to the wedding?

                         MICHAEL
          Alright, um ... say hello to New York.

Michael grabs his electronic tablet to reveal Michael's 'Best
Friend' on the screen.

                    MICHAEL (CONT'D)
          Say hello to David.

               MICHAEL'S BEST FRIEND
                    (thru tablet)
          Hello, David.

                         DAVID
Hi.
                    (chuckles)

                 MICHAEL'S BEST FRIEND
                    (thru tablet)
Er, I'm Michael's best friend.

                       MICHAEL
                    (into tablet)
Whoa, whoa, whoa, whoa, whoa, now that
kind of ...

                         DAVID
Really?

                       MICHAEL
                    (into tablet)
... territorial approach is gonna get
David a wee bit ticked off.

                         DAVID
Yeah.

                       MICHAEL
                    (into tablet)
Now why don't you fuck off back to your
party and your new wife, alright?

                         DAVID
Um, congratulations. Whoo-hoo.

                       MICHAEL
                    (into tablet)
Say bye to everyone.

They all say their goodbyes as Michael puts down the tablet.

                  MICHAEL (CONT'D)
                    (into tablet)
Bye, bye, bye, bye, bye ...

David swigs from a bottle of beer.

                         DAVID
So you dialled in in the end?

                       MICHAEL
It seemed appropriate.

                       GEORGIA
Did you do your speech?

                         ANNA
                    (hesitantly)
He got a bit nervous.

                       GEORGIA
Oh, did you?

                        MICHAEL
    No, I didn't.

                         ANNA
    Yes, you did.

                        MICHAEL
    No ... no ... I was fine.

                         ANNA
    After two whiskies and a packet of
    crisps.

                        MICHAEL
    Yes, well, we all have our methods,
    don't we?

                        GEORGIA
    What about Sweden?

                         ANNA
    We are going tomorrow.

                        GEORGIA
    Ahh.

                        MICHAEL
    Where are you?

David bursts into his best Welsh accent.

                         DAVID
    I'm in Cardiff, ain't I?!

                        MICHAEL
    Oh, of course.

                         DAVID
    Iechyd da!

                        MICHAEL
    Of course you're ... how was filming?

                         DAVID
    Yeah, it was fine.

                        GEORGIA
    What about the, you know ... flabbiness?

David cannot believe Georgia has brought this up.

                         DAVID
    That was ...

A beat.

                     DAVID (CONT'D)
    ... it's not a conversation we need to
    share.

GEORGIA
I think we've gone past that.
I think we share everything.

                                                DAVID
No, I was cool as a cucumber and that's
all you need to know.

Michael laughs.

                                          DAVID (CONT'D)
So, listen, how far away am I? How,
what's, what's the distance between
Cardiff and Port Talbot?

                                               MICHAEL
About forty minutes.

David reacts.

                                                DAVID
Come on, shall I come and visit?

                                               MICHAEL
Now?

                                                DAVID
Yeah. Shall I come and visit?

Anna and Michael turn and whisper to each other.

                                               MICHAEL
Yeah, nah.

                                                DAVID
Oh, you grumpy bastards.

                                               MICHAEL
No, it's, it's late. Come on.

                                                DAVID
I haven't seen you in months.

                                               MICHAEL
Yeah, and I know it's been very hard for
you, but ...

                                                DAVID
Oh, you're an infuriating human being.

                                               MICHAEL
Oh, and you're a very rude person.

                                                DAVID
I am not.

                                               MICHAEL
Just willy-nilly inviting yourself round
into people's houses. It's not like that
in Wales, David.

                           DAVID
            I ...

                          MICHAEL
            You're not in Scotland now.

                           DAVID
            Well, I am merely pointing out that I'm
            in the vicinity.

                          MICHAEL
            Well, point made. Thank you very much,
            nos da, goodnight, cheers.

They all gesture with their respective drinks.

                           DAVID
            Shove your leek up your arse.

They all drink.

8   EXT. FILM STUDIO LOT - DAY   8

DAVID hurries to GEORGIA sitting in her stationary car. He stops
and opens the PASSENGER door.

9   INT. GEORGIA'S CAR - DAY   9

GEORGIA watches as DAVID sits beside her wearing his mask.

                           DAVID
            Hi, baby.

He pulls it off.

                          GEORGIA
            Hi.

                           DAVID
            This is a lovely surprise.

He pulls off his baseball cap. They kiss.

                          GEORGIA
            Yeah, well I mean, I wanna say it's
            because I missed you so much.

                           DAVID
            Yeah.

                          GEORGIA
            But I just really needed to get away
            from our kids.

He turns to their youngest strapped in a child seat in the rear.

                           DAVID
            No, sure. Look, you brought this little
            one.

                    GEORGIA
        Yeah. Yeah, I have to bring that one
        otherwise my tits explode.

                    DAVID
        Of course. Is anyone looking after the
        other kids or ... ?

                    GEORGIA
        No, I just left them on their own with
        some stale bread and some candlestick
        stumps. They'll be fine.

                    DAVID
        Well, they're very resilient, yeah.

                    GEORGIA
        They are, yeah.

He stares lovingly at her.

                    DAVID
        Ahh.

                    GEORGIA
        I brought you a packed lunch.

She hands it to him in a children's coolbag.

                    DAVID
        Aren't you the perfect wife.

                    GEORGIA
        I am kind of, yeah.

He unzips it.

                    DAVID
        There's not actually anything in here.

                    GEORGIA
        No, well Wales is a really long way.

                    DAVID
        Of course, yeah. Yeah.

                    GEORGIA
        Yeah. Yeah.

A beat.

                GEORGIA (CONT'D)
        Do you wanna make out?

David checks his watch.

                    DAVID
        I'd love to. Unfortunately, I, I am
        supposed to have been in make-up four
        minutes ago, so ...

                              GEORGIA
          Oh. Okay, well I'll go home then.

                              DAVID
          I mean, stay and chat for a bit.

10 EXT. FILM STUDIO LOT — DAY   10

     We cut outside to GEORGIA's stationary car.

                              GEORGIA
          Okay.

                              DAVID
          What do you wanna talk about?

                              GEORGIA
          Books.

                              DAVID
          Books?

                              GEORGIA
          Books. I wanna talk about books.

                              DAVID
          Right.

11 INT. GEORGIA'S CAR — DAY   11

     The end credits start playing over this scene.

                              DAVID
          I don't historically have a lot to say
          about books.

                              GEORGIA
          Okay. Well let's give it a go.

                              DAVID
          Yeah.

                              GEORGIA
          What was the last book that you read?

                              DAVID
          Um, I don't know. What was the last book
          that you bought me?

                              GEORGIA
          No idea.

                              DAVID
          Cos I know that I definitely didn't read
          that one.

                              GEORGIA
          Excellent. Well, this is going well,
          isn't it?

Yeah.

David reacts to Michael banging on the passenger window.

DAVID (CONT'D)

Oh my ...

MICHAEL

Bloody useless.

DAVID

It's the old man of Port Talbot.

Anna is crouching by a pushchair in the background.

MICHAEL

I've been here for hours. Posing.

DAVID

Ahhh!

MICHAEL

Why?

DAVID

Look at you, in the flesh.

MICHAEL

Here I am!

DAVID

I can't believe it!

MICHAEL

All the bloody ... oh, I'm a listener,
to you, to me. I mean, I was here for
hours.

DAVID

There's very little actual charisma,
though. You sort ... you sort of just
disappear into a wall.

MICHAEL

I can't hear you, sorry.

DAVID

            (stutters)
Put your mask on, I'll wind the window
down. Put your mask on, I'll wind the
window down. Ah.

MICHAEL

Alright?

DAVID

There he is.

MICHAEL

Hello, Georgia. You alright?

                         GEORGIA
          Hi. I know.

                         MICHAEL
          How long have you got before you gotta
          go to work?

                         DAVID
          Um ... meant to have been in make-up
          eight minutes ago.

                         MICHAEL
          Er, right.

                         DAVID
          Yeah. When's your flight?

                         MICHAEL
          Er, we ...

Michael glances at Anna in the background.

                     MICHAEL (CONT'D)
          Yes, alright, alright, alright.
                     (to David)
          We are ... mmm, yes, quite late already.

                         DAVID
          Mmm, right. Okay. Okay.

                         MICHAEL
          Um, but, you know, you wanted to work,
          didn't you?

                         DAVID
          You wanted to travel.

                         MICHAEL
                     (softly)
          Yeah.

                         DAVID
          Here we are.

                         MICHAEL
          I guess that worked out then.

                         DAVID
          Look at you.

                         MICHAEL
          Yeah.

A beat.

                     MICHAEL (CONT'D)
          Er, yeah, I can't, I can't, I can't hear
          through these things anyway.

DAVID

No, don't worry. I'll, I'll ... yeah, I'll
...

MICHAEL

Alright.

DAVID

See you later.

MICHAEL

Lovely, lovely to see you, Georgia.

GEORGIA (O.S.)

You too, Michael.

David and Anna wave at each other.

DAVID

See you, Anna.

GEORGIA (O.S.)

Bye, Anna.

DAVID

Bye.

Michael goes to join Anna.

David closes the passenger window as he watches Anna and Michael in the background. He turns to Georgia.

DAVID (CONT'D)

Ah.

A beat.

GEORGIA (O.S.)

He looks like the Hobbit.

David watches as Anna and Michael walk off.

12 INT. GEORGIA'S CAR — DAY   12

GEORGIA and DAVID. He checks his mobile phone.

DAVID

Ah, it didn't record. Damn. Um ...

They check their equipment. Georgia points to another phone.

GEORGIA

Did it record here?

DAVID

Did we even slate it?

GEORGIA

For fuck's sake.

David points at the camera.

                              DAVID
              Is that ... have you turned it off yet?

                              GEORGIA
              I don't know. Cos I pressed the button
              and I don't know if I pressed it.

David continues checking his mobile. They peer at it.

                              DAVID
              It's still running.

                              GEORGIA
              It's still running.

They look into the camera.

                              DAVID
                         (to camera)
              Okay, so this is an end slate.

Georgia laughs.

                         DAVID (CONT'D)
                         (to camera)
              That was eleven ... seven eleven three.

David claps his hands together.

                              GEORGIA
              Which we might not have any sound for.

                              DAVID
              We've got it on there and we've got it
              on here. That's turned off.
                         (to camera)
              Good luck.
                                              BLACK SCREEN

Theme from *Staged* (intro)

It isn't unusual to hit your head against a brick wall for weeks – or longer – trying to find the right musical tone for a new project, especially at the very beginning of the process when everyone is still trying to figure it all out. I usually write at the piano, improvising and recording as I go (my muscle memory is terrible and I have lost, countless times, pieces of music that would no doubt have *defined* my musical career had I not bloody forgotten them). But for some reason, the theme for *Staged* came rather quickly, one spring afternoon. Straight off the starting block.

The only problem was, this particular bit of music didn't sound very… *Staged*. Should it sound more like it was made in lockdown? Should it sound more like a traditional sitcom? Was it funny enough? There was no EUREKA moment when it appeared, and its response from everyone, me included, was, a bit, *Okay, what else shall we try?*

It got put aside and I went to try and write some other options that *did* sound like a show made in lockdown. The only problem was, all the other ideas were completely pants.

So off we went, back to our unlikely hero, 'idea number 1', hiding in a hard drive somewhere for a week or more. I've only just gone and listened back to that first demo, and apart from a few minor tweaks, it hasn't really changed much at all from that first improvisation. It seems crazy now – I really can't imagine anything else accompanying David, Michael and all their guests along on this journey.

I was organising a Zoom call with some friends the other day and they jokingly requested a version of the theme played on the call. There have been countless messages on Twitter from people who have done that very thing, as well as people recording themselves playing it on the piano, or even in a full band from their homes during lockdown. It has somehow become 'a thing'. It was certainly never intended to ever be 'a thing'. But it, along with the show, that all started with Simon's brilliant words, has become something more than the sum of its parts. Which is pretty amazing really. All things considering. Because the theme tune could have been completely pants.

Alex Baranowski
London, 2021

Theme from *Staged* (intro)

Staged Series 1 & 2

Alex Baranowski

This bit is a lot easier with two people!

♩ = 80
Slow waltz

Credits

All original illustrations © Chris Glynn
www.chrisglynn.net

Photographs of David Tennant and Georgia Tennant, on pages 68, 91, 148, 381, 384–5: © Paul Stephenson
www.paulstephensonmedia.com

Photographs of Michael Sheen and Anna Lundberg, Series 2 location shots, on pages 60, 68, 80, 148: © Simon Ridgway
www.simonridgway.com

Theme from *Staged* (intro) © Alex Baranowski, Bright Notion Music Ltd.
www.alexbaranowski.com

Crossword © Geoff Iles

Answers to the crossword (page 355):

Michael – The Cross One
1. Adrian Lester   9. Useable   10. Viewers   11.&15. Judi Dench   12. Birds   13. Anna
16. Cedilla   17. Needles   18. Mochyns   21. Auction   23. Tool   24. U-boat   25. Part
28. Epicure   29. Avocado   30. Ugly customer

David – The Down One
1. Amended   2. Robe   3. America   4. Lived in   5. Seen   6. Eternal   7. Subject matter
8. Assassination   14. Plays   15. See 11   19. Cooking   20. Sub-menu   21. Adamant
22. In a pair   26. Lucy   27. Zoom

Acknowledgements

There are so many people to thank, but the *Staged* team would like to make particular mention of the following: Shane Allen, Joana Coelho, Simon Craddock, Kate Farquhar-Thomson, Dan Gage, Alfie Glynn, Harriet Hammond, Hilary Heath, Geoff and Bev Iles, Mary Jones, Rachel Kenny, Tony Maher, Charlotte Moore, Greg Phillips, Hannah Robinson, Andrew Rogers, Gregor Sharp, John Sivers, Robert Taylor and the wonderful teams at BBC, GCB Films, Infinity Hill, Onsight, Rainmaker and beyond.

Chris Glynn deserves special mention for the deliciously witty illustrations that have captured the very essence of the series and brought the book to life.

John Mitchinson and the publishing team at Unbound have brought unbridled enthusiasm and publishing wizardry to bear on the project. With our sincere thanks to editor DeAndra Lupu, head of production Lauren Fulbright, Cassie Waters, Aliya Gulamani, Mark Ecob, Julian Mash, Amy Winchester, Becca Harper-Day and Alex Eccles.

A Note on the Authors

Writer, director and co-creator **Simon Evans'** theatre directing credits include the inaugural season at Found111, productions for West End playhouses including the Donmar Warehouse and the Trafalgar Studios, and international venues including Dublin's Smock Alley and the Goodman Theatre, Chicago. His writing credits include *The Vanishing Man* and *The Extinction Event* (w. David Aula), *Bait* and *Seven Actor Dream*. Simon was Resident Assistant Director at the Donmar Warehouse, Staff Director at the National Theatre and Creative Associate at the Bush. He is a Founding Director of Myriad & Co., writing and creating work for clients including Disney, Microsoft, Lexus, BMW, Bombay Sapphire and Johnnie Walker Blue Label.

Producer and co-creator **Phin Glynn** has eight feature film credits over the last three years including *Mad to Be Normal* starring David Tennant and Elisabeth Moss, *The Doorman* starring Ruby Rose and Jean Reno, *Waiting for Anya* starring Anjelica Huston and Noah Schnapp and *You, Me and Him* also starring David Tennant with Lucy Punch. He is developing works by Stephen King, Graham Greene and Lawrence Osborne. Phin's first Spanish language feature as an Associate Producer, *El Prófugo*, played in competition at the 2020 Berlin Film Festival.

Completely Staged was compiled and edited by:

Producer **Victor Glynn** is an award-winning producer and writer. He has worked with such directors as Academy Award winners Juan José Campanella and Marleen Gorris, Oscar nominees Agnieszka Holland, Mike Leigh and David O. Russell. Actors in his productions include Academy Award winners Christoph Waltz, Judi Dench and Leonardo DiCaprio. He is a former senior executive at Sony and Pearson and for many years was CEO of Portman Entertainment, one of the UK's leading independent film and television producers and distributors.

Sophie Goldsworthy is a publisher, photographer and writer, currently working on her first novel. By day, she directs content strategy and acquisition across the global research publishing business at Oxford University Press.

Unbound is the world's first crowdfunding publisher, established in 2011.

We believe that wonderful things can happen when you clear a path for people who share a passion. That's why we've built a platform that brings together readers and authors to crowdfund books they believe in – and give fresh ideas that don't fit the traditional mould the chance they deserve.

This book is in your hands because readers made it possible. Everyone who pledged their support is listed below. Join them by visiting unbound.com and supporting a book today.

Leanne Abela
Bee & John Abraham
Kerri Adler
Rehza Aguilar
Nicole Ahner
Kaori Aikawa
Katarina Aiken
Julie Alderson
Laura & Michael Aldridge
Joy Allen
Kayleigh Allen
Nicola Alloway
Jane Andrew
Gary Andrews
Bernard Angell
Kirk Annett
Aono
Risa Arakawa
Luana Arfani
Maniwa Arisawa
Bridget Arndt
Angie Arnold
Adrian and Zoe Ashton
Fateh Badesha
Grace Baker
Hilary Baker
Susan Baker
Joanne Balharrie

Janni Ball
Scottie Ballard
Briony Barabas
Damien Barnard
Diana Barndt
Maureen Barndt
Holly Barnes-Wallis
Alessia Basile
Jemma Bastable
Adam Baylis-West
Emma Bayliss
Kay Baynes
Rachael and Rupert Beale
James Beckley
Véronique Bejaer
Susan Bell
Catherine Bellamy
Matt Bellbrough
Shannon Bellinghausen
Sue Benson
Julian Benton
Mariangela Berardi
Amanda Berendt
Heather Bertucci
Sabine Bey
Stefanie Beyer
Rachael Birchall
Kelly Birtwell

Kim Bissell
Gabriela Blevins
Paul Bolger
Kelsey Bomboy
Michaela Bos
Wendy Bosberry-Scott
Kate Boulton
Veronica Boutelle
Julie Bozza
Paul Brand
Walt and David Brecht
Nichola Brenchley
Ed Brenton
Catherine Breslin
Steve Brine
Marjorie Britt
Simon Bromley
Ann Brown
Lyn Browne
Lynne Brozynski
Ben Bruce
Stefan Budirahardjo
Nicole Bueermann
Martin Bull
Erica Bullivant
Kate Bulpitt
Ashley Bunney
Kimberly Burke

Maddy Burns
Petra Burrell
Caroline Busby
Richard Busby
Marcus Butcher
Edward Butler
Gordon Butler
Noel Butterworth
Rik Byatt
Pia C
Kristin C.
Alan Calder
Alistair Canlin
Anna Capcarrere
Olivia Cardosi
Wendy Carey
Lucas Cargill
Carrie-Anne Carruthers
Ande Case
Michael Casner
Cathy
Emily Chan
Louise Chantal
Helen Chapman
Sharon Charlton
Andrea Chettle
Jody H.Y. Cheung
David Chrichard
Sansarlat Christine
Paul Clark
Galit Cohen
Chris Collingwood
Karen Colohan
Lora Colver
Jacqui Connell
Amanda Cook
Sarah Caroline Cook
Joanne Cooke
Emyr Cooper
Andrea Copano
Blanca Corbelli

Rachel Cordes
Mike & Rosie Corlett
Simon A Craddock
Matthew Craig
Anthony J Crowley
Simon Curtis
Iris D.
Dave (EOL)
Rosie David
Amy Davidoff
Cat Davies
Karen Davies
Georgia Davis
Joshua Davis
Mary Davis
James Davison
Elijah Day
Jesse De Goeij
Charlie De Santa
Kim DeCina
Susan Deines
Mags Delaney
Claudia DeMent
Samantha Derr
Sheila Dettmann
Miranda Dickinson
Samuel Dickinson
Karl Djemal
Yuval Dohn
Seth Dong
Stephanie & Allan Donsig
Stacey Dores
Chris Douglass
Beth Drake
@DrMikeFraser
Lauren Dumont
Sheila Dunn
Anne Dunne
Inna Dvorecka
William Dyson
Ken Ellington

Steven Elliott James
Rosie Elvidge
Erika
Jennifer Estlund
Brioney Euden
Angie Eustice
Marcia Evans
Nadia Evans
Diane Eyre
Margret Fabis
Jerome Fagan
James Fairley
Orsolya & Alex Faisst
Kate Farquhar-Thomson
Megan Farr
Steven Feeney
Andrea Felix
Jack Fenwick
Louise Ferreira
Jeanne Fielding
Heather Fitzpatrick
Kathy Flynn
Chris Fosten
Sabine Foster
Nicki Fox
Tracey Frances Jones
Kimberly Freeman
Annie Friedlein
Karen Friend
Yuko Fujii
Mel Fuka
Paco B. Garcia
Nikki Gateson
Annie Gianunzio
Daniele Gibney
Samantha Gibson
Julie Giles
Jessica Gioia
Chris Glynn
Maureen & Christopher
    Glynn

Victor Glynn
Bruce Goatly
Franziska Gohlke
Sophie Goldsworthy
Ari Gonzalez
Pravin Gorajala
Amanda Graham
Danni Graves
Deb Green
Karen Green
Rohan Green
Linda Greenwood
Molly Grist
Chris Guy
Misato H.
Rosamund Haddow
    Mendes
Daniel Hahn
Lucy Halcrow
Chie Hama
Jackie Hamilton
Beate Hammes
Harriet Hammond
Gina Hamon
Vorn Hancock
Josh Handley
Irene Hannah
Pat & Jan Harkin
Hilary Harley
Andrea Harman
Stephanie Hartman
Simon Haslam
Jason Haspel
Matty Hawke
Graham Hayes
Emma Haywood
Felicia Hees
Richard Hein
Vicky Hempstead
Jenny & Simon Hemsley
Jude Henderson

Theresa & Josh Hesse
Rhian Heulwen Price
David Hicks
Hideka
Catherine Hill
Cathy Hill
Cheyenne Hills
Alison Hobro
Tracy Hodgkins
Sarah Höfermann
Lisa Hollifield
Ann Holmes
Sam Holroyd
Trudence Holtz
Stacey Hopwood
Aiko Hori
Catherine Horton
Helen Hotchkiss
Catherine Howard-Dobson
Bob Howell
Heike Hüttemann
Sarah Hyam
Inga Iceman
Angela Idler
Yumi Ikeda
Geoff Iles
Sarah Ireland
Makiko Ishikawa
David Jackson
Millie James
Jennie Jarvis
Philip Jeffree
Alex Jeffrey
Fiona Jeffrey
Barbara Jeremiah
Bill Jerman
金悦 Jin Yue
Shelby Jirikils
Carolyn Joanne Roberts
Trish Johns
Andrea Johnson

Andy Jones
Dallas Jones
Julie Jones
Yoshida Jun
Kazuyo K.
Sandra Kabisch
Riona Kaneta
Kaori
Viktoria Karadeniz
James Kassapian
Jo Keeley
Zoe Kempf-Harris
Traci Kent
Dan Kieran
Kevin Kieran
Sayuri Kimoto
Patrick Kincaid
Kath Kirkland
Cynthia Klawitter
Karen Knierman
Cecilie Knudsen
Sumire Kojima
Marie Kollinger
Leander Kreltszheim
Marion Kruhm
Auri Kuisma
Mio Kumamoto
Noma Kura
Duncan Ladkin
Kathryn Lagana
Allison Lahikainen
Mit Lahiri
Jon Lambourne
Anja Lampesberger
Adam Lane
Cheryl Langsjoen
Fjodors Latiskevics
Fion Lau
Léa.P
Duncan Leatherdale
Nat Lecoq

Courtney LeCount
Jillian Levine-Sisson
Kathryn Lewis
Stewart Licudi
Alison Liddle
Jonathan Light
Kristina Lihan
Jim Linning
Starry Liu
Patrick Lonergan
Aisling Longbottom
Sarah Longstaff
Judith S. Loukides
Emma Love
Ella Lovely Kennedy
Serene Low
Eric Lowmiller
LukeluvsccWL5
Jose Miguel Vicente Luna
Mike Lynd
Frances Lynn
Samantha Lynn Esposito
Nao M.
Rowan MacBean
Helen MacDonald
José Machado
Oliver Maclean
Christine Madden
Debeauquenne Maeva
Diana Maier
Katie Mallinson
Carolynn Manlove
Karen Mapplethorpe
Claire Mardlin
Missa Marmalstein
Helen Marsh Jeffries
Jane Marshall
Aziliz Martin--Levant
Karen Martin-Bond
Natalia Marusza
Hiroko Masuda

Yoshimi Masuoka
Scott Matthewman
Mick Mayes
Nicole Mazza
Liam McBey
Carol McCollough
Megan McCormick
Jemima McCue
Amber McCulloch
Ian McDonald
Kellen McGee
Taramichelle McGeown
Alastair McKie
Karen McKie
Peter McMinn
Julie McNally
Lynn McNally
Benjamin McQuigg
Leslie McQuigg
Robert Meade
mei_R_M
Mallory Melton
Anita Mihaly
Alis Millar
John Mitchinson
Deena Mobbs
Ayana Mochizuki
Christine Moellenberndt
Ania Moir
Alastair Monk
Rebecca Monk
Maurane Monnier
Sophie Moore
Laura Morales Corpa
Saki Morikawa
Ben Moruzzi
Shirley Moth
Bernard Moxham
Ramona Mühleisen
Yvonne Müller
Lauren Mulville

Clare Mundell
Rebecca Murray
Sarah Murray
myan-kichi
Kelly Nagle
Ai Nakamura
Moeko Nakasaka
Jamie Naragon
Carlo Navato
Kathleen Neary
Mary Nelmes
Katie Nickolaou
Siobhan NiLoughlin
Aya Nishizumi
Ayaka Niwa
Katherine Nixon
Hiromi Nonaka
Jo Norcup
Kathy Notarantonio
Vicki Novajosky
Mary O'Hanlon
Fiona O'Neill
Paul O'Connor
Akiko Ochiai
Lucy Oconnell
Saerom Oh
Leslie Ohanian
Satomi Ojima
Omshall
Asako Ono
Ingrid Oomen
Makiko Oono
Joanna P.
Lev Parikian
Adam Peake
Orange Peel
Judith Pengelly
Reishen Perdomo
AJ Perrigo
Sandy Peters
Kris Phillips

Megan Phoenix
Anne Piltz
Alice Platzer
Justin Pollard
Wendy Pond
Reecy Pontiff
Ana Portugal
Deborah Pun'kin Rutson
Q
Delayna Ravenstone
Simon Ray
Colette Reap
Remembering Calum
    Downes
Andrea Richardson
Nelleke Rietvink
Elga Riman
Stefania Rizzotto
Jane Roberts
Sue Robertson
Dave Robinson
Becky Robinson Fox
Morgan Robinson Fox
Claire Roderick
Emma Rodgers
Nicholas Rusbatch
Paul Russell
s.fusa
Saho
Aiko Sakai
Sakey
Katarzyna Sambierska
John Sanders
Liana Sanders
Ken Sankey
Helene Santi
Itziar Santín
Lisa Sara Bird
Alex Sargent
Hideko Sawami
Leah Scheble

Chris Schilling
Anja Schmidt
Stacy Schmidt
Sarah Schoonover
Nicole Schrader
Janette Schubert
Gemma Scott
Matthew Searle
Rebecca Seibel
Bonnie Seinfeld-Hoch
Sandra Selin
Jaime Sens
Christine Sexton
Christine Shanks
Dominique Gracia & Nick
    Shearer
Cathriona Sheehan
Isobel Sheene
Vi Shiau
Maki Shima
MIki Shima
Carol Shreeve
Rahel Sidler
Nicole Siemer
Victoria Sigsworth
Aline Silva
Bettina Silveira
Katie Skidmore
Keith Sleight
Sarah-Jane Smart
Fraser Smith
Jacqueline Smith
Neil Smith
Anastasia Soloveva
Mee Song
Stefany Soto
Angela Southall
Glynis Spencer
Zoe Spinks
Treva Stack
Wendy Staden

Karen Steel
Rosalind Stern
Hugo Stevenson
Sharon Steward
Barbara Stiller
Carolyn Strahan
Elizabeth Stuard
Chrissy Stump
Lesley Styles
Hiromi Sudou
Mizuki Sugihara
Sayuri Sugimoto
Callie Sullivan
Fabiola Superina
Chris Suslowicz
Fiona Suter
Jane Sutherland
Paulina Szuba
Caroline Szumigalski
Makiko Tachibana
Yuko Takakura
Amy Tan
Jeremy Taylor
Paul Taylor
Peter Taylor
Eliza J. Tem
Carrie Thompson
Jenny Thurston
Sophie Timms
Gold Toeman
Skye Toor
Cheryl Tortorici
Autumn Trapani
Greg Trawinski
Asami Tsuji
Sahoko Tsuji
Kate Tudor
Ian Tuffnell
Barbara Ulber
Akane Uno
Anna Vagner

Mark Vent
Mo Venus
Kathy Virasith
Dawn Wade
Bella Wagner
Tanja Wagner
Chris 'Woodstock' Walker
Carol & Robert Walport
Siân Walters
SY Wan
Tanya Warren
Sophie Webster
Duncan Wefan-Donnchadh McPhee
Zoe Welch
Courtney West
Josh White

Nicholas White
Christopher Wickham
Charlotte Widdows
Zoe Wigmore
Rachel Wilcoxson
Lynne Wild
Georgie Williams
Dawn Winskill
Stephen Wise
Laura Witte
Hayley Wong
Vivian Wong
Nat Wood Fox
Rebecca Woods
Rachel Woodward-Clark
Harriet Wulff
Frederike Wunsch

Tokuko Yabu
Akiko Yamada
Ikumi Yamamoto
Yuko Yamamoto
Mayuki Yamane
Luka Yamashita
Carolanne Ybarra
Stephen Usins Yeardley
Yukiko Yoshioka
Peter Young
Iva Žáková
Yisan Zhao
Shannon Zinda
Larry Zinn
Elizabeth Zwicky
茜雯 林
熊